A HISTORY OF THE STATE OF VERMONT

FROM
ITS DISCOVERY AND SETTLEMENT
TO THE
CLOSE OF THE YEAR
MDCCCXXX
[1830]

Nathan Hoskins

HERITAGE BOOKS
2022

HERITAGE BOOKS
AN IMPRINT OF HERITAGE BOOKS, INC.

Books, CDs, and more—Worldwide

For our listing of thousands of titles see our website
at
www.HeritageBooks.com

A Facsimile Reprint
Published 2022 by
HERITAGE BOOKS, INC.
Publishing Division
5810 Ruatan Street
Berwyn Heights, Md. 20740

Copyright © 1994 Heritage Books, Inc.

Originally published by
J. Shedd
1831

— Publisher's Notice —
In reprints such as this, it is often not possible to remove blemishes from the original. We feel the contents of this book warrant its reissue despite these blemishes and hope you will agree and read it with pleasure.

International Standard Book Number
Paperbound: 978-0-7884-0114-5

DISTRICT OF VERMONT, TO WIT:

BE IT REMEMBERED, that on the twelfth day of February, in the fifty-fifth year of the Independence of the United States of America, NATHAN HOSKINS and J. SHEDD, of the said District, have deposited in this office, the title of a book, the right whereof they claim as proprietors, in the words following, to wit: "A History of the State of Vermont, from its discovery and settlement, to the close of the year 1830. By Nathan Hoskins.— 'Illi, libertate adepta, floruerunt.'" In conformity to the act of the Congress of the United States, entitled "an act for the encouragement of learning, by securing the copies of maps, charts, and books, to the authors and proprietors of such copies, during the times therein mentioned."

JESSE GOVE,
Clerk of the District of Vermont.
A true copy of record, examined and sealed by me,
J. GOVE, *Clerk.*

Gamaliel Small, printer.

PREFACE.

History is indeed the store house of experience, the mirror of duties, the source of morality, and the foundation of virtuous conduct. It informs us of those events which the triumphs of time have obliterated from the visible operations of the world. It unfolds to view the proceedings of antiquity, and gives us a knowledge of the illustrious dead, by setting forth their transactions, their virtues, and their faults. Without its aid, the boundaries of our own observations, and the limited sphere of our own prejudices, must always keep us in a state of infancy and ignorance. The utmost extent of human longevity is an imperceptible point, in comparison with the series of ages that have rolled back into obscurity since the commencement of Creation. And all we can know is confined to this point, unless we call to our aid the study of

PREFACE.

History. Impressed with such ideas of the advantages and happiness acquired from historical researches, the author of this work has attempted to give a general and correct History of Vermont. Under this title, however, a complete developement of all the proceedings which may have had an influence upon the formation of national character, or the establishment of the liberty and independence of our country, cannot be expected within our present limits. Much embarrassment has been experienced in designating such military or political matters of the general government, as have an immediate or remote influence upon the History of this particular State. The events which have succeeded, since the shores of Champlain were first viewed by civilized man in this and the other hemisphere, have presented the most brilliant epoch in the annals of time. Every empire or government on the globe has shared in the sufferings or participated in the benefits which the conquests of two centuries have produced. From the reign of William III. to the recent peace with Great-Britain, the waters of this Lake have been a common highway for contending nations. Hence

PREFACE.

the territory lying within the present limits of this State, was, anterior to any settlement in the same, a scene of war and bloodshed. It becomes therefore necessary to embrace so much of the account of the French and Indian wars as eventuated in the limits of the State. My aim has been, in giving a narrative of the most important events in the History of Vermont, to place those principles of civil and religious freedom for which our ancestors contended, in the most conspicuous light, and to record those multiplied instances of patience, bravery, and patriotism, which have honored their names; and to effect by the tenor of a narrative, rather than by moral reflections, impressions of patriotism and virtue upon the mind of the reader. There will doubtless be many imperfections in the work, which the author would very kindly receive corrected by an intelligent public.

THE AUTHOR.

Vergennes, February 1, 1831.

CHAPTER I.

Situation—Extent—Mountains—Rivers—Lakes—Bays—Climate—Forest Trees—Esculent and Medicinal Plants—Quadrupeds—Birds, Fishes, Insects, Mineralogy and Geology.

The first and most perfect accounts we have of the discovery and settlement of countries, furnish but a partial representation of the real character of the times. The features of particular transactions are unknown by the colorings in the picture of recorded events. During the period of the first settlement of Vermont, the events of the American revolution, and the extensive conquests in Europe by the arms of the French, gave a powerful impulse to the patriotism and enterprise of the people. Such causes have established a highly prosperous and respectable character for the State. The situation of Vermont on the terraqueous globe, is between 42 degrees 44 minutes and 45 degrees of North latitude and between 3 degrees 31 minutes and 5 degrees and 24 minutes east longitude, from Washington. It is entirely an inland State, being separated at the shortest distance about eighty miles from any part of the ocean. This State is bounded on the south by Massachusetts. This is part of the divisional line, being 40 miles in length, as established by a division of George the II. between Massachusetts and New Hampshire, and was surveyed by Richard Hazen, in February, 1741. Conneticut river forms the eastern boundary of Vermont. This line by pursuing the course of the river, is about 215 miles in length and is derived from a decree of George the III. by which the western bank of the aforesaid river was declared to be the boundary line between the Provinces of New Hampshire and New York. The north line of the State runs on a parallel of 45 degrees north latitude, from Connecticut river to lake Champlain. This line, dividing a portion of the United States from Canada, is 90 miles long, and was surveyed in 1772 by I. Collins and I. Carden, but very erroneously afterwards Doct. Williams made some observations for determining it, and it was again surveyed by commissioners appointed by the United States and Great Britain, under the treaty of Ghent. The western boundary was settled by the government of Vermont and New York, at the termination of their controversy in 1790. Beginning at the south west corner of the State, this line runs northerly along the western boundaries of the towns of Pownal, Bennington, Shaftsbury, Arlington, Sandgate, Rupert, Pawlet, Wells and Poultney to Poultney river; thence down the same through the middle of the deepest channel of said river, East Bay and lake Champlain, passing easterly of the islands called the Four Brothers, and westerly of Grand Isle and La Motte to the 45th degree of north latitude. The length of this State from north to south is 157 1-2 miles, and its medium width from east to west is about 57 miles, containing an area of 9000 square miles, or 5,760,000 square acres. The surface of this State is very diversified and uneven, mountains, hills and rising grounds, are its general outlines, and a green verdure the apparent covering of the distant landscape—considerable plains of fine level country border upon the rivers, which at no great distance from them rise into a collection, and chains of high mountains intersected with deep and extensive vallies. Vermont is the most mountainous State in the Union, and in no part are the plains so extensive as to remove the prospect of mountains and hills from the view of the spectator. The Green Mountains extend from south to north through the whole length of the State, keeping about a middle direction from Connecticut river on the east, and lake Champlain on the west. The mountains commence near the sea coast, and after running through Connecticut, Massachusetts and Vermont, a tract of not less than four hundred miles in length, terminate in the Province of Canada. This range is one continued chain or collection of mountains. Their width is generally from ten to fifteen miles, and among them is frequency of vallies, an abounding of springs and an unbroken covering of woods. From the southern boundary of the State to Washington county, the range continues; but here the mountains separate into two ranges, the eastern is called the height of land, which separates the waters falling from this part of the State and Connecticut river from those which flow into the lakes Champlain and Memphremagog. The western range is interrupted and broken through by the Onion and Lamoille rivers; Cam els Rump or Hump, and Mansfield mountains, the loftiest eminences in the State, are in this range; the height of the former above tide water is 4188 feet, and that of the latter is 4279 feet. There are several other considerable eminences in the State, some of which do not belong to the chain above described. The tops of these mountains are generally composed of rocks and covered with moss and pine, spruce, hemlock, and other species of trees called evergreens, intermixed with bushes and winter grass, which constitute the principal varieties of vegetable productions that nature brings forth on the tops of these mountains. Upon ascending the summits of these mountains, the powers of creation regularly degenerate, and the trees in their dimensions are only shrubs of two or three feet high, whose branches are so thickly interwoven as to prevent passing between them. A view from the summit of one of them has been described in the following manner : on the east side of the mountain—every where all around, you have rocks frowning upon rocks an imperial elevation, and dark depths such as nature alone can excavate—you can see through the mists, which almost perpetually surround them, hugh masses so high, so rugged in their outlines and yet so heaped and wedged together that it is difficult to distinguish the large and bold cliffs and ravines among which their foundations have been pitched. At such a place as this there is no want of enthusiasm; the whole surrounding country appeared like the delineations upon a map—mountains, hills, vallies, rivers and lakes completed the enchantment of the scene—here the works of man seemed like a speck in the solitude of the ocean, the loftiest edifice was lost in the blueness of space, and villages, humbly catching the shadows of the mountain, looked like the dwellings of pigmies perched upon the bulwarks of creation. The situation of Vermont is such, that all the rivers and smaller streams have their origin within the limits of the State. Eleven of the largest of them have an easterly course, and fall into the Connecticut river. About ten flow westerly and discharge their waters into Lake Champlain. Two running in the same direction fall into the Hudson river, and three have a northerly direction, falling into Lake Memphremagog and pass off by the River St. Francois, through the

Province of Lower Canada. The largest of those on the west side of the mountain, are Missisque river, which rises in Kellyvale, and pursues a northeasterly course until it crosses the line of the State into Canada, and then turning re-enters the State near the south east corner of Richford, and falls into Missisque Bay at Highgate. This river is navigable as far as Swanton Falls, and is seventy five miles in length, including all its windings. The river Lamoille originates in Greensborough, and after running a westerly course of 75 miles discharges itself into Lake Champlain at the north west corner of Colchester. This is a fine smooth stream, and upon its banks border pleasant and fertile tracts of interval. It was discovered by Champlain in 1609. Onion river proceeds from a pond in Cabot, flowing in a northwesterly direction about 70 miles; it then falls into Lake Champlain between Colchester and Burlington, five miles from Burlington village, north. Its principal tributaries are Kingsbury and North Branch, Mad, Waterbury and Huntington rivers, and Muddy Brook. The several channels which have been worn in the rocks by this river, are a great curiosity.— One of these, at Middlesex, is about 80 rods long, sixty feet wide, and thirty feet deep. Another at Waterbury, is still more grand and sublime, being 65 feet in depth; a third channel is between Colchester and Burlington, of the same depth of that at Waterbury. Otter Creek is the longest, and one of the most useful streams in Vermont. It heads in Mount Tabor, runs northwesterly 90 miles, falling into Lake Champlain at Ferrisburgh. From Pittsford to Middlebury, a distance of twenty-five miles, it is navigable for boats, and from Vergennes to its mouth, a distance of eight miles, the Creek is navigable for the largest vessels on the lake. The rivers that run northerly into Lake Memphremagog, and those which unite with the Connecticut river, on the east side of the mountain, are much smaller than those on the west. Among them, White river is the most considerable stream. This river rises in Kingston, and flows in a southern direction about fifty miles, until it unites with Connecticut river, at Hartford. West, and Pasoomsuck rivers are near the size of White river. The Connecticut, so highly celebrated as the Nile of New-England, has its source among the mountains of Lower Canada, and coming within the jurisdiction of New-Hampshire, forms for some distance the boundary between New-Hampshire and Canada, and for the whole length of the states the boundary between New-Hampshire and Vermont, it runs through Massachusetts and Connecticut, which with the former part of its course amounts to four hundred miles, and empties into the ocean at Seabrook. The breadth of this river when it first enters the state, is 150 feet, in the course of sixty miles increases to 390, and its meridian width through Massachusetts and Connecticut may be calculated at 725 feet.— With respect to its length, utility and beauty, this is one of the first rivers in the eastern States. In the opening of the year, it overflows its banks, and for 300 miles increases and fertilizes an extensive tract of fine interval. This river is navigable for vessels requiring 10 feet of water 36 miles, to Middletown—for sloops 50 miles, to Hartford; and for boats two hundred and fifty miles, to Barnet: except the falls, which are now made, and making navigable by means of locks and other improvements. Lake Champlain, into which the rivers from one half of Vermont flow, and from them are discharged to the north west, by the St. Lawrence into the Atlantic Ocean, was the first large body of fresh water, discovered in the interior of North America. This lake lies between the States of Vermont and New-York, but more than one half of it comes within the limits of this State. It extends from Whitehall to Alburgh, a distance of 105 miles, and thence 24 miles to St. Johns, in Lower Canada; it varies in width from 1 to 15 miles; but its medium is almost 4 1-2 miles; an area of 970 square miles. The principal rivers that flow into it from Vermont, are Poultney river at Whitehall; Great and Little Otter Creeks and Lewis Creek at Ferrisburgh; Onion and Missisque rivers at Colchester, and Lamoille river at Swanton. A large number of rivers and streams fall into it from New-York and Canada; considerably exceeding those of this State. The waters, therefore, which form Lake Champlain, seem to be collected from a country of greater extent than the whole State of Vermont. The river Sorell, after a course of 60 miles, conveys the water of the Lake to the St. Lawrence, about 45 miles below Montreal. The shores of this Lake, are indented with numerous bays, among which are East Bay at Whitehall, Button Bay in Ferrisburgh, Selburn, Burlington and Colchester Bays, in the same towns: also Belamaqueens at St. Albans, McQuams Bay at Swanton, and Missisque at Highgate.— Some of the principal Islands scattered through the Lake, are South and North Hero and Vineyard. No Lake in the United States for the importance of the events, in the colonial and national wars of our country, is so highly interesting and justly celebrated, as Champlain. In the early settlement of North America, the rude craft of the savage was wafted on its surface, in his excursions for plunder, and in the war between England and France, and the more recent struggle betwixt the United States and Great Britain, its waters have been crimsoned with the blood of those who suffered, or perished in their successive encounters. The name of Lake Champlain, in the eventful periods of history, stands in connection with some of the most remarkable events in the annals of our country. At Ticonderoga, 20 miles north of Whitehall, was a fort, of the same name: and it was here the British army under the command of General Abercrombie, were repulsed in their attempt to take the fort from the French, with the loss of 1941 men; and on the succeeding year it was surrendered to General Amherst. This fort was taken from the English by Col. Allen in 1775, and retained until 1777; when it was evacuated upon the invasion of General Burgoyne; Crown Point fortress at Moriah, 14 miles north of Ticonderoga, was built by the French, in 1731, surrendered to Gen. Amherst in 1759, and held in the possession of the British until the capture of Burgoyne. Fortifications were erected during our last encounters with Great Britain, at Plattsburgh, where the American fleet, under Commodore McDonough, gained a signal victory over the British squadron, on the 11th of September 1814, and at Burlington, which is now in disuse. The northern line of this State passes across Lake Memphremagog, dividing it into two parts, so that about 8 miles comes within the jurisdiction of the States, and 32 miles in the Province of Canada.— This Lake discharges its waters by the river St. Francois into Lake St. Peters, about 15 miles below the mouth of the river Sorell. It is surrounded with a rich soil, and fine level country. In addition to this description of our rivers, and lakes, something may be added respecting the alluvial deposits, vegetable and organic remains, which abound in many places. The interval lands, which border upon the numerous streams in the State, incontestably demonstrate that nature has, by slow and silent operations, performed great and wonderful revolutions. From thirty to fifty feet in depth the soil has been changed by attrition. Remains of different substances have very often been removed, which have lain imbedded for centuries at a great depth in the earth. These alluvial deposits have a claim to antiquity far anterior to any knowledge the Europeans possessed of the American continent. Such changes have undoubtedly been effected by the high lands, rocks and earthy substances, being worn down and removed by the force of the streams precipitating from the hills and mountains. Thus in the low grounds, vegetable and other loose substances have accumulated to a great depth. The alluvial lands are the best in the State, being of a very strong and durable quality, and suffering but little from rains or drouth. There are many indications that lake Champlain was once much more extensive than it now is, and covered with its waters a considerable proportion of the land, which is now greatly elevated above its surface. Shells and clams are found in the highest parts of the islands in the lake, imbedded in the marl, or incorporated with the stones; and on the continent they are scattered at heights of forty or fifty feet above the level of the lake. The soil also, in many places, exhibits the appearance of being deposited in regular strata on the subsiding of the water. These layers or strata are extensively composed of substances varying in size and quality. Some are large pebbles, and others fine silicious sand, which has been cleansed of all earthy particles by the attrition of overflowing waters. The obstructions to the outlet of the lake were probably somewhere near St. Johns, and it appears it was not reduced to its present level at one time, but at three or four distant and distinct periods. The strongest indications of this, are, a succession of banks, one above another, which have every appearance of being for a long period washed and beaten by the waves. Probably the outlet of the lake was opened on a scale the most stupendous and sublime. The extremes of high and low water are about eight feet. The waters of Vermont, particularly on the east side of the mountain, are soft, and free from foreign substances. On the west side, many are impregnated with iron, carbonate of lime, and epsom salt. Several springs in the State possess the quality of chalybeate water, or a strong infusion of sulphur. Those at Alburgh, Clarendon, Tunbridge, Newbury, and some others, have been considerably resorted to by invalids.

Climate, Temperature of the Weather, Snow, Wind, and Rain.

Vermont, lying within the same parallels of latitude with Spain, France, Italy, Turkey, Tartary and China, would, if corresponding situations could produce similar climates, be a very warm and temperate region. The cold and sudden changes of weather so frequent here, would be succeeded by a temperature as felicitous to health, and productive in animal and vegetable varieties as the fertile fields of France, or the exuberant vallies of Italy. The manufacturer might acquire a profit from an adventure in the fabrication of silks, and the farmer gather a reward for his labors in the cultivation of the grape and the olive. And Vermont, an inland and the only entirely mountainous State in the Union, would, like the elevated regions of Spain, be covered with a crown of perennial verdure, or as the champaign parts of Turkey, be abundant in her harvest of rice. On comparing the American climates with those of the same latitude in Europe, a difference of 12 degrees should be allowed for the peculiarities of the American Continent. The cause of this difference is such a predominance of cold as subjects the American, in north latitude 45, to an equal degree of cold with the European, residing in north latitude 57. The climate of Vermont is on a medium between that of the warm and frigid latitudes. It resembles the former in the degree of its summer heat, and the latter in its sudden changes. The extremes of heat and cold are 100 degrees above, and 27 below zero; and the mean annual temperature, according to the observations that have been made, is about 44 degrees. December, January and February are the coldest months; June, July and August, the hotest; May, the wetest, and September the pleasantest. November is uniformly the most dreary season in the year. The sky is generally enveloped with clouds, and a freezing and thawing state of weather ensues. From observations made by Doctor Saunders, at Burlington, it appears that the mean temperature of the climate for five years was on a medium 43 degrees and one third. From 1701, observations of the weather, the result appears to stand thus: 1025 fair days, 676 cloudy, 289 rainy, 117 snowy, 19 foggy, 45 thunder, aurora borealis, hail and hazy none. As the season advances, the coldness of the air increases rapidly, and winter usually commences the first of December, and continues until April. The ground is generally frozen during this period, and sometimes covered with snow. The seasons, however, are milder and more variable than they were on the first settlement of the State, and the atmosphere is often rendered dark and obscure by smoke arising from the spontaneous decay of vegetation. The frost usually ceases in May, and comes on again in September. The winds in this State are of a variable kind, and their courses follow the direction of the different ranges of the mountains. Sometimes they continue to blow from one point for several days, but usually change courses once or twice in twenty-four hours. In 1682, observations made at Burlington by the gentleman above mentioned, the wind blew from the north 739 times, from the south 826, from the east 19, from the west 43, from the north east 11, from the south east 1, from the north west 18, and from the south west 25. The eastern part of Vermont is more exposed to the north east winds than the vicinity of lake Champlain, and they are there more experienced. The cause of the wind being so variable in this State is occasioned by the heat and cold expanding and condensing the atmosphere. Whenever the agitation of the air ceases, and a calm ensues, the electric fluid imparts heat, and rarifies the surrounding atmosphere, this becalmed strata becomes lighter than the circumambient fluid, and consequently ascends when the cold air rushes in from opposite directions. Thus at a distance of twenty or thirty miles, the wind may blow from the north and south in opposite directions. Violent and destructive winds rarely occur. Storms of thunder and lightning are common here in the summer months, and usually proceed from the west and south west. The quantity of rain which falls in North America, has been found to be double of that which falls in the same latitudes in Europe. The average depth of water which falls annually in the United States is about forty-eight inches, and in Vermont about forty-two inches. Although many parts of the Union suffer severely from drouth, yet it is not often the case in Vermont. The soil is naturally moist, the mountains are productive of rain, and the heat of the sun is not so intense as suddenly to disperse the vapors, dry up the waters or parch the lands. The summer of 1816 was the coldest ever known in Vermont. In 1826, no rain fell at Vergennes, and so through the greatest part of the State, from the 4th of July until about the 28th of September. The ground was completely parched, and vegetation entirely dried up.— Springs and wells generally failed of affording water.

Forest Trees, Esculent and Medicinal Plants.

The natural history of a country is so intimately connected with the civil, that an omission of it would render the latter less certain and useful. Without a knowledge of this branch of history, the condition of that period when the earth was covered with woods, and the hills and vallies shaded with a variety of plants, flowers and trees, as ancient as the powers of nature, would be forgotten and unknown. The memorials of that period, when nature's bounty furnished protection and sustenance to the animals of the forest, are but a sad lesson of extirpation and decay! The first settlers of the United States were furnished with a living and employment by means of agriculture, which had a great influence in the formation of their habits and character. An understanding of this part of history, becomes, therefore, necessary in deliniating our national customs and pursuits. In an inland State like this, where agriculture is the principal business, the original growth of the soil is mutilated and destroyed with a progress as rapid as the increase of its inhabitants. The forests, which had for centuries been maturing, were regarded as an incumbrance, rather than estimated for their value. Thus by gradual improvements, and cultivation of the lands, Vermont has been stripped of her native grandeur. The white pine, the greatest ornament of this, and probably of any forest on the American Continent, is principally destroyed. It was often found six feet in diameter, and two hundred and fifty feet in height, with a beautiful foliage, perfectly suited to the stem which it adorns. The oak, so highly valuable for strength and durability of its timber, remains but in small quantities, and those mostly in such situations as discovery has not reached, or neglect has preserved. The sugar maple affording a luxury from its saccharine juices, and great convenience in its timber and fuel, has been so diminished by the progress of cultivation, that groves of this majestic and valuable tree, once overspreading a large proportion of this State, are now found only on unfeasible, or mountainous lands. A similar destruction has been made of many other valuable species of trees, and some of which are entirely extirpated. The different situations and qualities of land peculiar to the growth of different kinds of forest trees, range in this order. The intervals along the large rivers were formerly timbered with oak, butternut, elm and walnut. The plain lands were generally covered with pine. On the medium land, the timber was usually beach, birch and maple, often intermixed with spruce, hemlock, elm, ash, bass, butternut, cherry and hornbeam. In some parts of the State are swamps which afford a plentiful supply of cedar. The sides and tops of the mountains are covered with evergreens, mostly hemlock, spruce and fir. Respecting the small trees, or shrubs, vines and vegetables, which grow wild and without cultivation, the following are some of the esculent vegetables: red, yellow and thorn plumbs; black, red and choke cherries; hazlenut, black currant, wild goseberry, whortleberry, barberry, mulberry, black grape, fox grape, black raspberry, red raspberry, upright blackberry, cranberry, strawberry, artichoke, groundnut, long red potatoe, wild onion, wild hop, the latter of these are only valuable for their roots and seeds. Those possessing medicinal qualities are considerable numerous, but not very powerful. The whole number of indiginous plants, together with the most common exotics in the State, amount to something more than six hundred and fifty. The ginseng was discovered in this part of the country about 1750. It grows to great perfection in the north part of this State, and has been a considerable article for exportation. The Indian turnip is a valuable and harmless medicine when dried, but taken green, is a most violent poison, producing spasmodic affections, and sometimes immediate death. The balsam obtained from the bark of the fir tree, which abounds in our mountains, possesses healing virtues highly valuable as a medicine.— The extract obtained from the bark of the butternut, is a very good cathartic. To these are added some others, which operate as poisons. The thorn apple, henbane, nightshade, ivy, creeping ivy, swampsumac and baneberry. There is also the bayberry, distinguished for its beautiful green wax, and fine perfume. The prickly ash, for its uncommon aromatic properties. The witch hazle, which blossoms after its leaves have been destroyed by the frost. And the sumac, celebrated for its medicinal qualities, and for dyeing. The great variety, extent and number of our plants and trees, together with their rapid increase and duration, denotes a power and energy which nature has never exceeded in the same climate, in any other quarter of the globe.

Quadrupeds.

Upon settling a new country, or state, the advantages derived to society from such settlements are valuable, as they extend the boundaries of civilization, and increase the subsistence and numbers of mankind, but they are detrimental to the existence of wild animals, and consequently they are almost exterminated from the soil. The wilderness, untouched by the efforts of industry, and untrod by the footsteps of man, is their only secure and peaceful dominion. A destruction of many species, and a diminution of those that remain, on settling this State, are among the most important events in the progressive stages of natural history. The deer no longer ranges over the rough and craggy tops of our mountains, or browses upon the green verdure of our vallies. The moose has been obstructed in his pathway, and his lofty mien is no longer seen in the covert of our forests. The hoarse and terrific howlings of the wolf have ceased, and that most ingenious, harmless and industrious animal, the beaver, has been extirpated, the fraternity of his united and social intercourse prostrated, by the success of our improvements. But these are not the only animals which have shared the hard fate of extermination. The rivers and streams which water this State, were formerly stored with fish in abundance, the bubbling brooks were darkened with crowds of speckled trout, and the delicate salmon resorted in great numbers to our rivers; but the places of their resort and protection are swept away by the changing channels of the streams, so that the size and number of the former are too diminutive for notice, and the latter have entirely deserted our waters. The soil of Vermont, in an uncultivated state, was rich and fertile, and the powers of vegetation extremely vigorous: it was overspread with an unbroken forest, and a great variety and number of animals, which lived on its surface. The productions of animal life, appeared in the various forms of quadrupeds, birds, reptiles, fishes and insects, which in their increase and growth, were numerous and rapid. Of the native quadruped in Vermont, thirty-six different kinds may be numbered, some of the most common and largest, are the moose, bear, wolf, deer, fox, raccoon, porcupine, skunk, woodchuck, cat, martin, rabbit, weasel, squirrel, mole, mouse, together with the amphibious animals, the beaver, otter, muskrat and mink; all of these animals, except the beaver and otter, still continue. The birds which are common to the inland parts and lakes of northern climates, are found in this State; and those most distinguished for the variety of their notes, and the melody of their sounds, termed singing birds, are the robin, thrush, thrasher, boblincoln, yellow and blue bird, wren, black bird, sky lark, cat bird, goldfinch, hanging bird, and spring bird. The birds of passage are those which appear in the middle of April, and depart in the middle of September: the house, barn and ground swallows, the black martin, wild pigeon, wild goose, and snow bird; the last of which appears the 20th of November, and departs the 1st of April. Of those birds which generally resort to ponds, rivers and lakes, called water fowls, are the heron, goose, teal, gull, crane, loon, stork, water hen, and duck. There are many kinds of these. The birds which winter in our climate, are the partridge, crow, forked tailed hawk, owl, snow bird, and wood pecker. There are other kinds of birds, not belonging to those above mentioned, such as two species of eagles, three of hawks, two of crows, and seven of wood-peckers, king bird, cuckoo, whippoorwill, humming bird, and many others; some of which have never been enumerated and described. The bat, a mammillary biped, is very common, and forms the connecting link between the beast and bird.

Fishes.

The variety of Fishes in the waters of Vermont, of the most consequence, are the salmon, trout, shad, pickerel, bass, sturgeon, perch, pout, eel, shiner chub, sucker, and dace. Some of them were formerly very abundant in the State.

Serpents.

The Serpents are the black snake, rattle snake, green snake, striped snake, and adder. The striped snake is very common, and harmless; but the bite of the rattle snake is poisonous, and fatal. The amphibious reptiles are two kinds of toads, six kinds of frogs, turtles, and lizards. Many instances are related of living frogs being found inclosed in the wood of trees, in solid rocks, and the bowels of the earth, where they must have lain in a torpid state for a long period of time. At Burlington, Castleton and Windsor, living frogs have been found in the solid earth, from 6 to 30 feet below the surface.

Insects.

The Insects are numerous, but the most common are the grasshopper, cricket, spider, ant, butter-fly, beetle, wasp, hornet, musquetoe, bumble and honey bees. From all accounts, respecting the honey bee, in Mexico and South America, there is no doubt of its being indigenous and common to North and South America. They live in hollow trees in the woods of Vermont, from year to year, are vigorous, attain their full dimensions, and plentifully supplied with honey. They were found by the earliest settlers, along the shores of lake Champlain, more than one hundred miles from any permanent English or French settlement.

Mineralogy.

An examination of the Minerals found in this State, has not till recently received much attention. Iron is very abundant. In some parts of the State, lead, zinc, copper, manganese, copperas, garnets, and kaolin clay, have been discovered. The various mineral substances abounding in the mountains, might be turned to very profitable account, both for useful and ornamental purposes at home, and as profitable articles for exportation abroad, was a sufficient attention bestowed upon the subject, to ascertain their properties, and acquire a competent skill in working and selling them to advantage. Iron, so indispensible to the arts, commerce and agriculture, and even the continuance of civilized life, has been wrought in considerable quantities, and of a superior quality, from the ore abounding on the west side of the mountain; and could, by proper attention, be made a very general and lucrative article of trade. Timber, for coal, is, and will continue to be, very abundant upon the broken lands. Convenient water privileges, for erecting works, flow near the mineral localities, and a water communication from New-York reaches within short distances of the places where the articles would be fabricated. Encouragement only is wanted to bring these vast resources into an immediate public advantage. Business so propitious to the rising interest of the country, requires nothing more for its promotion than the active enterprise of the people. Had the same attention and spirited exertions been given to manufacturing, there has to agriculture, and the inveterate habit of considering manufacturing establishments schools of iniquity, and calculated to exert a demoralizing influence on society, no doubt the prosperity of the business would augment the commercial resources of the State, and hold the artizans of Europe at defiance. So far from the assertion being supported by facts, that vice and immoral habits are the consequent inmates of manufacturing establishments, that industry and business habits of the workshop, are among the best methods of checking the intemperance of the indolent and licentiousness of the profligate.

Geology.

The eastern shore of lake Champlain, from ten to fifteen miles distance, the rocks belong to the transition class, and on the rivers are very considerable tracts of alluvial deposits. The ranges on the west side of the mountain, are, beginning at the lake,—1. Old red sand stone—2. Grey wack—3. Transition lime stone, alternating with Transition Argillite—4. Transition or Caciferous sand stone—5. Transition Argillite—6. Primitive Argillite—7. Sparry lime stone—8. Granular lime stone—9. Granular quartz, containing hematitic ore and manganese, and lying at the base of the Green Mountains, on the west side—10. Hornblende rock—11. Gneis, with alternating layers of granite,—Micha slate, constituting the middle ridge of the Green Mountain range, and extending in many places a considerable distance down the eastern side. On the east side of the mountain, the geological features are not so well known as on the west. Lime stone is found in many towns near Connecticut river; also argillaceous slate, which is extensively quarried at Vernon, Dummerston, and many other towns.

HISTORY OF VERMONT. 23

CHAPTER II.

The Discovery of Vermont.—Situation of Indian Tribes. —Indian Character.—Battle between the Algonquins and Iroquois.—Expedition against the Mohawks.—Discoveries, grants, and settlement on the American continent.—New-England and other colonies founded.— King William's War.—Destruction of Schenectady in 1790.—Queen Anne's War.—Burning of Deerfield in 1704.—Crown Point built in 1731.—Incursions of the French and Indians in the War of George the II. declared in 1744.—Encroachments of the French upon the English colonists, from Maine to the Mississippi.— Expedition against Canada, by William Johnson.—Massacre at Fort William Henry in 1757.—Change of British Ministry in 1758.—Abercrombie's Invasion and Defeat at Ticonderoga.—General Amherst takes the command of the American forces.—Captures Ticonderoga. —Expedition against the village of St. Francois, by Maj. Rogers.—Surrender of Canada to Great-Britain.

The first discovery of the interior of North America, by civilized man, was by Samuel Champlain, who sailed up the lake which now bears his name, in 1609. At that period, European settlements, in this part of New-England, had not commenced, nor were they until the English colonists arrived at Plymouth, in 1620, when the shores of New-England were first inhabited by civilized beings. The Indians occupied the whole country, for raising corn, hunting, and fishing. Their habitations and cultivated grounds were usually upon the rivers and plains, while the hills and mountains were resorted to for the chase; and to this use they appropriated the wilderness of Vermont. The Mohicans, a minor tribe of the Iroquois, whose principal residence was at Albany, claimed the jurisdiction, and had an occasional residence in Vermont. Antiquities of an Indian character are discovered in many parts of the State, particularly upon the largest rivers, and lake Champlain. On the island of South Hero, they had a settlement near the sand bar that crosses the lake into Milton; and another in Colchester, on what are denominated the Indian fields. Arrows and other utensils are frequently thrown up, on breaking the soil. The St. Francois Indians had a settlement of about fifty huts, and a considerable quantity of cleared land, on which they raised corn, in Swanton. They had also quite a station at Coos, now called Newbury, on their passage from the tribes in New-England to those upon lake Memphremagog. The settlers of the town of Clarendon derived their title from the Indians; and this was the only grant obtained from them in the State.

The principal tribes of Indians at this time, located in New-England, were those of the Pawtuckets, and their auxiliaries, the Agawams and Piscataquas: these had their principal residence near the mouth of the Merrimac river. The tribes inhabiting Massachusetts bay, were the Neponsetts and Nashuas—the Acumtucks resided at Deerfield. The eastern part of Rhode-Island, including Cape Cod, was inhabited by the Pokanockets. Here the grand Sachem lived, on the arrival of the English, holding his seat near mount Hope, in Bristol. On their coast the pilgrim fathers first landed, and were at one time charitably sustained by their kindness and attention, while at another, they were nearly destroyed by their valor. Various other tribes were scattered through New-England. A short time previous, to the arrival of the New-England Colony, a terrible pestilence, conjectured to be the yellow fever, had swept off more than half of their numbers. This event, so destructive to the natives, was very favorable to the Europeans establishing themselves, upon the American shores. The Tarateens or Abenaquies were located upon the Penobscot, Androscoggin and Saco rivers, in the north part of New-England. They removed afterwards, and settled on the river St. Francois, and were said to be the first Indians who become acquainted with the use of gun powder and fire arms. The Five Nations, who took their stations before the commencement of the English settlement, possessed the country from the eastern limits of Lake Erie to Lake Champlain. From the Kittatinny mountains, and the highlands, to Lake Ontario, and the Cataragui, or the St. Lawrence. The Mohawks settled on the Mohawk river, and held their chief residence about

18 miles from Schenectady, being the tribe adjoining those who passed the territory of Vermont. The Indians residing in Canada, when it was first discovered, were the Abgonquins, along the banks of the St. Lawrence, from Quebec to Montreal; and the Hurons, who were dispersed about the Lake, which bears their name. Those were some of the principal tribes and their allotted territories, who were engaged, in the controversies between the French and English colonies, and usually effected a passage, in their hostile encounters upon the waters of Lake Champlain.

The origin of the Indians cannot be determined by history, nor will calculation ever arrive at a probable certainty. Some writers have declared, that they were indigenous, whilst others maintain the opinion of their migration; but consider them the extremes of human depravity, and outcasts of the world. Criminations have been thrown upon them, they have been driven from their possessions, and the quietness of their dwellings have been interrupted by insolent invaders. Dissipation, introduced among them by their civilized neighbors, has brought on the pain of disappointment, and the conflict of barbarity.

The Indians are well formed, of a copper complexion, with long black hair, and high cheek bones. Their language is composed chiefly of natural sounds, and is deficient in such as are arbitrary. From a want of copiousness, it requires to be illustrated by many gestures; and abounds in metaphor, and allusion. They seem to be delighted on all possible occasions to make their meaning known by significant gestures. Hence hostilities are proclaimed, by sending their adversary some weapon of war. Among the Indians, the women were treated as brutes, rather than the companions of human beings. The contract of marriage was in fact a purchase, and so was considered by themselves. The savage, without tenderness, or refinement, does not look for pleasure, in the beauty, chastity and affection, or in the attachments, conversation and refined manners of the female, but in the labors and menial services she is able to perform. The character of the Indians may be properly compared to the aspect of an uncultivated country; whose pleasing variety and dreary

3

wildness alternately delight and amaze us. The Indian, unacquainted with civilization, exercises his inventions only for the immediate conveniences of life. He has no contested beauty to win by his gallantry, and no applause to expect from his refinements. His renown is placed in the hazard of his undertakings, and the success of their execution. To a mind fierce and implacable, and a resolution bordering upon desperation, the barren and inhospitable region, has no discouragement for his ambition; distance, no mitigation for his resentment. The Indian, accustomed to the speed of the chase, is active and enduring; the mountain, the river and the forest, are the scene of his delight, and the harvest of his wants. His body is weak for want of laborious exercise, which in civilized countries invigorates the mind, and gives energy to the system. In this rude condition, he scarcely exercises his reason, his ideas are confined to a narrow sphere, his intellect is limited and his emotions languid. His attention is employed about a few objects, which are only conducive to his present enjoyment. Thus, where nature's gifts are spontaneously bestowed, he dozes away his time, in spiritless apathy or senseless stupidity. His political regulations are few and unimportant, for the extension of his rights are no greater than the possessions of his toil. His lands are not cantoned for cultivation, but remain a wild for animals and game. He engages in war, not so much for interest as revenge; the desire of vengeance, which inflames the savage, resembles the instinct of a brute rather than the passions of man; he turns with fury upon the weapon which wounds him; as though endowed with sensensibility and life. His military operations are different from those of civilized nations. The glory of the soldier, is not in the attack of an open force—to surprise is the chief merit of the commander, and the pride of his followers—success obtained without blood, is considered a disgrace to a veteran savage. The torture which is inflicted upon a prisoner exceeds the utmost pains of sickness or natural decay. Insult and violence, which would shock the heart of depravity, are offered and endured without a look of pity or thought of regret. The burning stake, with all the horrors of dissolution, is welcomed, without a groan.

A display of fortitude in so dreadful a situation, is the noblest triumph of the Indian warrior. Freedom is the pride of his feelings. With him slavery is unknown, and like the Apostolic union, all things are possessed in common. His religion, like that of many of the eastern nations, consists in worshiping some visible objects, to which he ascribes the attributes of a God. The Indians in the territory of the United States, made no advances towards the discovery of letters. The only things they seemed desirous of recording, were the deeds of their warriors.—Whenever they were victorious, they made rough figures and imitations upon the trees, to represent the direction of their march, and the numbers they had captured and slain of their enemies: sometimes, their inscriptions were made upon rocks, but were confined to warlike affairs. Where West river, in this State, forms a junction with Connecticut river, several of these inscriptions remain. They are irregularly placed and rudely scratched upon a rock, and sunk but little below its surface; four of these represent the wild duck, and the fifth was probably designed to represent a fox or wolf. Ten or twelve figures of a superior workmanship, are wrought into the surface of a rock, at Bellows' Falls, in Rockingham. The heads of men, women and children, and some animals, are represented by these inscriptions. The outlines of these figures are awkward and badly executed; being sunk into the rock at least one third of an inch. What transactions they were intended to represent, tradition gives us no account. At the time Champlain founded the colony at Quebec, and circumnavigated the Lake which now bears his name, the Algonquins, a tribe inhabiting Canada, whose principal seat was at Hocklega, were at war with the powerful nation of the Iroquois. Champlain and his party of Indians of the Huron tribe, who had suffered severely from the inroads of the Iroquois, and two Frenchmen went on an expedition through Lakes Champlain and St. George, to avenge themselves upon their enemies. Being discovered upon the shores of the Lake, a skirmish took place. The Frenchmen were armed with muskets, which was the first time, probably, that the Iroquois had ever seen the effect of gun-powder, and the victory obtained over them, was complete. Fifty were killed and the remainder put to flight. This transaction gained for the new settlers the friendly attention of their Indian neighbors. The colony at Quebec, by reason of the Five Nations regaining their former ascendency over their ancient enemies, were full of apprehensions, that the time was not far distant, when they should be forced to abandon their country. The court of France interfering in their distress, sent a detachment of four hundred troops, which in the course of two years were reinforced with a regiment more, and went out on an expedition against the Mohawks, one of the Five Nations, in 1665. This detachment marched by the way of lake Champlain, on snow shoes, and came very near perishing, when they accidentally fell in with a settlement at Schenectady, and were saved by the interposition of Corlear, one of its inhabitants. After another expedition into the country of the Mohaws, attended with great expense and fatigue, but with little advantage, a general peace was concluded in 1667. During this season of peace, M. Courcelles, the Governor of Canada, was not inactive.— He foresaw that peace with savages would be of short duration. Accordingly he made preparations for the future defence of Canada. To prevent the irruptions of the Iroquois into his province by the way of lake Champlain, he built, in 1665, the forts Chambly and Sorel. Such were the inhabitants of America at the time of its discovery and settlement: a race of uncivilized and ferocious savages. The first attempts at forming a settlement within the present limits of the United States, was by the French, in 1562. This colony, commenced by Jasper Coligni, at Port Royal, was probably designed as an asylum from religious persecution, which then raged in France. Fifty years after the discovery of America by Christopher Columbus, and forty-seven years before the discovery of lake Champlain and the green mountains of Vermont, by Samuel Champlain, this settlement was commenced, which, however, was entirely broken up. The first permanent settlement commenced in the United States was under the direction of Christopher Newton, at Jamestown, in Virginia, 1606. The Dutch began the colonization of New-York in 1614; and the Pilgrim colonists, consisting of 120 persons, began their settlement at Plymouth, in 1620, under the direction of Mr. Carver. The whole number of inhabitants among all the colonists, in 1620, did not exceed 2600. A general convention of the English colonies was held at Albany in the year 1684. Their object was to guard against the incursion of the French, and against the Iroquois tribes, who were under the influence and instigation of the French Jesuits. The storm was averted by a treaty of peace, trade, and alliance, entered upon by Howard, president of the convention, and the Five Nations. In treating upon the events which transpired within the limits of the New-Hampshire grants, it will be necessary to describe the transactions of the colonies, which led to the frequent navigation of lake Champlain and traversing the then wilderness region of the green mountains. The wars occasioned by the vices and follies of the Kings of England and France, produced most of the controversies and sufferings experienced by the early settlers. The colonists engaged in warfare whenever the European governments were at issue with one another. Thus they had not only to share the troubles of the mother countries, but also the barbarism and vengeance of the savages.

The affairs of the colonies were always in confusion until a pacification between France and England took place. The first hostilities between the settlers of Canada and the British Colonies, originated on William's accession to the throne of England, in 1689, which terminated in the peace of Ryswic, in 1697. Queen Anne's war, so called, commenced in 1702, and continued to the peace of Utretcht, in 1713. The third controversy was declared by George II. in 1744, and continued until the preliminaries of peace were signed between France and England, at Aix-la-Chapelle, in 1748. The last conflict between these powers, anterior to the American revolution, was formally declared by Great-Britain in 1756, and was reciprocated the same year on the part of France. Louis XIV., king of France, in attempting to support the fugitive sovereign of England, kindled a war between his country and Great-Britain. The French in Canada directed their arms against New-England and New-York, and instigated the Indians to join in these hostilities. In 1689, three expeditions were fitted out in the dead of winter; one against New-York, a second against New-Hampshire, and the third against Maine. That against New-York was put under the direction of D'Aillebout, who had under his command about two hundred Frenchmen and fifty Indians. Being well acquainted with the country, they proceded by the way of lake Champlain, and after a march of twenty-two days, in the most reduced circumstances, arrived in the month of January at Schenectady, a village upon the Mohawk. The inhabitants, although notified of the designs of the enemy, felt perfectly secure, considering it impracticable for any men to march from Canada at this inclement season of the year, bearing their provisions on their backs. On Saturday night, about 11 o'clock, February 8, 1690, they entered the village whilst the inhabitants were reposing in profound sleep, and invested with small parties every house at the same time. The noise and violence of the onset had scarcely awakened them before the most inhuman barbarities were perpetrated. They set fire to their houses, and men, women and children were dragged from their beds and inhumanly murdered. Sixty persons fell by the hands of the enemy, twenty-seven were carried away into captivity, and the remainder fled naked to Albany, through a deep snow, twenty-five of whom lost their limbs through the severity of the weather. They were pursued by a party of young men from Albany, who took twenty of their number prisoners. To avenge this atrocious and unprecedented outrage, an expedition was fitted out of 2000 troops to penetrate Canada, by the way of lake Champlain, and attack Montreal at the same time that a naval armament should invest Quebec. This plan, however, failed, without accomplishing any thing. The troops did not cross the lake, for want of boats and provisions. The undertaking terminating so unpropitiously, that the Five Nations received very unfavorable impressions towards the English colonies. To retrieve which, and keep alive their hostility towards the French, Major Schuyler, of Albany, placed himself at the head of a party of Mohawks, passed through lake Champlain, and made a vigorous irruption upon the French settlement on the river Sorel. In this encounter about three hundred of the enemy were slain. This invasion of Canada excited the veteran Frontenac to return them a call by the same way. Arriving January 15th, 1695, they attacked the Mohawk castle, lost thirty of their men, but carried the Indian fortress, with the capture of 300 Mohawks. The prosecution of hostilities in the reign of Queen Anne, was marked with the most savage brutality on the part of the French and Indians, in their excursion against Deerfield, in the winter of 1704.

A force of about three hundred, under the command of De Rouville and his two brothers, took their route by the way of lake Champlain, until they came to the French (now called Onion) river—passing up that stream, thence over to Connecticut river, on which they travelled upon the ice to Deerfield. This place was slightly fortified by two or three garrisons, which were nearly covered by snow drifts. The party approached on the 29th day of February, and embraced the opportunity about two hours before day, when the sentinels were all asleep, to rush on to the attack. Entering the house of Rev Mr. Williams, they seized and bound him, butchered two of his children and a black servant, before his eyes. Having conquered the place and killed forty-seven of its inhabitants, they set fire to it, and departed the same day in great haste. A skirmish ensued, but the enemy were completely successful, and carried 112 of the inhabitants of Deerfield into captivity.— Attempts were further made at the reduction of Canada; in one of which, the troops to attack Montreal advanced as far as lake George, under the command of General Nicholson; but returned, on account of the wreck of the fleet that was to co-operate with them on the French lines. A treaty of peace, concluded at Utrecht, put an end to the difficulties. France ceded Newfoundland and Nova Scotia to England, and stipulated that the subjects of France, in hostile to her, in Canada and other places, should hereafter give no hindrance to the Five Nations, nor any other nation of Indians who are at peace with Great-Britain. The French now determined on making nearer approaches to Albany, while the attention of New-York was engaged on the western lakes. Accordingly, in the year 1731, they sailed through lake Champlain with a considerable force, and erected a fort at Crown point. This was a well devised measure to promote their own interest. The lake had been a thorough-fare, through which their expeditions against Schenectady, Mohawk castle, and Deerfield, had been directed. In all attempts at the conquest of Canada, lake Champlain was the contemplated way for making such excursions. A fort at the straits of lake Champlain, securing the whole navigation of it, commanding a large portion of the English and Indian frontiers, furnishing a magazine of arms and ammunition to supply troops, providing an asylum for the Indians when retreating from their plundering and murdering expeditions against the English frontiers, was an establishment of the highest importance. The garrison was first stationed on the east side of the lake, now in the town of Addison; but afterwards they established it on a peninsula on the west side, now called Crown point. During the war declared by George the II. which continued four years, from 1744, the only achievements in the then wilderness vale of Champlain, were by scouting and navigating parties of French and Indians, who spread destruction and dismay, by plundering, killing and scalping wherever they could find defenceless individuals or settlements. At Charlestown, on Connecticut river, a fort had been built some time previous to the commencement of the present war, to protect the frontier settlements of New-Hampshire. In the spring of the year 1747, after having killed and captivated some of the inhabitants, and destroyed their cattle in this place, the enemy made attempts to take the fort and destroy the settlement. A large party of French and Indians, under the command of M. Debeline, commenced the attack.— Captain Stevens, a bold and successful officer, resisted their encroachments with effect. The next movement was to set fire to the fences, log-houses, and other buildings adjoining, and burn down the fort. For two days this method of assault was continued, and then they prepared a wheel carriage, and loaded it with dry faggots, which was moved before them to set fire to the fort. These attempts were frustrated by the bravery and discernment of Stevens and his men. Debeline urged the garrison to surrender, but was answered, that the fort would be defended to the last extremity. An offer was then made, that if Stevens would sell them provisions, they would depart; to which he replied, that he would give five bushels of corn for any captive they would bind themselves by a hostage to bring back from Canada. On receiving this answer, Debeline withdrew his troops to Crown point.— Sir Charles Knowles, of the British navy, presented Capt Stevens, for this distinguished act of bravery, with an elegant sword. Small parties of Indians continued killing and captivating the settlers, pillaging their property, and burning their dwellings, during the continuance of this war.

The most advanced fortress, at Williamstown, was besieged in 1746, by an army of 900 French and Indians, who continued the siege twenty-eight hours, until the garrison, consisting of thirty-three persons, had expended all their ammunition, and were obliged to surrender. Colonel Hawks, the English commandant, lost but one, and the enemy forty-five. At this time, encroachments were making upon Nova Scotia, a considerable part of which the French laid claim to, and were erecting fortifications in several places. Crown point was settling in the north, and in the west attempts were not only making to complete a line of forts from the head of the St. Lawrence to the Mississippi, but they were advancing far into Virginia. A circumstance, which served to bring on the war, was, the alledged intrusion of the Ohio Company upon the territory of the French. This company, consisting of individuals from London and Virginia, had obtained a grant of 600,000 acres of land on or near the Ohio river, for carrying on the fur trade and settling the country. The Governor of Canada, supposing they would deprive him of the this trade, and prevent communications between Canada and Louisiana, claimed, by a former grant, the country east of the Ohio river to the Alleghany mountains, and forbid encroachments by the English. The French Governor manifested his hostile determination, by seizing several of the English traders and carrying them away captives, which aroused the indignation of the Twightwee Indians, who, by the way of retaliation, took several of the French traders and sent them to Pennsylvania. Complaints were laid before Governor Didwiddie, who presented the subject to the Assembly, which ordered a messenger (George Washington, afterwards the illustrious benefactor of the United States, being the person chosen) to attend and settle the dispute; but the attempt proved fruitless, and all prospect of a reconciliation terminated. Hostilities were commenced without a formal declaration of war, which happened near the first settlement of Vermont.

Among the expeditions fitted out against different places upon the Canadian frontiers, was one against Crown Point, under Colonel William Johnson. The Provincial troops, to the amount of 6,000, were ordered to rendezvous at Albany. The command of the expedition was given to Generals Johnson and Lyman, who collected an army together before the first of June, 1757, and were joined by Hendrick, a Mohawk Sachem, with a considerable body of Indians. The main army under the direction of General Lyman, marched as far as the carrying place, four miles from the south end of lake George.— Fort Edward was built at the carrying place, where General Johnson arrived from Albany, with the provisions, artillery and batteaux, necessary for the enterprise, and they were in readiness to advance to the lake at the latter end of August. He proceeded from Albany to the south end of lake George, where all were engaged in making preparations for crossing the lake. The army was stationed on rising ground, having a thick woods on each side of them, the lake in the rear, and a breast work of trees in front. The Indian scouts, while matters were thus conditioned, brought intelligence that a large body of the enemy were advancing by South Bay, from Ticonderoga, to Fort Edward, where General Johnson had stationed a garrison of about five hundred troops, under the command of Colonel Blanchard. One of the expresses sent to Colonel Blanchard, returned in the silence of the night, with tidings that the enemy had advanced within four miles of Fort Edward. A council of officers was summoned, by whom it was concluded, that Colonels Williams and Whiting, with Hendrick, the Mohawk commander, and his Indians, should be detached, with a party of one thousand men, to intercept the enemy. The army of the enemy, for the purpose of cutting off the garrison at Fort Edward, marched from Ticonderoga under the command of Baron Dieskau, and received information that it was strongly fortified, but that the army at the lake were destitute of arms and cannon. He resolved to attack the main camp, which was discovered by the advanced parties, at the distance of three miles. An ambush was immediately laid to surprise the party, which was completely successful. Colonel Williams, Hendrick, and many other officers and men were slain. Those who escaped this fatal ambuscade made safe their return to the corps under Colonel Whiting, the successor in command. The victors pursued the fugitives within about thirty rods of the camp—made a little halt, and began the attack by a brisk and heavy firing of platoons. They fought with great resolution, after a few moments trepidation, and the reception of a few fires. The Canadians and Indians were so intimidated at the firing of the artillery, that they retired in confusion behind the trees and bushes. Baron Dieskau, finding that he could make no impression from any movement, to force a passage, was obliged to abandon the attempt. The provincials seeing the confusion of the enemy, leaped their breastworks, and attacked them with such resolution as to put them to an entire rout. About 700 were killed, and 30 taken prisoners. Baron Dieskau was found among the number who were slain. The loss of the provincials was about two hundred, principally from the detachment under Col. Williams, together with forty Indians. As a detachment under Captain McGinnes was marching the next day from Fort Edward, to reinforce the camp, when near the spot where Williams was defeated, discovered between 3 and 400 of the enemy, sitting by the ford. He attacked them with such impetuosity, that after a severe contest, they fled in the utmost confusion. The brave commander received a mortal wound in the contest. Nothing of further importance occurred at this place, except the erection of a fort at lake George, called Fort William Henry, and the completion of the works at Fort Edward. The troops returned to their respective colonies, except those retained to keep the garrison.

That part of the campaign for 1756, which related to the fortresses upon Lake George, was committed to the brave and active Montcalm. He concentrated his forces at Ticonderoga, consisting of Regulars, Canadians and Indians, during the absence of most of the British troops, and passing up Lake George, commenced the siege of Fort William Henry with 500 men. At this time, General Webb, with the English army consisting of 4 or 5000 men, was encamped at Fort Edward. Colonel Monroe, an English officer, had under his command at Lake George a force of 2200 regulars and provincials, a part of whom were stationed at Fort William Henry and the remainder at a fortified place afterwards made the site of Fort George. After some skirmishing, the batteries of the French were opened on the same ground where the village of Caldwell now stands. M. Levi and the Chevalier La Corne stationed two divisions of the army in the woods, south of Monroe's position, to cut off the communication with Fort Edward, and an advanced party lay on the road near an extensive morass, about five miles towards that Fort. Monroe defended his precarious situation from the 3d to the 9th of August, expecting relief from General Webb, at Fort Edward, who had received pressing solicitations for relief, from the besieged, which he treated with the most emphatic and inhuman indifference. Many of Monroe's guns burst, and his ammunition expended, he was therefore obliged to surrender. On the 9th, articles of capitulation were signed, the terms of which were, that the vanquished should retain their arms, and be escorted to Fort Edward. The possession of the works were immediately given up to the French; when the Indians rushed instantly over the parapet, and seized such articles as they could, with impunity; then they commenced their depredations upon the baggage of the officers, which was represented as a violalation of the terms of the capitulation. But, in contempt of this, the Indians attached to the French army, fell upon the defenceless prisoners, and massacreed whoever came in their way. The whole garrison, consisting of two thousand men, women and children, out of which fifteen hundred were killed or made prisoners, and many of them never returned. Major Putnam was despatched with a company of rangers to watch the movements of Montcalm; but he arrived at the shore of the Lake just after the French had embarked on their return to Ticonderoga. The prospect was awful and horrid in the highest degree. The fort was demolished—the barracks and out-houses were a heap of ruins—the cannon, stores and utensils were carried away—the fires were still burning, with smoke and stench suffocating and offensive. Numberless fragments of human skulls, bones, and carcases half consumed, were still broiling and frying in the decaying fires. Dead bodies mangled with scalping knives, in all the wantonness of Indian barbarity, were every where to be seen.

More than one hundred women, inhumanly stabbed and butchered, lay naked on the ground, with their bowels torn out and still weltering in their gore. Some had their throats cut, and with others their brains were oozing out, where the hatchet had cleaved their heads. Destruction and horror every where appeared—a spectacle too diabolical and horrid to be described or endured. A most fortunate change for the safety of the Colonies and the honor of the British arms, took place in the English Ministry in 1758. The celebrated Lord Chatham was now placed at the head of the administration, who animated the British council and invigorated the energies of the Colonies, that were exhausted and discouraged by a series of ill planned and unfortunate expeditions. The English met with success in almost every encounter, until Canada was entirely subdued. Circular letters were addressed to the Colonial governors by the prime minister, by which they were assured of the determination of the ministry to send a large force to America, and called upon them to raise as many troops as their numbers and circumstances would permit. Massachusetts and Connecticut together furnished 15,000 men, who were ready for service in May. An expedition was fitted out this year, 1758, against Ticonderoga, under the direction of General Abercrombie, commander in chief of the British forces in America.— His troops, amounting to 16,000 strong, were conveyed across lake George by means of one thousand and thirty-five boats, and landed under the cover of a heavy artillery, without opposition. The English General advanced towards the fort as the French retired through an impassable woods. On approaching the fort, Lord Howe was killed in a skirmish with an inconsiderable number of the enemy. The army pressed zealously on to revenge his death, when 300 of the French were killed and one hundred taken prisoners. Information was communicated to Abercrombie, that a reinforcement of 3000 men were immediately expected: therefore he determined to storm the fort, before the arrival of his artillery. The expedition was abandoned after four hours of severe fighting, with the loss, on the part of the assailants, of 1941. But few of the enemy were killed, and most of these were shot through the head; their bodies being defended by the breast work. General Amherst succeeded Abercrombie as commander in chief in the campaign of 1759. He led on his forces, the 22d of July, against Ticonderoga, which surrendered soon after his arrival. The enemy, afterwards evacuating Crown point, returned to the Isle Aux Noix. General Amherst, relinquishing his successful pursuit, marched his army back to Crown point, where he encamped for the winter. Measures were concerted, in the mean time, to make the enemy feel the resentment of the Colonies, on account of the brutal ravages of the Indians upon the frontiers. The St. Francois tribe, settled on the St. Lawrence in 1703, had for a long time committed their bloody depredations upon the provinces of New-Hampshire and Massachusetts. Major Rogers, a bold and successful officer from the province of New-Hampshire, was appointed by Gen. Amherst to proceed with two hundred men in batteaux down lake Champlain, and from thence to the Indian village, and there revenge themselves upon these merciless cannibals, who had so dastardly and promiscuously murdered men, women and children—burnt their dwellings and destroyed their effects. After several misfortunes by the way, they came in sight of the town on the evening of the 8th of October, 1759.— He then ordered his men to refresh themselves, while he, dressed in the Indian manner, took an interpreter, and went out to reconnoitre the town. Finding them engaged in a great dance, he returned at 2 o'clock. About 4 o'clock, on the breaking up of their powwow, Rogers rushed into the town, knocked down, shot and killed in real Indian style, all who came in his way. The settlement contained 300 inhabitants, of which 200 were slain and 20 were taken prisoners; every thing was destroyed or taken away that could be, and the place was reduced to ashes. Several hundred scalps were seen on poles, waving in the air; two hundred guineas, a silver image weighing ten pounds, together with a quantity of wampum, and clothing and provisions, were found. The assailants suffered greatly, from hunger, on their return by the way of Memphremagog to Charlestown. Some of their number were lost by the annoyance of the enemy, and thirty-six died. While Rogers was engaged in subduing the Indians on the St. Lawrence, General Amherst was preparing to march his army against the forts and settlements in Canada. The superiority of a naval force had as yet secured to the enemy the command of the lake. Amherst, on ascertaining their strength and situation at the Isle Aux Noix, directed Captain Loring to construct, with the greatest despatch, a sloop of sixteen guns and a boat sufficient for carrying six large cannon. These vessels, together with a brigantine, were completed and manned on the eleventh of October, when the army, with the commander, embarked in batteaux, to engage the enemy. The weather became so tempestuous, they were obliged to land the next day on the western side of the lake. Captain Loring, in the mean time sailing down the lake, discovered the French fleet. He gave chase to them, drove their vessels into a bay, where two were sunk and the other was run aground by the crew, who escaped into the woods. One of the vessels was repaired and taken away by Loring, who had so far succeeded as to leave but one schooner remaining to the French. The army again re-embarked, and proceeded down the lake; but the General, finding the season for action had elapsed, and the severity of the winter coming on, considered it impossible to engage in a new expedition without endangering his army or running too great a risk of not accomplishing his object. He therefore returned to the bay, where his men had been sheltered from the storm, and marched to Crown Point for winter quarters. A new fortress and three new out works were erected here, for the more effectual defence of the place. In concentrating the provincial forces, to proceed to Montreal on the last English campaign against Canada, in 1760, the business was committed to Colonel Haviland. To facilitate these operations, Amherst directed that a road should be opened from Number Four, on Connecticut river, across the green mountains, to Crown Point. Colonel Goff, with a New-Hampshire regiment, performed this service. The road was begun two miles north of the fort at Number Four, and completed for twenty-six miles, where they discovered a path which led to Otter Creek, and a good road from thence to the lake. On the 13th of August the forces under the command of Haviland proceeded down the lake and took the Isle Aux Noix. In effecting it, but little resistance was shown, and few were slain in the contest. The post was deserted and the forts at St. Johns and Chambly became an easy conquest. They then crossed over to Montreal, which surrendered on the 8th of September, 1760, together with all the French settlements in this part of America. During the continuance of six years war, but two battles were fought in the valley of lake Champlain. The first at lake George, where Dieskau was vanquished and Johnson successful; the second at Ticonderoga, in which Abercrombie was repulsed and Montcalm defended his post. The population of the British provinces, afterwards erected into the Republic of America, so far as enumeration had been made, amounted to 1,499,000. Boston was the most populous town, containing 15,000—New-York 12,000, Philadelphia 13,000, and Charleston between 5 and 6,000.

On reviewing the operations of the Colonial wars, a few remarks upon their rise, and moral and political effects, may be worthy of attention. The Europeans first settled their country with a determination to secure their rights and make a permanent residence on the lands of which they took possession. But the natives, alarmed at these encroachments, became jealous and resentful. Controversies about property gradually resolved themselves into open hostilities, attended with all that cruelty inseparable from the Indian passions and habits. The interest and mutual hatred between the French and English sovereigns, furnished another cause for these wars. Whenever they supposed it would be for their interest to involve their kingdoms in the calamities of war, the Colonies were required to join in the cruelties of those bloody contests.

The *moral* effect of these wars tended greatly to debase and eradicate every principle of justice, humanity and candor from the mind, and establish feelings of malevolence, revenge and injustice. Men who were endeavoring to destroy, could not possibly wish to assist one another: instead of this, they were continually cultivating a spirit of abhorrence and revenge. The effect of these wars on the settlement and agricultural prosperity, was still more detrimental. The people were obliged to observe a debilitating caution and slowness in advancing their settlements into the country; and so fearful were they of being destroyed in their advances on the frontiers, that a proposal for locating and settling a township at Coos, (now Newbury) in 1752, was abandoned, on the St. Francois Indians refusing this privilege to the public authorities of Massachusetts and New-Hampshire.

Their *political* effects operated very injuriously upon the Colonies, and kept them in a state of absolute dependence. The governments were embarrassed—necessary and useful manufactures were checked—commerce and trade were restricted; and finally, they were designed to keep the intellectual powers of the people in a state of imbecility and ignorance.

CHAPTER III.

A View of the Civil Policy from 1760 to 1775.—First Settlement in Vermont.—Grants from New-Hampshire.—Proceedings of New-York occasion disturbance among the settlers.—American War commenced.—Crown Point and Ticonderoga taken by Colonel Allen.—General Montgomery invades Canada.—Allen taken prisoner.—Surrender of the Forts at Chambly and St. Johns.—Montreal given up.—General Prescott taken.—Flight of Carleton.—Arnold and Montgomery arrive at Quebec.—Repulse at the seige of that City.—Disaster at the Cedars.—The Americans retreat from Canada, under General Sullivan.—Defeat of the Americans upon lake Champlain.—The English Army land at Crown Point, and return to Canada.—General Burgoyne appointed to the command of the British Army.—Invades the United States.—Invests Ticonderoga.—St. Clair leaves the works.—Hubbardton Battle.—The American Vessels destroyed at Skeensborough.—Opposition of New-England to Burgoyne.—Victory at Bennington.—Transactions at lake George.—Battle at Saratoga.—Defeat and Surrender of the Royal Army.

No settlements were made in Vermont until the inhabitants of New-England, New-York and Canada had proceeded by regular advances into its sequestered bounds. The Governor of New-York had made a grant of land to Godfrey Dellius, in 1796. This tract extended from the northern part of Saratoga to Willsborough, about 70 miles in length and 12 miles in width from Hudson's river on the east; but was afterwards vacated by the government of New-York. Another tract was granted in the south-east corner of the State, consisting of 100,000 acres, in 1716; but no settlement was made upon it until 1724, and this was nothing but a garrisoned station. At Crown Point a settlement was begun by the French, in 1731; yet it was continually exposed to ravages of hostile parties and the cruelties of the Indians, which rendered the settlement of this State very slow and uncertain. However, upon the reduction of Canada, the frontiers of the other provinces were no longer exposed to the ravages of the French and Indians. This afforded a favorable opportunity for settlers to establish themselves upon the new lands and advance their fortunes by clearing them up and raising produce.— The soil was very productive and prospects encouraging. Accordingly numerous applications were made for grants of new townships. The divisional lines between New-Hampshire and Massachusetts being established in 1740, the former concluded their jurisdiction extended as far west as Massachusetts had claimed; that is, within twenty miles of Hudson river. Fort Dummer, erected by New-Hampshire, on the west side of Connecticut river, was considered as coming within the jurisdiction of that State. Not doubting from these circumstances, that the jurisdiction of New-Hampshire extended beyond Connecticut river, the Governor made a grant of land, in 1749, of the township of Bennington, six miles square and twenty miles east of Hudson's river and six miles north of Massachusetts line. Several other towns were chartered in the course of four or five years. War breaking out between Great-Britain and France, put a stop to any further grants until the conquest of Canada. By frequently passing through these lands on the military road from Charlestown to Crown Point, their situation and fertility became very generally known, and under the direction of the Governor and Council of New-Hampshire, one hundred and thirty-eight townships of six miles square were granted on the west side of Connecticut river, extending within 20 miles of Hudson's river, and to the eastern shore of lake Champlain. Governor Wentworth received a large amount of money, besides a reserve of 500 acres of land in each town. These proceedings roused the feelings of the government of New-York, as they, by the grants of Charles II. to his brother the Duke of York, extended their claim to all the land west of Connecticut river and east of Delaware bay, and intended to have the profits arising from the disposal of the same. Governor Colden, of New-York, issued his proclamation in December, 1763, asserting the validity of the former grants and commanding the sheriff of Albany to make a return of the names of all the people who, under color of the New-Hampshire grants, had taken possession of any lands to the west of Connecticut river. The Governor of New-Hampshire issued another proclamation to prevent the effects of the foregoing manifesto and to quiet the feelings of the settlers, declaring the grant to the Duke of York obsolete, and that the diligent should be confirmed in their grants and disturbers of the peace punished. After such assurances, the honest purchasers had no idea the contest for jurisdiction would ever affect the property of individuals. New-York, as if distrusting the grant to the Duke of York, applied to the crown for a decision of the controversy. The King, on hearing the representation purporting to be made at the request of the settlers, concluded it would be for their advantage to be annexed to the colony of New-York, ordered, on the 20th of July, 1764, that the western banks of Connecticut river, where it enters Massachusetts bay, as far north as the 45th degree of north latitude, *to be* the boundary line between the provinces of New-Hampshire and New-York. This division, made without the sanction of any evidence, occasioned no serious apprehensions among the people. They concluded that it only gave the future jurisdiction of their territory to New-York; to which they would cheerfully acquiesce, but had no idea of its affecting the title of their lands, purchased under grants from the crown. The Governor of New-Hampshire, dissenting to the change, but finally yielding the contest, issued his proclamation to the settlers, recommending obedience to the authority of New-York. A construction very different from that of the settlers was given by the authorities of New-York. They claimed that the meaning of the order intended that which had been, as well as what now is, the western limits of New-Hampshire, and that the grants of New-Hampshire were void of course. In exercising their jurisdiction, the Governor of New-York divided it into four counties, Albany and Charlotte on the west, Cumberland and Gloucester on the east side of the mountain; and established courts of justice in each of them. A surrender of the charters from New-Hampshire was demanded, and new grants, at great expense, were ordered to be taken out from the authorities of New-York. Few, however, complied with the requisition. Grants were made to new applicants, who instituted actions of ejectment and recovered without opposition, in the courts at Albany. But to carry their judgments into execution, and eject the inhabitants from their houses and lands, was difficult, and met with a spirited opposition. The government perceiving how contemptuously their proceedings were viewed, called upon the people to assist the sheriff in the execution of his duty. But it was soon found that no dependence could be placed upon this force; for as soon as the settlers appeared in arms, the militia deserted and the sheriff found himself alone. The opposition, on account of these transactions, became so bold and universal that some of the officers became sufferers in attempting to carry their judgments into effect. At length no officer of New-York dared to dispossess any occupant from his farm. The courts at Albany continued to render judgments, which were never carried into effect.

Associations were formed among the settlers for the purpose of giving greater force to their resistance, and finally a convention of delegates from the towns on the west side of the mountain was called. This body, after consulting upon the subject, chose Samuel Robinson an agent to represent their grievances to the court of Great Britain, and if possible, obtain a confirmation of the New-Hampshire grants. The result of his mission proved favorable to their desires. The King and Council granted the request of the petitioners. By this, the Governor of the province of New-York was required and commanded, from the time being, not to make any grants of lands described in said report, until his majesty's pleasure should be further known concerning the same. This mandate gave them the fullest confidence that their lands would not be regranted. However, they were soon disappointed, for those orders were contemptuously disregarded. The Governor made an attempt to conciliate the minds of the people to his regulations, by writing to the Rev. Mr. Dewy, and the inhabitants of Bennington, desiring them to state the causes of their unlawful proceedings, and proffering to the settlers conciliatory terms, as the circumstances would justify, with safety to those they might send on the business, except Warner, Allen, and three others, who had been leaders in the opposition to New-York, and had stimulated the public mind by their writings and councils.— Answers were given by the excepted persons, in explanation of their motives and conduct, and two persons, James and Stephen Fay, were delegated to transact this business.— Much kindness was shewn them, and stipulations entered upon that all public and private prosecutions should be suspended until his majesty's pleasure should be known. While these regulations were advancing, certain persons settled upon Otter Creek were disturbed by one Cockburn, a noted surveyor, who undertook to make pitches of lands upon their possessions. The inhabitants pursued and overtook him and his party at Vergennes, where they dispossessed Colonel Reed and his coadjutor, one Benzell, of a saw-mill and other property, that was illegally obtained. But these persons were delivered up in conformity to the wishes of the government of New-York, and honorably dismissed. During this asperity of feelings, the government of New-York passed an act the most despotic and minatory of any thing which had ever appeared in the British colonies. It provided that if any offenders shall not surrender themselves pursuant to the Governor's orders, they shall be adjudged and attainted of felony by the verdict and judgment, without the benefit of the clergy. Albany was the place of trial for all crimes committed in the grants. A proclamation was issued by the Governor of New-York, proffering 50 pounds as a reward for apprehending Ethan Allen, Seth Warner, and six others. Such increased violence of proceedings terminated every prospect of reconciliation. Resolutions were adopted by committees at their meetings in the counties of Albany and Charlotte, declaring their readiness to defend those denominated rioters, and to use their best endeavors for keeping up the administration of justice. The persons proscribed announced their determination still stronger to kill and destroy every one who should presume to be accessary to their capture. About this time a scheme was concerted by Colonel Skeen, to evade the government of New-York, by uniting the settlers and forming a province under the authority of the King. He accordingly received a commission as governor of Crown Point and Ticonderoga, and in March, 1775, informed his agent that he should call on the inhabitants to ascertain their sentiments on the subject of submission to the royal authority.

On the meeting of Congress in 1774, they advised their constituents to maintain their liberty against British aggression, which stopped the prosecution of business in courts held by the authority of the crown. The officers of the court holden at Westminster, in Cumberland county, were refused admittance to the court house, which they, with the sheriff and an armed force, undertook to accomplish by violence about 11 o'clock at night, and in the contest one man was killed and several wounded by the assailants. This rash proceeding occasioned the assembling of a large concourse of people the next day. A jury of inquest returned a verdict that murder had been committed by the adherents of the court. Several of the officers were committed to jail in Northampton, Massachusetts, who were afterwards released from imprisonment by the chief justice of New-York. Resolutions were passed by the committees of the people assembled at Westminster, in April, 1775, stating that it was the duty of the inhabitants to resist the government of New-York, until such times as they shall have security for their lives and property, and an opportunity for representing their grievances to the King and Council, together with the remonstrance against such unlawful acts, and a petition to be removed from such an oppressive power, and either be united with some other state, or formed into a separate government, as might seem best.

At this stage of irritation between the settlers and their opponents, the American war commenced at Lexington, April 19th, 1775, which turned the attention of both parties from their own contest to one of more importance and grandeur. A long time before hostilities commenced, dissensions existed between Great Britain and her colonies. These difficulties arose on account of the absolute despotism in making laws to bind the colonists in all cases whatsoever, and taxing them without their consent. As soon as the controversy commenced, the necessity of securing the forts of Crown Point and Ticonderoga, for reasons that they had suffered much when these were in the possession of the French, and the probability that they would be equally as fatal in the hands of the English, became evident, and engaged the attention of many individuals in the province. The plan was projected by Messrs. Dean, Wooster and Parsons, of Connecticut, but they were in want of money to defray the necessary expenses of the expedition, which they obtained by way of a loan to the amount of 1800 dollars, from the government of Connecticut. Several officers proceeded to Salisbury, purchased a quantity of powder and ball, and went to engage Ethan Allen at Bennington, in the enterprise. Allen joined Dean and others at Castleton, having a small quantity of provisions, with a force of 270 men, and then took proper measures to learn the state of the works and strength of Ticonderoga.

Colonel Arnold, from Connecticut, received a commission and instructions to enlist 400 men for the reduction of Ticonderoga, then represented to be guarded only by 40 soldiers, and containing large stores and munitions of war. The situation of this fortress was ascertained by Capt. Phelps, who, attired in the dress of a poor man, enquired for a barber to shave him: he entered within the walls, and appearing very awkward, had an opportunity to discover the situation of things, and passed unsuspected.

They arrived at Champlain, opposite Ticonderoga, on the 9th of May. Allen and Arnold embarked with eighty-three men, and landed near the works. At the dawn of day a dispute arose concerning the right of seniority, when it was agreed, upon receiving the advice of their friends, that both should enter the fort together, with their men in the rear, which they accordingly did, and so unexpectedly was the approach of a hostile force that no other resistance was shown than the snapping of a sentinel's gun. Capt. De la Place, as soon as he appeared, was ordered to surrender. He demanded upon what authority they required it. "I demand it (said Allen) in the name of the great Jehovah and the continental Congress." Incapable of making any defence or resistance, the British Captain surrendered the garrison, which consisted of only three officers and forty-three privates. Colonel Seth Warner and a part of the men repaired immediately to Crown Point, which was garrisoned with but twelve men and a sergeant, who surrendered on the first summons. A detachment of continental troops seized the fortress at Skeensborough, captured Maj. Skeen, and took possession of his mansion house.

To secure the command of lake Champlain, an armed sloop must be taken. Arnold therefore manned and armed a schooner found at South Bay, then sailed and captured the armed vessel at the outlet of the lake. Thus, without bloodshed, two important posts, a British captain, sergeant, forty-three privates, and two hundred cannon, some mortars and howitzers, with a large quantity of military and naval stores, were taken. Gov. Carleton, surprised at the forwardness of the Americans in the defence of their country, endeavored to raise a force from the Canadians, by proclaiming martial law; but almost every man refused to interfere in the affray.

The Bishop of Quebec was next called upon to employ the influence of his sacerdotal character to rouse the people to arms, but he passed it off as being inconsistent with the canons of the catholic church. He in the next place attempted to bring the Indian rage and ferocity into the contest, but they did not wish to take up the hatchet and injure a people with whose affairs and quarrels they had no connexion. On the intelligence that the Canadians and Indians would not engage in the war, the American Congress concluded that the present was the most favorable time to destroy the British power and effect a union between Canada and the provinces, in the same revolution, as the Canadians could not sustain their neutrality any longer than the arrival of forces competent to force them to submission. The command of 2000 men fitted out for this expedition, was assigned to General Schuyler. Information was soon received that Carleton was prepared to oppose their undertakings, and that several armed vessels lay at St. Johns, filled with forces and munitions of war, which would probably get the immediate command of the lake. This project being communicated to Gov. Carleton, he despatched about 800 men to strengthen St. Johns on the river Sorel, a station commanding the usual entrance into Canada. Montgomery, a young officer of splendid talents, was ordered to move down the lake with his troops and prevent the passage of the vessels into the lake. General Schuyler pursued on from Albany, though in an ill state of health, and joined the forces at the Isle Aux Noix, in the vicinity of the British works, and from thence published proclamations addressed to the Canadians, assuring them that the American army had no design against their freedom, religion or possessions, but only against the British garrison. It contained an animated request for all the Canadians to join them in asserting their independence. The situation of St. Johns being found so much stronger than was expected, they landed about one mile and a half from the fort, and advanced to reconnoiter the works, when they were attacked by a company of Indians, and three of their number were killed, and eight wounded. The assailants retreated with a loss of five killed, and four wounded. Not proceeding to the attack for want of artillery, they returned to the Isle Aux Noix. Schuyler left for Albany, and the chief command devolved on Montgomery, who on receiving reinforcements, invested St. Johns, but was retarded in his operations by a want of powder and ball, and also by the insubordinate and undisciplined behaviour of his men. Colonel Allen, a subordinate officer under Gen. Montgomery, being sent with a force of 80 men against some hostile Indians in the interior of Canada, met Major Brown on his return, and made an arrangement with him for attacking Montreal. Allen was to land at the north part of the city, and Brown with two hundred men at the south. Allen succeeded in crossing the river, but Brown failed of performing his part of the undertaking. Instead of retreating, Allen, with great rashness, resolved to maintain his position. Carleton learning what Allen's situation was, met him with about forty regulars and some hundreds of militia and Indians. Fifteen of the Americans were killed, and the survivors being overpowered by numbers, were obliged to surrender, when their brave commander and his associates were loaded with irons and sent on board a man of war to England. While Montgomery was pressing the siege at Montreal, the revolting Canadians greatly assisted him. On the 8th of October, these Canadians, under Majors Brown and Livingston, entered upon the project of taking Chambly, situated below St. Johns, on the river Sorel: they passed safely down the river by the works at St. Johns, with their artillery, and gained possession of the fort with small loss. One hundred prisoners, with 120 barrels of powder, and a considerable quantity of other stores, were the fruits of this encounter. The besiegers having obtained a supply of powder, made vigorous advances toward the fort. Carleton, elated by his victory over Allen, collected 800 men, with the idea of raising the siege of St. Johns, and embarked at Montreal to pass over to the southern shore of the St. Lawrence, when Col. Warner, with 300 green mountain boys, watched their motions and prepared, under the covert of some bushes, to salute the enemy on their approach, which was done so effectually with grape shot that the flotilla returned in confusion to Montreal. Carleton was deserted by the Canadians, and McLean, one of his Colonels, made a precipitate retreat to Quebec. On the first day of November, the fortress at St. Johns was cannonaded by Montgomery.

Major Preston, hearing of Carleton's defeat, and McLean's retreat, could no longer delay the proffered capitulation, but surrendered his garrison on the third day, amounting to six hundred men and a considerable quantity of cannon and military stores. Montgomery hastened to Montreal, and having despatched Colonel Easton down the river Sorel, he secured the passage on the river St. Lawrence, with a number of cannon, boats and musketeers, so that vessels could not pass without danger of being sunk or taken. General Prescot, with 120 men, appeared, and was obliged to surrender. Eleven armed vessels were taken, with cargoes of provisions, military stores, and various other articles. The day before Montgomery entered Montreal, Carleton, considering this city not tenable, quit it in the night, and in a boat with muffled oars, was conveyed through the American squadron. General Montgomery, after engaging to allow the inhabitants the free exercise of their religion, and the possession of their property, with the privilege of governing themselves, entered the town with his army. By his generous behaviour, many of the Canadians enlisted under his banner. More, however, of his own troops, whose terms of enlistment had expired, insisted on returning to their homes. So dear to them were the delights of the domestic fireside, and so vividly were they riveted on the memory by the severe duties of their campaign, notwithstanding the high character of their commander, his address, his entreaties to induce them to proceed, availed nothing. With the remnant of his army, which consisted of no more than three hundred men, he began his march to Quebec, expecting there to meet another body of troops, sent to act in concert with him. On the 13th of September, Arnold set out with 1100 men, (of whose character it has been well said, as a soldier, he was vigorous, impetuous and fearless; as a man, over-bearing, avaricious and profligate) to meet Montgomery at Quebec. After enduring excessive hardships and distress in passing over rapid streams, deep swamps, mountains and precipices, and being reduced by hunger to the alternative of eating their cartouch-boxes, breeches and shoes, they arrived at Point Levi, opposite Quebec, on the ninth of November, with about seven hundred men, after having been thirty-one days out of sight of any human habitation, in a cold inhospitable wilderness, where not even the Indian presumed to tread.— The French were surprised to see a hostile force proceeding from a barren wilderness. On the 13th of November, Arnold passed the St. Lawrence, marched up the precipice which Wolfe had ascended before him, and arrayed his army, which, often enduring so great hardships, was reduced to 700, on the plains of Abraham. Being persuaded by the cannonade from the walls, that the garrison was ready for the combat, he was compelled to retire, and marched on the 18th to Point Aux Tremble, there to await the arrival of Montgomery. Carleton withdrew from Montreal, and reached Quebec immediately after Arnold left the place, and began to prepare his troops, amounting to 1500, for a vigorous defence.

Montgomery's arrival was on the first of December,

with three vessels and three hundred men, ammunition and provisions, for his army. It was a cause of great rejoicing to meet their companions in a foreign land, after a long absence, and after suffering every thing but death from the inclemency of the season, and to receive a supply of winter clothing. The united forces amounted to no more than nine hundred effective men. A flag demanding the surrender, having been previously sent out by Arnold, was fired upon by the enemy. They, therefore concluded to risk a general assault. Accordingly, on the morning of the 31st of December, during a heavy fall of snow, the troops were led on to storm the place.— The upper and the lower parts of the city were to be attacked at the same time, but those in the upper were only to give a false alarm, to divide the strength of the garrison. As Montgomery was leading on his men, a violent discharge of grape shot from a cannon fortuitously pointed, terminated the life of this brave officer, and several other officers and men who were with him. The men observing their leader fall, drew back. Colonel Campbell, on whom the command devolved, ordered a retreat for another part of the city already attacked by Arnold. He made a bold assault upon the other quarter of the city and carried a small battery. Soon a ball shattered his leg, and he was sent to the hospital. They continued the engagement about three hours longer, till they were convinced of the fall of Montgomery. Some retreated and others were unwilling to encounter another tempest of shot, surrendered as prisoners of war; about one hundred were killed in the engagement. The fall of General Montgomery was bewailed by the whole continent.— He was eminent for his zealous devotion to the cause of American liberty, and was endeared to the good by the exercise in war of the most amiable virtues. His soldiers adored him for his lofty spirit and daring bravery. The enemy respected him for his honorable conduct and distinguished talents. Until this bold enterprise, continued success bore testimony to the greatness of his mind, and defeat, when he was no more, confirmed the grandeur of his character. In 1818, his remains were removed from Quebec to New-York, his adopted state, where Congress had erected a monument to perpetuate his fame. Arnold had about four hundred men, stationed three miles from the city. This heroic band, though far inferior in numbers to the garrison, had so cut off the communications between them and the country, that they were very near starving for want of provisions, and the cold weather, with the small pox which prevailed in the army, reduced them to extreme sufferings. Although a reinforcement of troops had arrived from Montreal, Arnold could scarcely number more than one thousand effective recruits. When the disasters at Quebec were communicated to the American Congress, they ordered ten battallions to Canada, under the command of General Thomas. The most of the troops were on the march by the first of May; but on arriving at the city, their numbers did not exceed 1,900.— This force was soon reduced by that loathsome disease, the small pox, to about nine hundred men fit for duty.— The siege of Quebec, after many unavailing efforts, was raised by order of General Thomas, the very day that the British fleet reached the confines of Quebec, with reinforcements to the garrison. It was now found necessary to retreat with the utmost speed, as the fleet had intercepted all communication between the different parts of the American camp. The baggage, artillery and many of the sick, fell into the hands of the enemy. Much is due to Carleton for his generosity and kindness to the sick, who fell into his hands, as they were destitute of every necessary for convenience and comfort. He clothed, fed and relieved the soldiers and officers when prisoners at Quebec, and invited the latter to participate in the hospitalities of his own house. He discharged the officers on a parole of honor, and returned the soldiers to their respective provinces, furnished with every necessary for their convenience and happiness. Sorel was the first place at which the retreating party halted, where General Thomas with several regiments was stationed at their arrival.— Here their worthy commander died with the small pox, which yet prevailed in the camp. While the Americans were unsuccessfully exerting their valor against superior numbers at one place, they experienced a very severe misfortune in the pusillanimous conduct of certain officers in another. A party of three hundred and ninety Americans, posted at the Cedars, forty three miles above Montreal, with a few pieces of cannon, under the command of Colonel Beadle, were assailed by Captain Foster, descending the river with a detachment of forty regulars, one hundred Canadians and about five hundred Indians, who were armed only with muskets. Beadle leaving Butterfield, a subordinate officer, with the command, repaired to Montreal to procure a reinforcement. Butterfield, being destitute of valor, surrendered the fort on the intimation of Foster, that if an Indian should be killed they would, without the probability of his restraint, massacre the whole garrison. Sherburn left Montreal to assist the fort at the Cedars with an hundred and fifty men, and was taken prisoner by the savages before its surrender.— Twenty-eight were murdered, seven or eight carried into captivity, and the remainder, after being deprived of their clothing, were delivered to Foster. Arnold marched with nine hundred men to check the progress of such barbarity. Foster informed him that if he did not assent to the cartel agreed upon by Sherburn and others, he would suffer the Indians to put every prisoner to immediate death. Fearing he would resort to such measures, Arnold hesitated.— The business, was, however, concluded. The whole proceeding was highly censured by Congress, and Arnold's agreement was considered by them, nothing but a sponsion, which might be annulled or affirmed by them, as he had no power to make such stipulation. Beadle and Butterfield were cashiered and declared incapable of ever holding a commission in the American armies. A British armament of thirteen thousand men pursuing the fugitive army of the republicans up the rapids of the St. Lawrence, entered the city of Montreal a short time after Arnold evacuated it with his troops to cross the St. Lawrence for Chambly. The Americans, with great resolution and zeal, ascended the river, and preserved their artillery and stores. More than one hundred batteaux heavily loaded, were drawn up the rapids by the men in the water to their middle, and whatever stores they were unable to remove were destroyed. Having arrived at St. Johns, General Sullivan, the successor of General Thompson, in obedience to an order from Schuyler, continued his march to Crown Point, at the head of lake Champlain, which they just reached when the British took possession of St. Johns.—The retreat from Canada, under such disasterous circumstances as the American troops had to encounter, was highly creditable to the commander, Sullivan, and his associates, Stark, Poor, Wayne, and other excellent officers. Gates took the command of the army on their arrival at Crown Point, July 12, 1776, and of the regiments which were ordered to Canada, only seven thousand and six returned. The army had been greatly reduced by deaths and desertion at Quebec, Trois, Rivieres, the Cedars, and in their retreat from Canada. This terminated the campaign of 1775, which in its conception was singularly bold and romantic, and in its progress was displayed fortitude seldom equalled in military annals. The object of the expedition not being attained was a severe disappointment. Had it been accomplished, such an extensive and defenceless frontier to protect with a military force, would probably have been injurious to the cause of independence. It was now the business of the army to provide necessary accommodations and place themselves in a situation for defence. Mount Independence, east of Ticonderoga, was selected as the the most eligible situation to erect a fortification; and fort George, at the south end of that lake, for a general hospital. Six hundred men arrived in August, from New-Hampshire, and were active with the former forces in strengthening and extending the works for defence. Preparations for constructing the first naval force that ever fought on the lake, engaged their attention. But the timber was growing in the wilderness, and had with most of the materials for a naval equipment to be dragged by the men to the place of use over roads almost impassable. But amidst all these and other difficulties and embarrassments, such was the resolution, industry, and perseverance of the men, that one sloop, three schooners, five gondolas, carrying fifty-five guns, besides seventy swivels, were equipped by the 18th of August, and three hundred and ninety-five men, composed the armament, well fitted for action. This fleet was constructed with the most unparalleled rapidity, considering the disadvantages which the Americans had to encounter. The British had also been actively engaged at St. Johns, in building a fleet which would give them the superiority over the lake, and enable them to attempt the reduction of all the fortresses and country as far as Albany. Some of their vessels were constructed in England, which were taken in pieces, and brought by the rapids, then put together again upon the lake. Vessels, consisting of one gondola, weighing thirty tons, thirty long boats, several flat bottomed boats, and four hundred batteaux, had been dragged up the rapids. The whole flotilla of the British now in readiness for service, consisted of the Inflexible, Maria, Carleton, Thunderer, twenty gun boats, four long boats and some gondolas, mounting upwards of eighty cannon and some howitzers. These were followed by an extensive train of vessels, batteaux, and boats, built for transporting the royal army, with the military stores and munitions of war. Captain Pringle conducted the armament, and seven hundred prime seamen navigated the fleet. Every thing was in complete readiness on their part, the weight and strength of their guns and vessels was double to that of the Americans. Lake Champlain, whose waters had been celebrated as a seat of hostilities ever since the commencement of the European settlements, was in 1776, overspread with a fleet sufficient to compete with the defying squadrons of former ages. General Arnold, who had been a sailor in his youth, proceeded down the lake in the last of August, to gain intelligence of the enemy. On the eleventh of October, General Carleton sailed up the lake with the British fleet, and discovered the American squadron drawn up in a very safe and strong line of defence, in the passage between the island of Valcour and the western main. The situation of the American commander formed a safe retreat, and was discovered only by accident. After a short contest, the enemy, not being able to bring their whole force into action, retired. A continuance of unfavorable wind, induced Captain Pringle to withdraw those vessels that were engaged, from the action, and as the dusk of evening came on, formed a line as near the Americans as possible, to prevent their escape. The Washington galley, commanded

by General Waterbury, had suffered the most severely.—
Fortune seemed to favor the enemy, but not so much so,
as to give them any great degree of self-complacency; two
of their gondolas were sunk, and one blown up, with sixty
men. The Americans had one schooner burnt, a gondola
sunk, and several vessels much injured.

All hopes of success against a force so far superior,
were perfectly idle. The only way to save the American
fleet was to retreat to Ticonderoga under cover of darkness. This was accomplished with such promptitude that
the next morning the vessels were out of sight of the
British line. A renewal of the chase, together with a favorable wind, October 11, 1776, gave the British a successful chance of overtaking them at Ferris' Bay, in Panton. A spirited engagement ensued, the British pressed
with resolution, and the Americans made desperate resistance: one of the American vessels headed by General
Waterbury, had so many men killed, and was so shattered to pieces as to be obliged to surrender. After contesting for four hours for the pre-eminence of the lake, Arnold finding it impossible for the exertions of skill or courage to endure the force and fire of the enemy with safety
to his men, dexterously covering the retreat of his vessels,
ran them ashore, saved his men, and blew up the fleet.
The Americans had now, of every description, but six armed vessels upon the lake. Having been unsuccessful upon the water, they set fire to the fort at Crown Point, and
marched their army to Ticonderoga. The fortifications
were strengthened and an army of twelve thousand effective men under the command of Gen. Gates, were posted
here. The British commander landed at Crown Point, and
after continuing there one month in examining the direction of the channel and sounding its depth, re-embarked
his army for Canada, without making an attempt at the reduction of Ticonderoga. The militia were dismissed
from service the same day. The Colonies had long endured the oppressive measures and misrule of the British
government—years multiplied their afflictions, and their
remonstrances were answered only with insults. The
public mind revolted at such treatment and determined to be free. Cruelty produced the revolution, patriot-

ism and knowledge estimated the extent of its advantages. As a prelude to independence, Congress recommended to those colonists that had no constitutions, to adopt indefinitely such governments as might best conduce to the happiness of the people. The Colonies had been accustomed to consider themselves an independent government, and some desired that they should declare them as such; accordingly a declaration was prepared by a committee of Congress, and almost unanimously adopted on July 4th, 1776. We hold these truths (says the contex) to be self evident, that all mankind are created equal, that they are endowed by their Creator with certain unalienable rights, that among them are life, liberty and the pursuit of happiness, that to secure these rights governments are instituted among men, deriving their just powers from the consent of the governed that whenever any form of government becomes destitute of these ends, it is the right of the people to alter or abolish it, and to institute a new government, laying its foundation on such principles, and organizing its powers in such form as to them shall seem likely to effect their safety and happiness. An enumeration of the oppressions complained of by the Americans is closed by a representation of the character of the British King, who in their language is unfit to be the ruler of a free people. The ineffectual appeals to the English nation are also enumerated, with remarks upon their indifference to the voice of justice, and a determination to hold them like the rest of mankind, friends in peace, and enemies in war. In conclusion, they declared themselves absolved from all allegiance and political connexion with the British crown, and invested with the full powers of self government. The tempest of war lowering upon the continent, threatened the hallowed sanctuary of freedom with ruin. At the north, the Americans had been driven from Canada, and their fleet destroyed on the lake. General Howe had been successful in defeating them on Long Island and at New-York, in taking forts, men and magazines, and had also got possession of New-Jersey, and Newport, in Rhode-Island. Their only success had been in the defeat of Cornwallis on Sullivan's Island, and in the action of Trenton, where one thousand German troops surrendered to General Washington. The British were so far superior in their naval and military forces, and munitions of war, that whoever computed the issue of the controversy by the natural course of things could hardly avoid the conclusion that the Colonies would have to submit to the sovereignty of Great Britain. At the opening of navigation upon the lake, preparations were making for an invasion of the United States, from Canada. General Burgoyne, distinguished as a scholar and a courtier, having fought with some celebrity in Portugal, and served under General Carleton during the last campaign, had the command of Canada and the lakes assigned to him, instead of Carleton, who was by far the most able of all their Generals in America. A division of the states, effected by sending a powerful force from Canada through the lake to form a junction with the British army at New-York, was calculated upon as a direct means of subduing the states, by cutting off all communication between the north and the south, and thus their whole strength be turned against one part. The force allotted for this excursion exceeded seven thousand and one hundred men, exclusive of a corps of German artillerists, amounting to more than three thousand two hundred, besides a large retinue of Canadians and Indians. An excellent train of brass artillery was supplied, together with every thing which could add efficiency to the army. And for the assistance of the commanding General, were selected, Philips, Frazier, Powell, Hamilton, Reidsel, and Sperht, all officers who had distinguished themselves by former services. General Schuyler had been indefatigable in making preparations for defence, but the fortifications were commenced late in the spring, and only few troops were collected. Soon after Burgoyne's arrival at Quebec, he despatched Colonel St. Ledger with a force composed of regulars, tories and Indians, up the St. Lawrence, to Oswego, directing them to proceed to the Mohawk river and join him at Albany. With an army increased to ten thousand men, he proceeded up lake Champlain as far as the river Boquet, in New-York, a few miles north of Crown Point. Here he had a conference with a large number of savages, who had been persuaded to join the army. In conformity with the high ideas General Burgoyne entertained of himself and his army, he issued a most pompous proclamation, setting forth the cruelty that would be practiced upon those who continued obstinate to his invitations. Encouragements were offered to those who should assist the king in redeeming the colonies from oppression, and restoring them to the privileges of English liberty and laws. After terminating his addresses he moved on with his army to Ticonderoga. The old forts and out-posts had been strengthened, and on the eastern shore of the inlet opposite to Ticonderoga, Mount Independence had been fortified very securely. A bridge connecting the two posts was thrown across the inlet, supported by twenty-two pieces of large timber, fifty feet distant from each other. The side next to the lake was defended by a firm constructed boom.— This work for connecting the forts and cutting off all access by water on the northern side, was not completed.— The garrison, under the command of general St. Clair, had not a sufficient number of men to withstand so powerful a force. They, therefore, evacuated the station, taking with them the baggage of the army and such munitions of war as the hurry of the occasion permitted, on board of two hundred batteaux, convoyed by five armed gallies, to Skeensborough. The main army marching by land through Castleton, which is about thirty miles south of Ticonderoga, were directed to join the army at Skeensborough.— The number of continental soldiers and militia belonging to St. Clair's forces amounted to 3,446. About 3 o'clock in the morning, July 6, 1776, the troops were put under motion. The retreat would have been effected without the knowledge of the enemy, had not a house, contrary to orders, been set on fire by a French officer. This circumstance gave the enemy complete information of what was going on and a discovery of every movement of the American army. When the army arrived at Hubbardton, they halted for nearly two hours, where many having been unable to keep pace with their regiments, fell in with the rear guard. This body of the army was transferred from Colonel Francis, of Massachusetts, to Colonel Seth Warner, of Vermont, with orders to pursue the army as

6

soon as the whole came up, and to halt about a mile and
a half behind the main body. The place of destination
was reached by a part, who encamped at Castleton, and
Warner with the remainder tarried at Hubbardton. As
soon as the retreat of the Americans was perceived, General Frazier began a speedy pursuit with 850 men. General Reidesel, with a great proportion of the Brunswick
troops, joined in the pursuit. Frazier continuing the pursuit through the day, and received intelligence that the retreating army were not far distant, ordered his men to lie
on their arms through the night.

On the morning of the 7th of July, Frazier commenced the attack upon the three regiments commanded by
Warner, Francis and Hall. They formed at the distance
of sixty yards, but Hall being fearful of danger, did not
bring his regiment into action; he fled and was afterwards
taken prisoner by the British. Francis fell fighting with
great resolution and bravery, and Warner was left to sustain the battle, with about eight hundred men. The American officers and soldiers supported their gallant commander with such intrepidity and firmness that the British lines
gave way. Recovering, they formed again, and advanced
upon the Americans with their bayonets, but were soon
thrown into disorder. The issue of the battle was uncertain, until Reidesel appeared with his advanced column.
The Americans, overpowered by superior numbers, fled
at every point. Warner collected the most part of his
men and conducted them with safety to Fort Edward.—
The Americans lost in killed and wounded and prisoners
three hundred and twenty, and the enemy not less than
one hundred and eighty-three in killed and wounded.—
Frazier pursued the Americans by land, and Burgoyne
by water. The obstructions to the navigation being incomplete, were easily destroyed, and by nine o'clock the
vessels passed the works. Before the Americans arrived
at Skeensborough, they were attacked by the foremost
brigades of the enemy's gun-boats: and on the approach
of their frigates, two of the American gallies were taken
and the other blown up. The republicans not being sufficient to withstand the force of the enemy, set fire to the
works at Skeensborough, and retreated up Wood Creek

to Fort Anne, where they were joined by a party from Fort Edward. Colonel Hill was detached with a view to intercept the fugitives on Wood Creek, and secure Fort Anne. He was attacked with so well directed a fire that his only safety consisted in retreating to the top of a hill to prevent being surrounded. At this difficult crisis a party of Indians arrived and were answered in their war-whoops, by the British regiment, whom the Americans concluded to be a large reinforcement come to their assistance. They thereupon relinquished the attack, reduced the fort to ashes and retreated to Fort Edward. In their retreat they were peculiarly unfortunate: one hundred and twenty-eight pieces of cannon, batteaux, stores, magazines, 349,760 pounds of flour, 143,830 pounds of pork, and a large drove of cattle fell into the hands of the enemy. St. Clair, the commander of the Americans, after suffering much from want of provisions, and great fatigue upon a wretched road through Rutland, joined Schuyler on the twelfth of July. The people, not aware of the weakness of the army, attributed its retreat to connivance and treachery, and trembled at the dangers which threatened them from the British, Canadians and savages. The management of General St. Clair was generally condemned, and whatever might have been his excuses, his plans proved fruitless, and he did not seem to possess that genius which finds relief in instantaneous resource, decisive counsel and animating action. The united forces of St. Clair and Schuyler, at Fort Edward, did not exceed four thousand four hundred men. These were engaged in retarding the march of the British army, by falling trees in the road, tearing up buildings and throwing every obstacle in the way that was possible. With the loss of three hundred men the enemy penetrated into the heart of the country, and were from their past success calculating upon a speedy submission of the whole country to their arms. The first business of the British was to render Wood Creek navigable and the roads passable, to transport their artillery and stores, which was accomplished only at the rate of one mile in twenty-four hours. Burgoyne arrived at Fort Edward on the thirtieth of July. The joy of the army was inexpressible: they considered all their difficulties terminated, and nothing remaining for them but an easy march, through a fertile country, to take possession of Albany, and form a junction with the British army at New-York. Saratoga, and afterwards Stillwater, 25 miles north of Albany, became the chief seat of the Republican army, consisting only of four thousand regular troops and fifteen hundred militia, and these almost destitute of the habiliments of war. All the towns north of Manchester and Sunderland, were abandoned by the settlers who were seeking safety in the other states, or wherever they could find it. A meeting of the committee of safety was holden at Manchester, July 15, 1777, when it was agreed that they should collect all the forces in their power to oppose the enemy, and at the same time write in the most earnest manner to the states of Massachusetts and New-Hampshire, to send troops to their assistance, before the remainder of the inhabitants should be compelled to leave the grants for provisions and safety. The Assembly of New-Hampshire was convened, and during a session of three days, arrayed the whole militia of the State into two brigades, and placed them under the command of Generals Whipple and Stark. One fourth of Stark's brigade, and about one regiment from the other, were ordered to proceed immediately with Stark "to stop the progress of the enemy on the western frontiers." Stark proceeded to Charlestown with his men, amounting to eight hundred, and sent them forward to join the troops of Vermont, under Colonel Warner, at Manchester, then about six hundred. A difference of opinion between Schuyler and Stark, as to the best method of approaching General Burgoyne, led Congress to interfere upon the subject, and express their disapprobation towards the Council and Governor of New-Hampshire, for giving him instructions destructive of military subordination. Stark however assured Schuyler before the interference of Congress, that he would lay aside all private resentment, when it appeared in opposition to the public good. Massachusetts supplied a large quota of militia, over whom General Washington wisely judged that General Lincoln would prove an able and influential commander, and sent him forward for that purpose. Lincoln and Stark joined Schuyler with all their forces, except Warner's regiment. Arnold was also sent on by Washington, with a train of artillery, to assist Schuyler. General Gates was appointed by Congress to relieve General Schuyler, which was very encouraging to the New-England troops. The English commander, with fifteen days labor in removing provisions and stores from Fort George to the Hudson, finding they had not more than four days subsistence in store, resolved to furnish themselves at the expense of the Americans. He accordingly despatched a body of troops under the command of Colonel Baum, to surprise, and take a large quantity of provisions, guarded only by a force of militia. This detachment amounted to about seven hundred British, Canadians and Indians, with two pieces of light artillery. Another corps for the support of Colonel Baum, was posted at Battenkill, under the command of Colonel Breyman. Stark collected together his brigade and the militia that were present, and sent to Colonel Warner, at Manchester, to bring on his regiment. He also sent expresses to the neighbouring militia, to join him speedily. General Stark marched his troops on the fourteenth about eight miles, and met the enemy. Skirmishes were kept up through that and the next day, during which thirty of the enemy and two Indian Sachems, were wounded. On the sixteenth of August the Americans were led on to the attack of Colonel Baum, at his intrenchments upon the bank of the Hoosick river. A general action ensued, which lasted about two hours, and was like one continued roar of thunder. The German dragoons and their brave commander, after expending their ammunition, charged with their swords, but were soon repulsed. Two pieces of cannon were taken, Colonel Baum was mortally wounded, and all his men, except a few who escaped into the woods, were killed or taken prisoners. The militia dispersed in search of plunder, when a reinforcement under Colonel Breyman, arrived. At this juncture Colonel Warner very fortunately arrived, and instantly led on his men against Breyman. At sunset, the Germans were driven from the field with considerable loss, and made safe their retreat under the cover of darkness. The Americans took in these actions, about seven hundred prisoners, with their equipments, four brass field pieces, and a large amount of swords and other military stores. The loss of the British, in killed, was 207, and the number of wounded unknown. The Americans had thirty slain and forty wounded.

Fortune now began to favor the Americans. The decisive victory at Bennington diffused confidence and joy. The friends of independence, before dispirited by misfortune and defeat, were now animated by the prospect which suddenly burst upon them of a distinguished victory over an arrogant and once dreaded enemy. The greatest exertions and enterprise were every where displayed. To see the American militia without any military attire or weapons, except a farmer's gun, destitute of a bayonet, force entrenchments, kill and make prisoners of the royal troops, filled the enemy with indignation and amazement. Congress presented their thanks to General Stark, his officers and men, for their signal victory at Bennington, and appointed Brigadier Stark a Brigadier General in the army of the United States. The garrison at the junction of the Mohawk and Hudson rivers, having been increased to 5000 men, was marched from that encampment on the 8th of September, and proceeded on their way to Behman's heights, at Stillwater. While the Americans were greatly encouraged by the prospect of success, the feelings of human sympathy were excited by the brutality of Burgoyne's Indian allies. An instance of an awful kind happened in the murder of Miss McRea, a young lady of distinguished amiableness and virtue, who was engaged to a young officer of the British army. She was taken out of a house near Fort Edward, carried to the woods, and there scalped and disfigured in the most inhuman manner. The circumstances of her shocking fate were heightened by her being dressed to receive her promised husband, when she was met by those cannibals of British cupidity. More than one hundred of different sexes and ages perished in a similar manner, by the same ruffians, who were rewarded for their cold blooded murders by the facetious and accomplished General Burgoyne. Every circumstance and plan that could be made to bear, was resorted to for rousing up the minds and filling the ranks of the American army. General Lincoln, after receiving large reinforcements, determined to make a diversion in the rear of the enemy. He marched with a body of militia from Manchester to Pawlet. Colonel Brown proceeded from thence to the landing place at lake George, to destroy the enemy's stores, and release the American prisoners confined there. Colonel Johnson was stationed at Mount Independence, to annoy the enemy at the north end of lake George, and if an opportunity favored, to unite their forces, and attempt the reduction of Ticonderoga and Mount Independence. At the same time Colonel Woodbridge, with five hundred men, was ordered on to Skeensborough, thence to Fort Ann, and so on to Fort Edward. These expeditions were managed so discreetly, that by the 18th of September, all the out posts at lake George, part of Fort Ticonderoga, Mount Defiance and Hope, two hundred batteaux, an armed sloop and several gun boats, were almost instantly taken. Two hundred and ninety-three of the enemy were taken prisoners, and one hundred Americans, who had been captured, were set at liberty. Finding themselves unable to carry the works at Ticonderoga or Mount Independence, they made a safe and speedy return to the head quarters of the commander. During these proceedings, Burgoyne having secured provisions for thirty days, marched his army across the Hudson on the 12th of September, and on the 14th encamped at Saratoga, within four miles of the American army. Three thousand American troops marched out to attack the British, on the 18th of September, at 1 o'clock. The contest began between the scouting parties of the two armies, which were respectively and repeatedly reinforced until nearly the whole of each army were engaged. The battle now became general, and both armies appeared to conquer. The fire was kept up for three hours. They alternately drove and were driven by each other, a blaze of fire was constantly to be seen. The British line broke, the Americans then pressed in from the woods which lay between the camps, and drove them to the high lands, where their flanks being sustained, they recovered, charging in their turn. The Americans were then driven back with a dreadful fire, and again the British were dispersed. The artillery fell into the hands of the Americans as often as they were repulsed by the assailants, but they could neither remove nor employ it against the enemy. Night put an end to the conflict. This bloody and undecisive contest proved a loss to the British of more than five hundred men in killed, wounded and captured, and to the Americans, in killed, wounded and missing, of three hundred and nineteen. Each claimed the victory, but the consequences of defeat were felt by the British alone. The English commander tried in vain by his maneuvering to allure the disquieted feelings of many in his army; but the brutality of the Indians had not been gratified with the usual amount of plunder, and disliking the hard service and the checks they received for their wanton murders, at Fort Edward, deserted in large numbers, some to the woods, and some to the army of General Gates. The Canadians and American loyalists quit in considerable bodies. General Burgoyne's expectation of meeting Clinton upon the Hudson river, was now completely frustrated, as the American army had surrounded him, and cut off all his supplies. General Lincoln joined Gates on the 29th of September, with two thousand troops.

In the beginning of October, General Burgoyne found his provisions growing too scanty to last until they should receive assistance from New-York, ordered a diminution of the soldiers rations, which was patiently submitted to by the troops. The foraging party of the British army suffering from scarcity, Burgoyne found that it could only be relieved by making a movement of his army to the left of the Americans. For the accomplishment of this design, 1500 regular troops were ordered out, with a train of artillery. Burgoyne commanded in person, assisted by Generals Philips, Reidesel and Frazier. These were some of the best Generals and troops that now belonged to the British service. The distance of the embodied armies was only three quarters of a mile. General gates being informed of the march of the royal army instantly put his troops in motion. About four o'clock, the American column approached the enemy and was fired upon by their artillery. The Americans, disregarding their fire, rushed impetuously to the assault, and being reinforced, the British left was entirely overpowered and obliged to give way. The Americans chased them nearly two miles, and stormed their camp through a severe fire of grape shot. That part of the assault conducted by Arnold did not succeed in forcing the intrenchment, but Colonel Brooks in another quarter entered the fortifications sword in hand, completely routing them, with the loss of their baggage, tents and artillery. The Americans maintained their ground, and nothing but the approach and darkness of night, put an end to the action, or left quietness to the remaining part of the British camp. Two hundred of the enemy were made prisoners. This action was more furious, obstinate, and bloody than any that had ever been fought in America. The British now found in the Americans, an unshaken resolution to defend their country and capture the royal army. The situation of the British forces was such, that General Gates designed to surround, rather than attack them, and to effect this, large detachments were posted at Saratoga and Fort Edward. Burgoyne perceiving his plan, determined to prevent it, by removing his camp to Saratoga, which was accomplished in the evening, leaving the sick and wounded, amounting to three hundred. On their arrival here, a large force of Americans were stationed, not far distant, with whom, they thought not best to enter upon an engagement; therefore, a retreat to lake George was ordered. But the difficulties of the way, and the American garrisons stationed on every practicable route of retreat, prevented all possibility of escape, and Burgoyne was obliged to recall an escort which had been sent out for that purpose. All that was now wanting to complete the reduction of their army, was to cut off their supply of provisions, hitherto carried up the Hudson river to Saratoga. Not a single batteaux of provisions was received secure from the annoyance of the Americans. Such were the losses of the enemy that a council was called for attempting a retreat by night, at the fords near Fort Edward.—The Americans, they learned, were strongly intrenched there, so that maneuver was abandoned. No hopes of assistance from Clinton, to whom urgent application had been made, now remained. Burgoyne called his principal officers for a council of war, whilst a cannonade pervaded the camp, and the grape shot fell in every part of their lines. There was not a spot of ground in the whole encampment, secure for holding a council, for while they were deliberating an eighteen pound ball crossed the table around which they sat. By the unanimous determination, a negociation was opened on the 17th of October.— On the intelligence of this glorious victory, universal joy pervaded the country. Past injuries were forgotten in the elevation of prosperity. The number of troops surrendered by General Burgoyne, were 5752, which being added to those of the sick and wounded, in the hospital, and those lost in battle, in sickness and desertion, made an entire loss to Great-Britain, of 9213, together with forty-two pieces of cannon, and five thousand muskets. From feelings of regard towards the prisoners, General Gates kept his forces within the lines, whilst the captured were piling up their arms. Both soldiers and officers were treated with great kindness by the Americans. The cruel depredations committed by them upon the defenceless inhabitants, were not retaliated upon the prisoners, on their march to Massachusetts. A regiment of Green Mountain Boys, under the command of Colonel Warner, proceeded with General Gates' troops down the Hudson river, to check the desolating ravages of Vaughan and Wallis.— These exterminators hearing of their approach, retreated with their troops to New-York. The garrison at Ticonderoga, on hearing of Burgoyne's defeat, rendered their cannon useless, and returned to Canada, leaving the northern frontier in perfect tranquillity. Those who had by the ravages of war, been driven from their habitations, returned. The benefits of agriculture, so far as a crop of grain or hay remained, were attended to and collected together even in the months of November and December. After an engagement in their domestic concerns, the people of Vermont found it necessary to establish such a constitution and laws, as would silence the claim and controversies of New-York, establish their independence, and secure to them protection and the administration of justice.

HISTORY OF VERMONT. 71

CHAPTER IV.

Indian depredations upon the early settlers.—Destruction of Royalton.—Political Affairs in Vermont, from the commencement of the revolution in 1775, until its termination in 1783.—Meeting of Conventions.—Declaration of the Independence of Vermont.—Transactions of New-York.—Acts of Congress.—Controversy and Claims of New-Hampshire, New-York and Massachusetts.—Commissioners open a negociation with Vermont.—Proceedings of Vermont.—Measures pursued by Congress.—Management of the British Agents.—Resolutions of Congress.—Transactions between Vermont, New-York and New-Hampshire.—Washington's communication.—Congress defer the admission of Vermont into the Union.

The settlers of Vermont were occasionally annoyed by the Indians, from the commencement until the termination of the revolutionary war. Their encroachments were made by scouting parties, whose pursuit was for the acquisition of plunder and riotous entertainments, while their unwelcome visits were obtruded among the distressed inhabitants. The northern hive of Indians residing upon the Canadian frontier, poured in upon the wilderness territory of New-England, throughout the French and American wars, carrying many of the settlers into captivity. Such accounts of these depredations as have been preserved, will be concisely noticed in our narrative. The inhabitants in the south-east part of Vermont encountered in their early settlements, all the dangers of the Indian wars and hardships incident to the frontier improvements. The settlers confided their safety to fortified places, of which there was upon the banks of the Connecticut river, one at Brattleborough, called Dummer's, and Bridgman's, and Sartwell's Forts, at Hinsdale, now Vernon. But these were insufficient to shield the inhabitants from the incursions of the savages.

In 1746, a party of twenty Indians attacked a number of men at Bridgman's Fort, killed and wounded four, and made two prisoners. The next year they burned the Fort,

killed and carried several away into captivity. Eight
years after this outrage, in the month of July, they ambushed Caleb Howe, Hilkiah Grout and Benjamin Gaffield, as they were returning from their labor. Howe was
killed, Gaffield was drowned in attempting to cross the
river, and Grout escaped unhurt. Their wives and children were carried away as prisoners into Canada. The
number of captives was fifteen. They were marched
through this state, then a wilderness, in eight days, to a
place on the lake fifteen miles from Crown Point : proceding then with them to St. Johns, where they were sold
to the French, or distributed amongst the Indians.

On the 30th of August, 1754, they surprised Charlestown, New-Hampshire, and made prisoners of Messrs.
Labaree, Farnsworth and Johnson, with his family.—
These savages proceeded to the wilderness, and encamped with their prisoners within the present limits of the town
of Cavendish, when Mrs. Johnson had a daughter born,
whom she called Captive. Mrs. Johnson was compelled
to continue her march over the green mountains, a distance of two hundred miles. After enduring many hardships in captivity they were ransomed and returned again
to their friends and the society of their native State.—
A battle was fought at New-Fane, in 1756, between a party of thirty soldiers on their way from Charlestown to Fort
Hoosac, in Massachusetts, commanded by Captain Melvin and a superior force of Indians. Being overpowered by numbers, the captain and his men retreated from the
field, leaving two killed and one missing. Repairing to
Fort Dumner for assistance, the next day he returned to
the battle ground, and found that the Indians had departed:
he then proceeded on his way. There were numerous
other instances of savage depredations upon the lives and
property of the settlers at this period. So great were their
fears of these merciless cannibals, that the hallooing of a
hunter, which the people supposed was the yell of savages, roused all the inhabitants to arms. They fled without preparations, seeking only for the safety of their lives.
These fearful apprehensions were, however, soon corrected
on hearing their mistake. In the revolutionary war, the
Indians, though under different masters, continued their

irruptions upon the inhabitants. George and Aaron Robins were killed by them in 1777, in the town of Brandon: most of the inhabitants were made prisoners and their dwellings burned. Among the captives were Joseph Barker, his wife and child. Mrs. Barker, on account of her peculiar situation, was with her child set at liberty, and on the following night became the mother of another child, with no other convenience than the comfortless solitude of the forest. Mr. Barker made his escape at Middlebury by feigning himself sick. After the capture of Burgoyne, and previous to the evacuation of Ticonderoga, a party of men from Otter Creek, entered and plundered the house of a Mr. Prindle, inimical to the American cause—not being the owner of the house, he set it on fire, retreated on board a British vessel on the lake, and implicated his neighbor, Mr. Stone, in the robbery and burning of it.— The accused undertook to secrete himself, but was discovered and taken prisoner to Ticonderoga, where he remained three weeks. In November, 1778, Major Carleton collected 39 men and boys at Bridport, from the adjoining towns, and carried them away prisoners to Canada. Two of the prisoners, Elijah Grandy and Thomas Hinkly, were discharged to carry the women and children to the Americans, while the husbands and elder sons were detained. The prisoners arrived at Quebec on the 6th of December, and were detained 16 months and 19 days. In the spring after, several had died, they were removed 30 leagues down the river to work. On the night of the 13th of May, 1779, eight of them escaped, and crossed the river, here 27 miles wide; by noon the next day, they reached the opposite shore. They separated into two parties of four each. Messrs. Sturdifit, Ward and Smiths, composed one company, and proceeded up the river, for Sorell.— Most of the people treated them with kindness, until the 20th, when nearly opposite Quebec, the river was so swollen that they durst not attempt to cross it, and therefore, requested the aid of a Frenchman, whom they saw in the field. He conducted them to his house, where they were made prisoners by a French officer. All of them, except Sturdifit, effected an escape, who remained a prisoner until the close of the war. Ward was separated from the Smiths a week, when he accidentally fell in with them. Two days after they came together, four Indians, with their guns and dogs, come upon them, whom they outrun through the night, and the next day till noon, when they were taken by the Indians, about six miles from the Three Rivers, and imprisoned. One side of the prison, where they were committed, was wood, through which they cut a hole with an old jack knife, and in a week made an escape by a rope formed of their bed clothes, by which they let themselves down from a window, into a room adjacent to the prison. Fourteen days they eluded the search of the Indians by travelling in the woods. Having crossed over from the north side of the St. Lawrence, they reached the Sorell in the night, and the next day ascended the Chambly mountains, to take observations for directing their course through the forests of Vermont. They arrived at Missisque Bay, after four days travel, through swamps and a dreary wilderness. During the whole route they subsisted entirely on what flesh they killed and cooked in the woods. At Panton, they fell in with a scout of three Americans, who readily supplied their wants. In Bridport, they were entertained at the house of Asa Hemingway, the only one that was not destroyed in the ravages of war. The day following, they reached the picket forts at Pittsford. Of the prisoners who were carried away into captivity, Messrs. Nathan Smith, of Bridport, Joseph Holcomb, of Panton, Nathan Griswold, of Waltham, and Mrs. Grandy, whose husband was released to collect and carry the women and children to the Americans, and many others who shared in the sufferings of those calamitous times, are still living.

The transactions of Lieutenant Benjamin Everest, during the first settlement of Vermont, furnish a pretty fair example of the bravery, fortitude and sufferings of the people. Mr. Everest, soon after his father removed to Addison, in 1769, was engaged with Colonel Ethan Allen in suppressing Benzell, and other Yorkers, in their intrusion upon the inhabitants of Panton and New-Haven. Receiving a commission from the Continental Congress, he was engaged at Hubbardton battle in Colonel Warner's regiment, and at Bennington, in the regiment commanded by Colonel Herrick. The next year he had the command of Fort Vengeance, at Rutland, and after this, was taken by the British as a spy, and confined nine days in prison, from whence he was removed on board of a prison ship for Canada. Perceiving that death was his inevitable doom if he did not succeed in making an escape: accordingly he conceived the plan of having his irons taken off and himself placed upon the quarter deck by his entreaties, then to overcome the guard with a generous supply of liquor, and escape to the shore by swimming the lake from the vessel. All this he accomplished, but with much suffering. He passed through the Indian encampment as a British officer, and travelled in the night over west mountain through the snow a foot and a half deep, to Westport. From this place he passed over the lake and through the wilderness to Castleton. Afterwards he was surprised by seven Indians, when on a scouting party, and taken a prisoner. They delivered him over to General Powers, who confined him in irons. From these he extricated himself and fled to the covert of the woods. The whole encampment were rallied in searching after him, but he eluded their grasp by concealment in a thick growth of vegetation, lying near the whole day in plain sight of an Indian guard. He proceeded to lake George in the night, and through that to Fort Edward. During the whole time of his flight he was pursued by the Indians, and entirely destitute of food for three days.

A scout of twenty-one Indians, on the 9th day of August, 1780, entered the township of Barnard, and made prisoners of Messrs. Wright, Haskell and Newton. Two of whom made an escape the spring following, and the other was exchanged some time afterwards. They suffered many severe hardships while prisoners, but all of them returned and lived on the same farms from which they were taken. In October 16th, 1781, five men proceeding from the fort in Corinth, on a scout down Onion river, were fired upon in the town of Jerico, by a company of sixteen tories. Three of the number were wounded, one mortally, who died within 40 hours, and was buried in Colchester. The others were taken to Quebec, and detained till the next spring, when they were permitted to return. Major Breckenridge, with a scouting party of twenty men, after annoying the settlers of Newbury, killing one man and taking another prisoner, marched to Corinth, where they obliged the inhabitants to take the oath of allegiance to the king of Great-Britain. The settlement at Peacham, on Hazen's military road, was, when the soldiers had left the forts, invaded by a party of French and Indians, who took Colonel Elkins and several other prisoners.—Elkins was sent a prisoner to England, with 150 others, and confined in mill prison. In 1782 they were exchanged for the troops of Cornwallis; when the Colonel returned to his residence. The lives and safety of the settlers upon the New-Hampshire grants were exposed to the depredations of the Indians and tories—many were killed or tortured, having all their property destroyed, and others lived in constant fear of being brought to a like situation. Royalton, a township upon White river, containing three hundred inhabitants, and some of the towns adjacent, were invaded in 1780 by two hundred and three Indians and seven white men, under the command of Lieutenant Horton, who had proceeded up Onion river, on an expedition against Newbury, for the purpose, as was supposed, of taking Lieutenant Whitcomb. who had wantonly shot General Gordon, an English officer, in July, 1776, between St. Johns and Chambly, and took from him his sword and watch. The British, resenting this act as unjustifiable and mean, were anxious to avenge themselves on Whitcomb. While on their way, falling in with some hunters, they were informed that the people of Newbury were expecting an attack and prepared for defence. This turned their attention towards Royalton. They accordingly proceeded up Stevens' and Jail branches, then down the first branch of White river to Tunbridge, where they lay in their encampment during the Sabbath, and on Monday, the 16th of October, they commenced their depredations at the house of John Hutchinson, living near the line between Tunbridge and Royalton. After taking him and his brother prisoners, they proceeded to Robert Havens', where they killed Messrs. Button and Pember; from thence to Joseph Kneeland's, took him, his father, Simeon Belknap, Giles Gibbs, and Jonothan Brown prisoners. Proceeding to Elias Curtis', they took him, John Kent, and Peter Mason prisoners. Thus far they had gone with the greatest silence, and when they arrived at the mouth of the branch, they made a stand, sending out small parties in different directions to plunder and bring in prisoners. By this time the alarm had become general, the inhabitants were flying for safety in every direction, and the savages filling the air with their horrid yells. One party extended their ravages down the river into Sharon, took two prisoners and burnt several houses and barns. Another party proceeded up the river, made prisoner of a young lad, plundered and set fire to the house of General Stevens, and advanced about three miles in that direction, killing the cattle, plundering and setting fire to the buildings as they passed. After finishing their work of destruction, they returned with their booty to the place of their attack in the morning. They then proceeded across the hills to Randolph, where they encamped for the night, on the second branch of White river. In the course of the day, they had killed two persons, taken twenty-five prisoners, burnt upwards of 20 houses and about the same number of barns, killed 150 head of cattle, and all the hogs and sheep that fell in their way; having suffered no loss themselves, and scarcely met with any opposition. So sudden and powerful was the attack that the people took no measures for their defence. The alarm, however, spread so soon that several hundred marched from the towns on Connecticut river, by evening, to the place where the attack commenced. They organized themselves under the command of Captain John House, an experienced officer in the Continental army, who began his march with this brave and undisciplined corps, in quest of the savage army, who by this time were encamped seven or eight miles ahead.— With great animation they pursued on their way, in a dark night, guided only by a few marked trees, amidst logs, rocks and hills, until they arrived where the last houses had been burnt. Apprehensive that the enemy were near, they now proceeded with more caution. The Indian sentries were placed nearly half a mile in the rear, behind some trees near the path. When the van was in a short distance of the sentries, they were fired upon and one man was wounded. The Americans returned the fire, killed one Indian and wounded one or two more. House proceeded within three hundred yards of the Indian camp and halted, to await the approach of day light. The Indians were alarmed at this intelligence, but they soon devised means for their safety. An aged prisoner was sent out to inform the Americans that if they proceeded to attack them, they would instantly put all the prisoners to death. Savage barbarity had consigned over two of the prisoners, to be scalped and tomahawked—one on account of his refusing to march, from an expectation of relief from the Americans, and the other, by way of retaliating the death of the Indian who was slain. The Indians hastily retreated, covering their rear with their warriors. Having consummated their plans, they quickly crossed the stream, marched up the west side into Randolph, took one prisoner, proceeded through the west part of Brookfield, thence to Onion river, and by that route to St. Johns and Montreal. House and his forces, not apprehensive of the enemy's departure, waited until day, when they were all gone. This delay deprived them of the opportunity of attacking the enemy, whom they pursued five miles into Brookfield, where they found all quiet. Considering by this, that any further attempt at a pursuit would be unavailing, they, therefore, returned to their own habitations. At the time of the attack upon Royalton, the Indian character seemed to have undergone considerable change: although they plundered, burnt and destroyed every thing that came in their way, yet they killed only those who attempted to escape, or opposed them. The women and female children, in particular, were treated with lenity and forbearance, such as had not been exhibited upon any former aggression: and it appears they were well aware of it, by the manner in which they conducted themselves toward the savages.— One woman had self-possession enough to address them in spirited terms, telling them that if they had the spirits and souls of men they would cross the stream, go to the fort and fight with the men. They tamely bore her remarks, and only replied, "Squaw should not say too much."— Yet more bold and praiseworthy encounters were performed by others who received but little repulsion, particularly by an elderly matron. They had taken her little boy, but she followed with her other children and importuned them to return him. Unwilling to contend with her, they yielded, and by her further earnest solicitations, released ten or twelve belonging to her neighbors. At length, wishing to be rid of her, and being tired of her importunities, an Indian very politely offered to carry her over the stream upon his back. She without hesitation accepted, and he safely carried her to the opposite bank, after passing through the water up to his middle. When she had succeeded in getting the children across, she directly returned, to the great surprise and exultation of their parents and friends. On their way to Canada, the prisoners were not treated with severity. When they arrived at Montreal, several of them were sold to a British Colonel, at the price of eight dollars a head. One only of the twenty-six that was taken off, died in captivity: the remainder were liberated, and returned to their friends the next summer.

The New-Hampshire grants had co-operated with the general government in furnishing men and provisions for carrying on the war of independence, and following up a rigorous prosecution of the contest, with as great zeal and fidelity as those who were members of the confederated states. Whatever was thus done in aid of the general cause of American liberty, rested entirely with the will of the state. The government of Vermont was then, in relation to the general confederacy, as independent of its power or control, as any kingdom in Europe. Their proceedings, however, as a body politic, had scarcely the form of a civil government. They had no other method of transacting business, than to follow, when collected together, the general advice of the most vigilant and ambitious of their leaders. When called upon for supplies, the people assembled to determine what was best to be done, and when a vote had passed upon any subject, there was no other power to carry it into effect than the consent and inclination of each individual. Custom alone, gave the force of law to their proceedings. "The sentiments and maxims derived from the opinions and feelings of the neighbours and leaders, were all the powers that subsisted to put any restraint on the most vicious, or to preserve the lives or properties of the inhabitants." Such a state of society was found to be incompatible with the safety and prosperity of the people. The attention of the public had been so much engaged in the concerns of war, that the controversy of New-York had almost ceased. The government of Vermont was then vested in town meetings and councils of safety, which gave directions in all matters of public concern. Business which related to a whole community could not be conducted with any despatch or certainty, so long as the general voice could not be taken in one place, either by the whole people or by a delegated power. Combinations on a more general plan were necessarily introduced among the several towns, to be holden at different times and places in the grants. A general state government had not been attempted nor ever thought of; nor had the independence of Vermont as yet been contemplated. Without any government or plan of proceedings, the people seemed to have approached nearly to a state of nature: combining together only so far as necessity required to promote their common interest and safety. In the latter part of the year 1775, some of the principal men went to Philadelphia, to obtain the advice of Congress, and on their return, dispersed several letters containing the advice of that body upon the subject of their affairs; which was, that the people should form a temporary government, by committees and conventions, as the circumstances of society might require. In compliance with this advice, a convention assembled at Dorset, January 16th, 1776, and a petition from that body was forwarded to Congress. They avowed their willingness to render every possible assistance in prosecuting the American war, whenever they should be called on by government for that purpose, but expressed an unwillingness to put themselves under the provincial government of New-York, lest it should be construed as an act of submission to their authority. They concluded by requesting of Congress, should it find their services necessary, that they should not be styled inhabitants of New-York, or be subject to the limitations, restrictions, or regulations of that province; but as settlers of the New-Hampshire grants, and that whatever commissions were issued, they might so be regarded.

The Committee entrusted with this business recommended to the petitioners to submit, for the present, to the government of New-York, and contribute their assistance in the present contest with Great-Britain, and that such submission ought not to prejudice their rights to the lands in controversy, or be construed to affirm or admit the jurisdiction over it whenever the present hostilities are ended. At a time when the fate of America was problematical, the committee could not but desire that all internal controversies might terminate. To prevent a decision the petition was withdrawn. The settlers on the New-Hampshire grants had never been recognized by the crown as holding a distinct jurisdiction, nor invested with separate powers. They had never enjoyed the privilege of a regular organization, under which they could act with system and effect. They had no other bond of union to stimulate them, than a common interest in opposing the claims of New-York, and necessity, which urged them to resistance, operated to give the force of law to the recommendations of their committees and conventions, while a few adventurous spirits gave impulse, energy and system to their operations.

The affairs of the settlers were thus peculiarly situated, when the memorable declaration of Independence was published to the world, July 4th, 1776, by the Congress of the United Colonies. Their situation at the dissolution of the Colonies with Great-Britain was unprecedented. Colonel Skeen had received a royal commission to be governor of Ticonderoga, Crown Point, and an uncertain extent of country bordering thereon. The possession of their lands was originally had under royal grants from the governor of New-Hampshire: but New-York now claimed the jurisdiction and the right of the sale. The settlers had petitioned the crown for an adjustment of their dispute, and when there was indication of a favorable decision between the contending parties, the connection between the crown and the colonies was dissolved. There was no power recognized by the parties as superior, or possessing the right of deciding the controversy. All claims by New-Hampshire to the grants were renounced. The convention of New-York now reviving the controversy, unanimously declared on the 2d of August, 1776, that all quit rents formerly due to Great-Britain, are now due and owing to this convention, or such future government as shall hereafter be established in this state. The situation of the settlers was such as would naturally suggest to them the right and expediency of declaring themselves independent. The claims of New-York had never been admitted, and allegiance to the crown was no longer acknowledged: therefore the time had now arrived, and regard to their own safety required their assumption of the power of self-government. A variety of opinions originated from the difficulties. With some a union with New-Hampshire was considered expedient, and others thought a submission to New-York would be their only safety.— But those who were the most determined, considered that the powers of government might as well be assumed, and the consequences arising from such a measure, be hazarded at the present time. Accordingly a convention was called, by notices from some of the most influential individuals, to ascertain what the general voice of the people would be on this subject. This body, consisting of delegates from thirty-five towns, assembled at Dorset July 24, 1776. A resolution was passed in this convention, that they would defend their liberties to the utmost of their power. The people were inclined to think that an entire separation from New-York would be altogether best.— The convention met again September 25, and unanimously resolved to declare the New-Hampshire grants a separate district, and that no law or laws should be accepted from any other source. This body were again convened at Westminister, January 15, 1777, and there passed a resolution that their only safe course was to form themselves into a new State, and assume all the powers of government: with this view the following sentiment was declared. "This convention, whose members are duly chosen by the voice of their constituents, do hereby proclaim and publicly declare that the district of territory comprehended and usually known by the name and description of the New-Hampshire grants, of right ought to be, and is hereby declared forever hereafter to be considered a free and independent state, called, known, and distinguished by the name of New-Connecticut, alias Vermont. And that the inhabitants who at present are, or may hereafter become residents within said territory, shall be entitled to the same privileges, immunities, and enfranchisements, which are, or which may hereafter at any time be allowed to the inhabitants of any free and independent state in America. And that such privileges and immunities shall be regulated by a bill of rights, and by a form of government, to be established at the next adjourned session of this convention. Having come to this decision, they drew up a declaration and petition to Congress, addressing them as the Supreme Power of the land. "That they should hereafter consider themselves as a free and independent state, capable of regulating their own internal police, in all and every respect whatever, and that the people possess the sole and exclusive right of governing themselves in such manner and form as they in their wisdom should choose, not repugnant to the laws of the general government. And further they declared their readines to act in conjunction with the people of the United States, in contributing their full proportion towards maintaining the present just war against the fleets and armies of Great-Britain. A petition was also raised and forwarded, requesting Congress to receive their declaration and secure to this territory a free and independent situation among the confederated states, and also the privilege of a delegation in Congress. To this declaration and petition are subscribed in behalf of the inhabitants, the names of Jonas Fay, Thomas Chittenden, Heman Allen and Reuben Jones, statesmen of high respectability and talents. The character of most of the leading men in Vermont was at this time conspicuous for wisdom and stability. The measures they took, placed Vermont in a commanding situation; it inspired others with confidence and increased firmness among themselves. An appeal corresponding so well with the spirit of the times, could not be otherwise than approved of by the neighboring colonies. A willingness was manifested by New-Hampshire to admit Vermont to an independent government; Connecticut and

Massachusetts also approved of the measure. But to New-York, her conduct appeared to be a renewal of previous opposition and a rebellion against lawful authority. Apprehensive of bad consequences from such proceedings, the committee of safety for the State of New-York, then in session, (January 20th, 1777,) investigated the matter, and directed the president to communicate this information to Congress, that certain designing men, by their arts and influence, had prevailed on a portion of the State of New-York, to revolt and disavow the authority of its legislature. The evidence received by them produced the conviction that persons of great influence in the neighboring states have encouraged these divisions, and even some members of the honorable Congress were implicated in the scheme, but decency required a suspension of this belief. The commission conferred upon Colonel Warner, with the power of selecting the officers of his regiment, to be raised within the present disputed tract of country, which lately declared its independence, and supported by the general government, has given too much weight to the insinuations of those who predicted that Congress was determined to support these insurgents, especially as this Colonel Warner has been outlawed for his opposition to the legislature of New-York. For the satisfaction of justice and the conviction of these deluded people, that Congress has not been prevailed on to assist in dismembering a state, which of all others, has suffered most in the common cause, the commission given to Colonel Warner must absolutely be recalled. In pursuance of the same subject, another representation was made to that body, March 1777. In this the convention of New-York declare that they depended upon the justice of that honorable house to suppress by some proper means, the mischiefs which must ensue to the general confederacy from the unjust and pernicious designs of such of the inhabitants, as merely from selfish motives, have fomented the dangerous insurrection. That notwithstanding all the arts of the seducers, Congress may now be informed that the spirit of defection was by no means general. The county of Gloucester, and a large portion of Cumberland and Charlotte counties, continued steadfast in their allegiance to the government of New-York, and that there was not the least probability that Colonel Warner could raise such a number of men as would be an object of public concern. A general attention had now began to be given to the introduction of regular forms and proceedings in Vermont, and for their encouragement in the formation and adoption of a government, Thomas Young, of Philadelphia, sent a printed paper to the people of Vermont, to which was prefixed a resolution of Congress, passed May 15, 1776, recommending to all bodies of people who look upon themselves as returned to a state of nature, to adopt such a form of government as would conduce to the happiness and safety of their constituents.— The address gave it as the sentiment of several leading members of Congress, that Vermont had nothing further to do than to take up a government in every township in the district, and invite the inhabitants to meet in their respective towns and choose members for a general convention, to meet at an early day, for choosing delegates for the general Congress, and to form a constitution for the state; at the same time telling them to make the experiment, and he would insure them success. And further, that they had as good a right to choose how they would be governed, and by whom, as others had. The people of New-York were highly indignant that publications espousing the cause and calculated to establish the independence of Vermont, should be circulated. The president of the New-York council of safety, wrote on the 28th day of May, 1777, to the President of Congress, that a report prevailed, and daily gained credit, that the revolters were privately countenanced in their designs by certain members of Congress, and for fear of injuring the reputation of that honorable body by imputations so disgraceful and mean, they esteem it their duty to give this information on the subject, unwilling that suspicions so disrespectful to any member of Congress should be entertained, yet the fact is that numbers of the people in this state do believe the report to be well founded.

The representations of Thomas Young, were laid before Congress on the 23d of June, to bring the matter to some decision. The papers and letters which had been received from the Convention of New-York, and from the people of the New-Hampshire grants, were refered to a committee of the whole, who, after several adjournments, acted on them June 30. This body declared that the design of their creation, was for defending the several states against the oppressions of Great-Britain, and, therefore, it was not intended that Congress would countenance any thing injurious to the rights and jurisdiction of the several communities which they represent. They further resolved that the inhabitants of the New-Hampshire grants, can derive no countenance or justification, for declaring themselves an independent government, from the act of Congress declaring the united Colonies, independent of the crown of Great Britain, nor from any other act of Congress. The petition of Jonas Fay and others, that their declaration, styling themselves a free and independent State, might be received, and that delegates from the same be admitted to seats in Congress, were dismissed. Congress disclaimed all intentions of giving any encouragement to the claims of the people for an independent state, by their commissioning Colonel Warner to raise and command a regiment of Green Mountain troops; but the design was to reinstate many officers of the different states, who had served in Canada, in the army of the United States. In concluding their strictures upon the affairs of Vermont, they declared Young's letter to be derogatory to the honor of Congress, and a gross misrepresentation of the resolution therein refered to, and tended to deceive the people to whom they are addressed. These resolutions appeared to be dictated by the influence of New-York, from the most favorable construction that could be given them, and the people of Vermont concluded that they should have to support their independence with the same firmness with which it had been declared. This furnished an occasion for the people to become more acquainted with the nature and origin of their rights. New-Hampshire had conceded more in favor of the independence of Vermont, than any other State. The American army posted a Ticonderoga, was compelled to leave that station on the 6th of July, 1777, by the British, under Burgoyne. Most of the people on the west side of the mountain, left their habitations in great consternation and trouble. The council of safety in Vermont, requested assistance from the council of safety in New-Hampshire, and assured them that if none should be granted, they should be under the necessity of putting themselves under the protection of the enemy, and others adjoining would be obliged to do the same. They declared at the same time, their willingness and ability to support an army and do every thing in their power to establish the independence of the government. By an order of the General Assembly of New-Hampshire, a large force of militia were put under the command of General Stark, with orders to repair to Charlestown, on Connecticut river, there to consult with a committee of the New-Hampshire grants, respecting his future operations, and the supply of his men with provisions, to take the command of the militia and march into the grants, and to act in conjunction with the troops of that new state, or any other of the states, or of the United States. About the same time, Mr. Weare, President of New-Hampshire, sent a communication to Ira Allen, Secretary of the State of Vermont, on the subject of the forces being supplied for the aid of the frontiers, couched in a style and form of expression acknowledging Vermont as a free and a sovereign, but a new State. There was no doubt but that New-Hampshire had conceded the independence of Vermont, and would use her influence to have Congress do the same. A new controversy now arose amongst the inhabitants of New-Hampshire, which produced a very serious difficulty with that state. New-Hampshire was originally granted as a province, to John Mason, and was circumscribed by a line drawn at the distance of sixty miles from the sea. The original bounds of New-Hampshire were well known to the inhabitants on the east side of the Connecticut river, who were now anxious to unite with the people on the west side of the river, in forming a new state. With these views it was an easy matter to offer reasons in justification of their proceedings. The original limits of the province of New-Hampshire extending only sixty miles from the sea coast, and the additional towns being annexed lately by virtue of the royal commissions, which could operate no longer than the power of the crown subsisted, were urged, together with the cessation of all obligations to New-Hampshire, on their denial of the authority of the crown. These, they asserted, gave them the full liberty to join whatever government they chose. Success attended the propagation of such ideas in the towns near the river; conventions assembled, and in a few months sixteen towns declaring themselves in a state of nature with regard to their internal police, requested Vermont to receive them into union with herself. This application was perplexing to the government of the states, a majority of which were opposed to the projected union.

Those towns contiguous to Connecticut river, were in favor of receiving the towns from New-Hampshire, and proceeded so far as to propose withdrawing from their connexion with Vermont and forming a new state. The question for altering the jurisdictional bounds of the state rested with the people, and great activity was shown by the party in favor of the union, for securing a majority of members in the next assembly. On the meeting of the legislative body a vote was obtained in favor of the confederation and an admission of any other town, on the east side of Connecticut river, on their producing a vote of the majority of the inhabitants, or sending a representative to the assembly of Vermont, was also agreed to. The sixteen towns withdrew from New-Hampshire, and announced their separation, and requested a divisional line between them and the state. Justly alarmed at this proceeding, Mr. Weare, then President of New-Hampshire, wrote to Governor Chittenden, claiming those seceding towns as a part of the state before the revolution. He gave information also that a minority in those towns had claimed protection from that state, which the assembly of New-Hampshire viewed themselves as bound on every consideration to afford. He desired the Governor, for the sake of public tranquillity and peace, to relinquish so improper and dangerous connexion.

The delegates in Congress from New-Hampshire were urged by Mr. Weare to take the advice and procure the interposition of Congress, stating at the same time as his opinion, that this probably was the only method of settling the controversy without the effusion of blood, as all attempts at reconciliation had proved fruitless. On the reception of this intelligence, the Governor and Council of Vermont requested General Ethan Allen to repair to Philadelphia, and ascertain in what light their proceedings were viewed by that body. The agent reported on his return that Congress was unanimously opposed to the union of those towns with Vermont, and if the proceeding were disannulled no member of Congress would oppose their independence. The Legislature on hearing the report of Congress, took up the subject of the union. At their session in Windsor, October 13th, 1778, a question was moved whether the towns on the east side of Connecticut river, which had been admitted into the union with Vermont, should be erected into a county by themselves. The question was decided by 23 in the affirmative, and 31 in the negative. After ascertaining the feelings of the assembly on this subject, the members from fifteen towns on Connecticut river withdrew from the house, and with them proceeded those from the sixteen towns in New-Hampshire, together with the deputy governor and two assistants. The assembly of Vermont consisted of sixty members, two-thirds of which were necessary to make a house to do business. This was just the number left when the seceding members had retired.

The business was pursued and finished by the remaining members. But the arrangements with New-Hampshire were referred over for the instructions of the people. The legislature was now adjourned to meet again on the second Thursday of February next, and an order was issued to the constables of the several towns, whose representatives had withdrawn to lead them to another choice. The seceding members immediately assented and entered upon a plan for calling a convention of delegates from the towns along the valley of Connecticut river. The real object of this movement was now well understood and it proved very injurious to Vermont. The plan was to form a new state with the seat of government upon Connecticut river, which would effectually dismember Vermont.— This convention met at Cornish, N. H. on the 9th day of December, 1778. They agreed first to unite generally, without any regard to the original line assigned by New-Hampshire, and to make the following proposals to that government:—either to agree among themselves as to the divisional line or submit it to Congress; or to arbitrators mutually chosen. If neither of the above proposals should be accepted, the convention concluded to connect themselves with New-Hampshire and become a state as it was before the settling of the said line in 1764. The design of these towns, eight of which were represented in the convention, was now apparent. The people of Vermont were fully awake to their danger. The injustice of aiding in the dismemberment of New-Hampshire become too evident to admit a doubt as to the course proper to be pursued.

If their scheme should succeed, the government of one or the other of the states must be broken up. To get rid of this dangerous connection, the union was dissolved on the 12th of February, 1779 by an act of the legislature.—These difficulties about the division of the states, induced several of the leading members of the New-Hampshire assembly to lay claim to the whole of the lands. New-York also put in her claims for the jurisdiction of the same. It was not to be doubted now, as New-Hampshire could make no legal claim to the premises, that it was a contrivance amongst the leading men in the two states to divide Vermont between them. A natural division would be formed by the range of the Green Mountains running through the state, between New-Hampshire and New-York, which would fully terminate all the controversies of the people of Vermont, as to their limits, the validity of their grants, or the powers of the government which they had assumed, had no other state laid a claim or interfered in the controversy. But Massachusetts extended her right to a large portion of Vermont: whether her designs were earnestly expressed, or whether it was a manœuvre she employed to disappoint the views of New-Hampshire and New-York, did not appear. The claim of Massachusetts appeared much more plausible than that of New-Hampshire, because the line between these states might be considered settled; but that between Massachusetts and New-York had never been. In treating upon the controversy with New-York, it will be necessary to return to the proclamation of Governor Clinton, February 23, 1778, from which it appears that New-York, though claiming jurisdiction over the contested territory, had evidently changed her policy towards Vermont. The overtures for reconciliation, after enumerating the causes of disagreement, were, that all persons should be quieted in possessing and improving lands acquired by title under grants from New-Hampshire or Massachusetts; that persons holding or possessing lands not granted by either of the three governments, should be confirmed in their possessions, and have a quantity of land contiguous to their possessions, sufficient for a convenient farm: that all controverted cases concerning lands cannot be decided by rules, exhibited in the articles aforesaid. The legislature of New-York will provide for the determination of the same, according to the rules of justice and equity, arising out of such cases. That quit rents shall be reduced to what they were originally, under the grants of New-Hampshire and Massachusetts. That the aforesaid regulations and directions must be observed at the peril of the people. There was an appearance of fairness in these propositions which might have deceived those who were not very perceptive and jealous of their rights. But the people of Vermont were not to be deceived by such presentments of condescending authority. No relief was perceived in these overtures by those who had long been accustomed to a thorough investigation of every point in the controversy. The idea kept strengthening with the progress of the difficulty, that the claims of New-York were entirely groundless. Under such convictions, they declared their independence and proceeded to organize a government. The supremacy of New-York they utterly disavowed. Colonel Ethan Allen published an answer to this proclamation, in August, 1779, observing, after he had replied to the overtures in that document, that the principal inducement he had in answering them was to derive full proof from the same, that the best way for vacating the interposing grants of New-York, is to maintain inviolable, the supremacy of the legislative authority of the state of Vermont.— This will put it in the power of the people to enjoy the great blessings of a free and independent government. In a correspondence with one of the inhabitants of Vermont, Governor Clinton observed that he should earnestly recommend a firm and prudent resistance to the drafting of men, and raising taxes, and the exercise of every act of government under the ideal state of Vermont, and in such towns where the friends of New-York are sufficiently powerful for the purpose, would advise the entering into an association for the mutual defence of their persons and estates, against this usurpation. In a communication to Congress on their controversy with Vermont, he affirmed that the violence of the inhabitants would soon bring on a civil war, and that all the troubles of the people in this district, arose from the former, not the present government of New-York. A difficulty of a more serious aspect, originating among certain persons disaffected towards the government of Vermont, in the south-east part of the State, ensued.

Some of these persons who were commissioned by Governor Clinton, asserted that they had a regiment of five hundred men, and that the county committee was opposed to the authority of Vermont. The government of this state found their associations so direful in their consequences, that Colonel Ethan Allen was directed to raise a part of the militia to suppress them. On this intelligence, a person under a commission from New-York, sent a communication to Governor Clinton, for his advice and direction, stating the propriety of having the Albany militia in readiness to attack any armed force that should assemble for that purpose, and that it would be an easy matter to give information by employing some of their inimical townsmen in Vermont. In answer to this application, general firmness and prudence were recommended, and in no instance acknowledgement of the authority of the State of Vermont, unless there was no alternative between submission and inevitable ruin:—assuring them at the same time, if any attempt was made at their reduction, the militia should be ordered out against the enemies of the State of New-York wherever they might be found.— At this critical juncture, a convention was organized from the different persons in Cumberland county, who met at Brattleborough, May 4th, 1779, which gave a new impulse to the controversy of New-York. They represented their aggrievances to be a destitution of the regular means for punishing the most atrocious offenders or of obtaining private justice; that the officers of the pretended State of Vermont, have exercised authority over those who continue loyal to the State of New-York, and have quite lately taken away our cattle with their illegal orders, and took a magistrate a prisoner, who was acting under the authority of New-York, in a matter which no way concerned them, and placed him under bonds of 1000 pounds for his appearance at the next court. Demand was made, on the authorities of New-York, to carry their solemn engagements, entered upon with the loyal inhabitants, into immediate execution. Fearful of civil commotions, Gov. Clinton informed the President of Congress, that matters were approaching to a very serious crisis, which nothing but the immediate interposition of Congress could possibly prevent; that he should be obliged to defend by force those who adhered to New-York. Congress was reminded of the consequence of submitting the controversy, especially at that period, to a decision of the sword, and also that the justice and faith of government, the peace and safety of society, would not allow them any longer to be the familiar spectators of the violence committed on their fellow citizens. On the 29th of May, 1779, these and various other papers relating to the disputes with New-Hampshire, were laid before Congress, and by them referred to a committee of the whole. Immediately after, Congress resolved that a committee be appointed to examine into the reasons why the people in the New-Hampshire grants refuse to continue citizens of those States, which heretofore exercised jurisdiction over them, and that every prudent measure should be taken to prevent animosities so prejudicial to the Union and every measure adopted to promote a settlement of difficulties. Hostilities ensued between a party of green mountain boys, under the command of Colonel Allen, and a militia officer, acting under the authority of New-York. Relief was immediately sought of Governor Clinton, who represented the same to Congress. The committee who had been appointed to confer with the inhabitants, was highly disapproved of, and a delay in their journey, until a resolution of Congress could be taken on the subject, requested. Congress ordered the officers deprived of their liberty to be immediately freed from arrest, and that, on the arrival of the committee, all matters would be investigated. But two of five of the committee, Dr. Witherspoon and Mr. Atle, attended. On entering Vermont, many enquiries were made and several conferences held, both with those in the interest of Vermont and New-York. Written answers were given to some of their interrogatories. They seem to have endeavored at a reconciliation between the parties; but no part of the business for which they were sent appeared from their report to be accomplished.

The various claims of of New-York, New-Hampshire, Massachusetts and the settlers, to the disputed territory, became so serious a matter that alarming consequences were justly to be feared. It therefore became Congress, to whom all parties appealed, to intespose in a matter which seemed essentially to affect the common interest of the Union. Accordingly, on the 24th of September, 1779, a resolution was unanimously passed, requesting the states of New-Hampshire, New-York and Massachusetts to enact laws, expressly authorizing Congress to hear and examine into all the disputes and differences relative to the jurisdiction aforesaid, between the said three states respectively: and it was further resolved, that it was the duty of the people in said district, to abstain from exercising authority over any power or any inhabitants who profess themselves to be citizens or owe allegiance to any, or either of said states; and also that the three states aforenamed, ought to suspend exerting their laws over any of the inhabitants of said district, except such as confess the jurisdiction of the same; and finally, that all unappropriated lands or estates which are or may be adjudged forfeited or confiscated, lying within said district, ought to await the final decision of Congress in the premises to be sold or granted. The evasions of Congress evidently showed that the union and affection of New-Hampshire, New-York and Massachusetts was considered by that body of more importance to be preserved, than the existence of Vermont. This evasive policy was probably best at a time when the bonds of union might be severed by the disaffection of one of these states. Acts in compliance with the recommendations of Congress, were passed by all the states, except Massachusetts, who withheld probably to save Vermont from dismemberment. The resolutions of Congress establishing four separate jurisdictions in the same territory and at the same time, was impossible, and such as the people who had assumed the powers of government could not comply with. A constitution, laws and courts of justice were already settled, and civil authority fully exercised.

The plan of encouraging a system of espionage, was inconsistent with the existence of Vermont. She was literally struggling for an existence, but happily, her citizens possessed resources of mind equal to the emergency of the occasion. Five agents were appointed by the Legislature of Vermont, to agree upon, and finally settle certain articles of union and confederation, between this State and the United States, which should be binding upon the inhabitants in all cases whatever.

Governor Chittenden sent General Allen, October 28, 1779, to wait on the Council and General Court of Massachusetts, and be informed over what part of the State they extended their claim, and to what extent they should endeavor to carry their pretentions into execution, in the trial at Congress. Every necessary step was there promised to be taken, in order to bring about an equitable accommodation of all difficulties, agreeable to the strictest rules of justice and equity; but this could not be done without an acknowledgement of the independence of the State. The reasons for supporting their independence were fully exhibited, nor did they, in the least measure, evince a disposition to abandon it. After the aforementioned resolutions of Congress, communicated to Governor Chittenden, were laid before the Council, he replied, "that they could not view themselves as holden in the sight of God or man, to submit to the execution of a plan which they had reason to believe, was commenced by a neighboring state, for the purpose of suspending their liberties and privileges, upon the arbitrament and final determination of Congress: when, in their opinion, they were things too sacred, ever to be arbitrated upon, and what they were bound to defend, at the expense of their possessions and lives." They also denied the right of Congress to intermeddle in the internal police and government of Vermont—a government, which existed independent of the United States, and was not accountable to them for liberty—the gift of the beneficent Creator. She was not represented in Congress, and therefore could not submit to resolutions passed without her consent, or even knowledge, which put every thing valuable at stake.— They declared their willingness to assist with their blood and treasures in supporting the war with Great-Britain, but were not so lost to all sense and honor, as that after four years' war with Great-Britain, that they would yield every thing worth contending for; the right of making their own laws, and choosing their own form of government, to the arbitrament and determination of Congress.

The business of settling the controverted claims upon the territory of the New-Hampshire grants, was not taken up on the first day of February, nor on the 21st day of March, as was ordered by Congress, but the business was postponed. Nine States, exclusive of those who were parties in the question, were not represented. On June 2d Congress resolved that the proceedings of the people in the New-Hampshire grants, were highly unwarrantable and subversive of the peace and welfare of the United States, and they are hereby strictly required to forbear and abstain from all acts of authority civil or military, over the inhabitants of any town or district, who profess allegiance to any other State. The question was again defered to the second Tuesday in September.

These resolutions being communicated to the Governor of Vermont, he declared that however Congress might regard them, the people of Vermont viewed them as subversive of the right they have to independence and liberty, as well as incompatible with the principle on which Congress grounded their own rights to independence, and their tendency went directly to the subversion of American liberty. Vermont being a free and independent State, had devised the authority of Congress to judge of their jurisdiction, and were not included in the thirteen United States. Therefore they were at liberty to offer or accept terms of a cecession of hostilities with Great-Britain, without the approbation of any power, on the supposition that neither Congress nor the Legislature of those States which they represent, will support Vermont in her independence, but devote her to the usurped government of any other power. She has not the most distant wish to continue hostilities with Great-Britain and maintain an important frontier for the benefit of the United States, and for no other reward than the ungrateful one of being enslaved by them. Yet, notwithstanding the usurpations and injustice of the neighboring governments towards Vermont, and the late resolutions of Congress, from a principle of virtue and close attachment to the cause of liberty, as well as from a thorough examination of their own policy, they were induced once more to offer union with the United States of America, of which Congress was the legal representative body. The claims of New-Hampshire and New-York to the jurisdiction of Vermont, were brought forward for a decision. Ira Allen and Stephen R. Bradley, Esq'rs, agents for Vermont, presented themselves, but were not considered as the representatives of any state or country invested with legislative authority. Yet they required of Congress to be notified whenever any subject relating to the independence of Vermont came before them. In September, being cited to appear, the agents of New-York furnished evidence to substantiate their claims to the New-Hampshire grants, and that the settlers had no right to a separate and independent jurisdiction. Vermont, having never consented to submit the question of her right to an arbitrament of Congress, was very much disconcerted on finding that Congress was admitting testimony to decide the controversy without considering her as one of the parties or her agents in any other capacity than that of private persons. A feeling of obligation for the character and destiny of Vermont, constrained the agents to enter a remonstrance to the proceedings of Congress. The towering spirit of independence was not checked by this repulse They declared it would lead to their own abasement and betray the trust reposed in them, to sit any longer as idle spectators. They professed their willingness to furnish their full proportion of troops and money for the American war, until that should be terminated, and readiness to submit their dispute to the mediation of one or more disinterested States, for final determination and adjustment.—But they reprobate the idea that Congress should sit as a court of judicature to settle the dispute by virtue of any authority given to them by the acts of the States, which make but one party.

The evidence of New-Hampshire being heard, Congress delayed for further consideration. This delay of a decision in the national legislature did not meet the approbation of the people of Vermont, although it furnished pretty conclusive evidence that the situation of the State had made some impression upon Congress. However, the immediate recognition of her independence, and admission into the Union, could not be expected. While the pertinacious adherence of New-Hampshire and New-York to their claims buffetted their designs and roused their resentment, they determined upon a different kind of policy. Congress were fearful of deciding against them, knowing that the leading men would rather have Vermont become a province under the British government, than submit to the authority of New-York. Therefore a decision upon the controversy of Vermont was wisely avoided, which would have been as dangerous as to have done the same against New-Hampshire or New-York. Congress avoided a decision upon the constitutional question, whether they had the power to form a new State within the limits of the Union. The repulse Vermont received on being refused an admission into the Union, and the alarm she had taken from the measures pursued by New-Hampshire and New-York, roused her to persue the same measures that the other States had, in claiming jurisdiction beyond the settled boundaries of their governments. A majority of the inhabitants of the western parts of New-Hampshire were still desirous of uniting under the government of Vermont,—others were wishing to support the claims of New-Hampshire over the whole territory of Vermont.— A meeting of delegates from several towns in New-Hampshire was held at Walpole, and a committee was appointed to report their views upon the subject of uniting Vermont with New-Hampshire, which reported that a convention ought to be called from the towns on both sides of Connecticut river, to settle the controverted claims of New-Hampshire and Vermont. On the 16th of January, 1739, representatives from forty-three towns repaired to Charlestown; but to the great disappointment of those who moved the measure, a majority of the convention was in favor of joining with the government of Vermont. A committee was appointed to consult with the legislature of Vermont, on the subject of the proposed union; and they reported to the legislature, then sitting at Windsor, February 10, 1782, that the convention were desirous of uniting with Vermont in one separate and independent government, upon such principles as should be mutually thought to be equitable and beneficial. In pursuance of the desires of the convention, the legislature resolved, on the 14th day of February, "that in order to quiet the present disturbances and enable the inhabitants on both sides of Connecticut river to defend their frontier, the legislature of this State do lay a jurisdictional claim to all the lands whatever, east of Connecticut river, north of Massachusetts, west of Mason's line, and south of latitude 45 degrees. The articles of union were agreed on by the convention of New-Hampshire, then in session at Cornish, opposite Windsor, and the assembly of Vermont, which were declared sacred and inviolable.

A number of the inhabitants in the adjacent parts of New-York had previously petitioned Vermont to receive them into union, and afford them assistance for the defence of the frontiers; informing them likewise, if their petition was rejected, they must retire into the interior of the country for protection and safety. This petition of the inhabitants, the necessity of defending the frontiers, and the measures New-York was pursuing to subdue Vermont, were considered by the legislature as sufficient reasons for receiving the petitioners into her union. Accordingly a resolution was passed on the 14th of February. The legislature of Vermont determined to lay a jurisdictional claim to all the land north of Massachusetts, and extending the same to Hudson's river, thence east of the centre of the deepest channel of said river to the head thereof, being extended to latitude forty-five degrees, and south of the same river, embracing all the lands and water to the present line of this state

Vermont now extended her claims into the jurisdictions of New-York and New-Hampshire, with more propriety than these States had in claiming the lands of Vermont. This policy was highly successful. The sixteen towns that had formerly connected themselves with Vermont, and those towns attached to New-York, immediately joined in the measure. Also most of the towns in the adjoining counties of Grafton and Cheshire, in New-Hampshire, declared for the union. Thirty-five towns were represented from New-Hampshire, at the April session of the general Assembly. A committee was appointed by Vermont to take into consideration the request of the people, in the eastern parts of New-York, and in May 15, articles of union were agreed on by the representatives of twelve districts in that state, and the committee from Vermont. June 16th, representatives from ten districts took their seats in the legislature of Vermont.

This bold and decisive measure pursued by Vermont in defending herself against the encroachments of the states, produced, if nothing more, a high estimation of the bravery and fortitude of the people. Their capability for self-government could not be doubted after so successful an experiment in organizing and administering the affairs of the state, and their loyalty and firmness in supporting the cause of American Independence. An infant settlement, destitute of the wealth of older communities, generously furnishing troops and provisions for carrying on a war with one of the most potent kingdoms in the world, merited the highest praise, and the full enjoyment of its rights. The union formed, with the parts of the adjoining states, added an extent of territory equal at least to the one over which she originally claimed jurisdiction. By this policy, she increased her resources, gained the confidence of her friends, compelled the respect of her enemies, united the disaffected at home, invited emigration, and laid the foundation for a large and powerful state.

The negotiation with Canada was a very fortunate expedient for obtaining from Congress an ultimate adjustment of their difficulties, and securing an extensive frontier against the cruel depredations of an invading enemy. At the time the business was pending, no people in America were more firmly attached to the cause of Independence than they, and none less liable to temptation; but sooner than yield to dismemberment, they would have joined the enemy and established a royal government for their protection. The report that the settlers were adherents to the British government, secured their favor, and such was their increase of population and power, that they had nothing to fear from the strength and policy of their opposers. The legislature of this state continued to make grants of land, although Congress had resolved otherwise, and they acknowledged no grants made by New-York:— From the estimate the British agents had formed of the people, they calculated upon a system of corruption, and believed they could seduce them from their attachment to the American cause, and induce them to unite with the British government; and that Vermont would be persuaded to become a British province. The first intimation of the kind was a letter from Colonel Beverly Robinson to Colonel Ethan Allen, dated March 30th, 1780, and delivered to him in July, in the street at Arlington, by a British soldier, habited in disguise. The business communicated, and tenor of the letter, were expressed after the following manner:—"I am now undertaking a business which I hope will be received with the same good intention it is made. By information from many of the inhabitants, I learned that the people were opposed to the wild chimerical scheme of the Americans, in attempting to separate this continent from Great Britain, and to establish their Independence. And that they would willingly assist in uniting America with Great-Britain, and in restoring that happy constitution which has so wantonly and unadvisedly been destroyed. If the information is correct, and such be your sentiments and inclination, an unreserved communication of your views on the subject shall be faithfully attended to and laid before the Commander-in-chief according to your directions, which doubtless will have as great effect from me as any person whatsoever. Proposals cannot be made until your sentiments are made known. Should a friend be sent here with proposals, he shall be protected and well treated and allowed to return whenever he pleases." On receiving this letter Colonel Allen immediately communicated the contents of it to the governor, and a number of gentlemen in Vermont, who unanimously agreed that it was best to return no answer. Colonel Robinson again wrote to Ethan Allen, in February, 1781, inclosing the former letter in his communication, and saying:—" The frequent accounts we have had for three months past from your section of the country, confirm the opinion of your inclination to join the King's cause and assist in restoring America to her former happy and peaceful constitution. This induces me to make another attempt in sending this to you, especially as I can write with more authority, and assure you of obtaining the terms mentioned in the above letter, provided you and the people of Vermont take a decisive and active part with us." And he further requested in what manner the people of Vermont could be most serviceable to the British, either by acting with the northern army, or in joining the army from New-York. No answer was returned to these letters by Allen; but they were sent in a communication to Congress, March 9th, 1781. He declared to that body that no person could dispute his attachment to and sufferings in the cause of his country; but he did not hesitate to assert, that Vermont had an indubitable right to agree on terms of cessation of hostilities with Great-Britain, provided the United States persist in rejecting her application for a union with the States. Vermont, of all people, would be the most miserable, were she obliged to defend the independence of the United States, and they at the same time at full liberty to overthrow and ruin the independence of Vermont. I am persuaded, when Congress consider the circumstances of this State, they will not be more surprised that I have transmitted these letters, than that I have kept them in custody; for I am as resolutely determined to defend the independence of Vermont, as Congress are that of the U. States; and rather than submit, will retire with the hardy green mountain boys into the desolate caverns of the mountains, and wage war with human nature at large. In the spring of 1780, the friends of certain prisoners, taken by scouting parties and conveyed to Canada, applied to Governor Chittenden to send in a flag and regulate their exchange. The business was accordingly made known to the commanding officer of Canada, and in July, General Haldimand's answer was brought by the way of lake Champlain to Governor Chittenden. A flag was sent to Colonel Allen, the commanding officer in Vermont, promising a cessation of hostilities with the same, during the negotiation for the exchange of prisoners. Allen consented to the proposal, on condition that it should extend to the adjacent frontiers of New-York.— After some hesitation upon treating with any part of America, but Vermont, the British officer agreed to the proposition.

Col. Ira Allen and Maj. Joseph Fay were appointed commissioners by the Governor, to treat upon a negotiation of an exchange of prisoners with the British agents, Capt. J. Sherwood and George Smythe. The interview afforded the British agents an opportunity to make proposals and offers to found a royal establishment in Vermont, and such a one as should be desired. The overtures of the royalists were treated by the commissioners with affability, though nothing decisive was concluded upon. They however considered the prospect fair, for effecting their purposes. About this time, the Indians unfortunately made a mischievous descent upon Royalton. High expectations were entertained the next year that their scheme would succeed, and it was for the interest of Vermont not to undeceive them. The continental troops in Vermont and parts adjacent, had all been ordered out of the territory, leaving the people, who were destitute of money and magazines, exposed to the northern army, consisting of seven thousand men. Vermont had no other way but to effect by policy what she could not by power. The executive council concluded that this kind of management was designed by Congress to force their submission to New-York: therefore they thought it best for their own safety, to manage the British attempt at seduction to their own advantage. Col. Allen proceeded to Canada, to complete a cartel for the exchange of prisoners, in May, 1781.— The whole business was accomplished in seventeen days, on a verbal agreement that hostilities should cease between the British and those within the jurisdiction of Vermont, until after the next session of the legislature of the State, and longer, if the prospects were agreeable to the commander in chief. The rage of party feelings ran so high against the tories and those in friendship with the British, that a person in Arlington, who had in this way rendered himself obnoxious to the people, would have had his house destroyed, if Col. and Capt. Brownson had not by their advice prevented the outrage. Col. Allen being entrusted with the matter, was fully competent to transact the business of his commission. Possessed of a ready talent at negotiation, the British agents were suffered to deceive themselves with the idea of their own success, and he completely effected his objects by inducing them to form an agreement that no hostilities should be commenced against the State of Vermont. An exchange of prisoners was effected with the enemy on lake Champlain, by Major Fay, in July; and in September, Fay and Allen had another conference with the British agents, and left them in high expectations of making a royal province of Vermont: so that the enemy avoided hostilities and returned the inhabitants who had been carried away into captivity. The news of Lord Cornwallis' surrender, October 19th, 1781, arrived at the time when the legislature of Vermont were sitting at Charlestown, New-Hampshire. General St. Leger, at the head of the British army from Canada, ascended lake Champlain, and encamped at Ticonderoga. At this time General Enos commanded the troops of Vermont, and had the head quarters of his army at Castleton. Although the General and a number of his officers understood the regulations with the British, yet it became necessary to keep up appearances by sending out scouts to Champlain, to observe the enemy. One of the scouts fell in with a party of General St. Leger's. Some shots were exchanged, when Sergeant Tupper was killed and his men returned. The British agents sent letters to the seat of government for the State, announcing their intentions, and offering to publish proclamations immediately among the people.

The news of Cornwallis' surrender, they were informed, would probably render such a step dangerous, and defeat every prospect of success; therefore their only prudent way was to await the disclosures of time. The disasters of the southern army disheartened them and they returned down the lake for winter quarters, without having done any injury to Vermont. In the winter of 1782, the British in Canada were anxious to know what effect the surrender of Cornwallis had produced upon the minds of the people, and two letters were written in February and April, requesting information on that subject, in the most urgent terms. My anxiety, (says the agent,) induced me to apply to his Excellency for permission to send the bearer with this letter, to which I earnestly request you to return me an answer in the most candid and unreserved terms, the present wishes and intentions of the people and leading men of Vermont, respecting your former negotiations, and what effect the catastrophe of Lord Cornwallis has on them. Will it not be well to consider the many changes and vicissitudes of war? However brilliant the last campaign may appear, the next may wear a very different aspect. I hope you will view the matter as I do, and I think you will consider it more than ever your interest to unite with those who wish to establish you a free and happy government. Will there be a proper time to send a proclamation? I repeat my request, that you will tell me without hesitance, what may be expected in future. Another communication of April 22, was addressed to the correspondents of the British in Vermont, urging the necessity of an immediate decision in the case, and proffering the aid and friendship of the government in securing to them the great privileges of peace and prosperity, should the people of Vermont acquiesce in their propositions.

Fearful about the event, and even anxious for an answer, on the 30th of the same month they wrote again, with still greater promises. "His Excellency," (observed the agent) "has never lost sight of his first object, and I am happy to be able in this to inform you that the General has lately arrived, by the way of Halifax, with full powers from the King, to establish in V———t a government including the full extent of the east and west unions, with every privilege and immunity formerly proffered to you, and he is likewise fully authorized, as well as sincerely inclined, to provide especially, for ——— and to make ——— Brigadier General, in the line ——— field officer, with such other rewards as your sincerity and good services in bringing about the revolution, may in future merit. In short, the General is vested with full powers to make such rewards as he shall judge proper, to all those who distinguish themselves in promoting the happy union, and as his Excellency has the greatest confidence in you, and ———, much will depend on your recommendations."— Two officers belonging to Vermont, were then prisoners in Canada. Allen was sent by Governor Chittenden, with a letter to General Haldimand, requesting their release.— All the arts of negociation were employed to persuade Vermont to become a British province, and to do it without bringing on a renewal of hostilities. Every species of argument was employed by the General to effect a treaty with Vermont, but nothing more was done than to suspend hostilities, and write a friendly letter to Gov. Chittenden, stating the liberation of the prisoners. "You may rest assured that I shall give such orders as will effectually prevent hostilities of any kind being exercised in the district of Vermont, so long as the public affairs are subject to my management. And you may have my authority to promulgate in such manner as you shall think fit, this, my intention, to the people of said district; that they may, without any apprehension, continue to encourage and promote the settlement and cultivation of that new country, to the interest and happiness of themselves, and their posterity." The war and these negociations terminated in producing the highest impressions of amity and friendship in Canada, towards Vermont. The last communication of the British, on this subject, was on the twenty-fifth of March, 1783, before the news of peace was officially known or relied on as such in Canada. An expression of their sentiments upon this subject may be infered from the letter of General Haldimand, in the spring of 1783: "I am commanded to acquaint you, that, actuated from the beginning, by the sincere desire of serving you and your people, as well as of promoting the royal cause, by re-uniting you with the mother country, his excellency never lost an opportunity of representing every circumstance that could be advanced in your favor to the King's ministers, in the hope of accomplishing a reconciliation. His excellency will continue by such representations to do all in his power to serve you, but what effect it may have at this late period is very uncertain. While his excellency sincerely regrets the happy moment which it is much to be feared cannot be recalled, of restoring to you the blessing of the British government, and views with concern the fatal consequences approaching, which he has so long and so frequently predicted, from your procrastination of rejecting the adoption of his desired measure.

In the present uncertain state of affairs, uninformed as his excellency is of what is doing or perhaps done in a general accommodation, he does not think fit, until the result shall be known, to give any opinion which may influence you, perhaps to the prejudice of your interest, or that might interfere with the views of government. Should any thing favorable present, you may still depend on his excellency's utmost endeavors for your salvation. In this manner terminated a correspondence which, on the part of the British, consisted of various attempts to induce the leading men of Vermont to desert the American cause and become a British province. The correspondence was, on the part of those in Vermont who were acquainted with the secret, a doubtful and evasive course of general answers and proposals, calculated to support the British hopes of seduction, by carefully avoiding the implication of government in such measures or engagements. The object of these transactions was a cessation of hostilities and security against an invasion from Canada, when Vermont was deserted and unable to protect herself. Thomas Chittenden, Moses Robinson, Samuel Safford, Ethan Allen, Ira Allen, Timothy Brownson, John Fasset and Joseph Fay were the only persons in Vermont who had any knowledge of the Canadian negotiation. And they, from the commencement of the war, were among the most sanguine for the independence of America: men who, through the whole of the correspondence, gave decisive proofs that they could neither be bribed by wealth or seduced by honors. The proceedings of the English government had become so odious that the people, under a suspicion of the communication with the British agents, rose more than once to demand explanations. Whether such a measure was justifiable at this crisis of affairs, reason best can determine. It may be said, that such a course of proceeding at a time when the Republic of America was liable to be vanquished, was unjustifiable; but on the other side, it may be urged, that thirty thousand people, neglected by Congress, distracted by intrigues and the policy of the adjacent states, had as good a reason for defending their liberty as the rest of the continent. Should it be found that the only alternative for Vermont was to be ruled by the power of their ancient enemies, their proceedings in this case will be applauded rather than condemned. The people could hardly be made to believe that they were under any moral obligation to destroy themselves, for the sake of securing the independence of those who had refused them admittance into their confederation. But however the propriety of such policy might be viewed, the event showed that a sound judgment had been formed respecting its effect.

The people of Vermont by this management were freed from hostilities; their prisoners were restored, and themselves considered as friends rather than enemies. Thus while the British Generals imagined they were deceiving and corrupting the people of Vermont by their superior arts and addresses, the wise policy of eight honest farmers disarmed the northern army, kept them quiet and inoffensive during three campaigns, opposed Cornwallis, protected the northern frontiers, and finally saved the state.

The British Ministry, as well as the Generals, considered that they had nearly accomplished the defection of Vermont, from the cause of the American Independence. A letter, written by Lord Germain, then at the head of the American department, was intercepted on the way to Sir Henry Clinton, and carried to Philadelphia. The purport of it was, " the return of the people of Vermont, to their allegiance is an event of the utmost importance to the King's affairs, and at the same time, if Washington really meditated an irruption into Canada, it may be considered as offering an insurmountable bar to the attempt. General Haldimand, who has the same instructions with you, to draw over those people and give them support, will, I doubt not, push up a body of troops to act in conjunction with them, to secure all the avenues through their country into Canada; and when the season admits, take possession of the upper parts of the Hudson and Connecticut rivers, and cut off all communications between Albany and the Mohawk country. How far they may be able to extend southward and eastward, must depend on their numbers and the disposition of the inhabitants." This letter was placed before the public, in the Pennsylvania Packet, a newspaper of that time.

The evidence that orders were given to the British Generals in New-York and Canada, to support the people of Vermont, was now publicly known, and the heads of the British government were apprised of this disposition. Nothing was wanting to prevent it but the admission of the State into the Union. After ascertaining the fact, that the leaders of Vermont were capable of accomplishing what they had undertaken with vigor and intrepidity in the American war, and in the contest for the independence of the State, public opinion was decidedly in favor of admitting Vermont into the Union. It was declared to be dangerous to risk the independence of the United States, upon a dispute with those who had shown that they deserved the blessings of freedom as much as their neighbors. General Washington was of the same opinion, which gave additional weight. The subject of her admission was acted upon in a style very different from what it had been before. In August 7th, 1781, Congress by a majority of its delegates, resolved that " the claims of the people inhabiting the New-Hampshire grants, to exercise the powers of a sovereign and independent State, and the rights which New-Hampshire and New-York have to extend their jurisdiction over the said grants, be refered to a committee of five persons, appointed to confer with such persons as may be appointed by the inhabitants of Vermont, in vindication of their said claims. And further to agree on such terms as may be proper for their admission into the confederacy of the States. Congress also recommended to the people to appoint an agent or agents to go and confer with the committee at Philadelphia, on the subject in contemplation, and decide upon the terms and articles of union and confederation with the United States of America, in case they shall be admitted into the union. A conference was had between the committee of Congress and an agent of Vermont, on the 18th of August following. It was afterwards, on the 21st of August, made by resolution of Congress an indispensable preliminary to the recognition of the independence of Vermont, and their admission into the Federal Union, explicitly to relinquish all claims to lands east of Connecticut river, and west of the towns granted by the Governor of New-Hampshire, and lake Champlain to the forty-fifth degree of north latitude, excepting a neck of land between Missisque Bay and the waters of the lake. These resolutions, with a verbal message, requesting explicit information what were the real intentions of the people of Vermont, were sent by Washington to Governor Chittenden. Whether the independence proposed by Congress would satisfy them, or if they had it in contemplation to become a British province. The Governor returned a decisive answer that no people were more attached to the cause of American independence than the inhabitants of Vermont; but sooner than be put under the government of New-York, they would submit to the crown of England. The resolutions were then laid before the General Assembly of Vermont, convened at Charlestown, October, 1781, but although Congress conceded all which Vermont claimed, still, upon debating the subject, the assembly voted that they could not comply with the resolutions, without destroying the foundation of the universal harmony and agreement that subsisted in the state, and violating the solemn compact entered into by articles of union and confederation. They however affirmed that they should continue steadfast in the principles on which the state first assumed a government, and hold the union of the different parts of it inviolate; and that they would not submit the question of their independence to the arbitrament of any power, but were willing to refer the question of their jurisdictional boundary with New-Hampshire and New-York to commissioners mutually chosen, and when admitted into the Union, would submit any such dispute to Congress. Though Vermont had not accepted the resolutions of Congress, yet they were considered by New-York as a virtual determination of her claims. The subject was brought before the legislature of that state, and a number of resolutions, with a protest against the proceedings of Congress, were passed, mentioning their claims to the disputed territory, and the former proceedings of Congress. They declared by their resolutions, that the federal government had no authority by the articles of union to intermeddle with the boundary limits of either of the United States, except in cases of dispute between any two or more of the states, nor to admit any, not even a British colony, excepting Canada, without the consent of nine states, and above all, to form a new state, by dismembering one of the thirteen states, without the consent of the whole. Should Congress attempt to carry their resolutions into effect, the legislature declared it would be an assumption of power and a manifest infraction of the articles of confederation, and against which their solemn protest would be entered, and their delegates were expressly directed and required to enter their dissent at every step which may be taken to carry the said acts of Congress into execution.

Among the early settlers of Vermont, no individual felt a stronger solicitude or used more unwearied exertions to confirm and establish the independence of the state, than Governor Chittenden. Perceiving the state to be in a very critical situation, he wrote to General Washington, stating their situation and difficulties. Placing the utmost confidence in the General, the Governor gave him an account of the proceedings with the enemy, and assigned for a reason that Vermont, drove to desperation by the injustice of those who should have been her friends, was obliged to adopt policy in the room of power, and further added, that Lord George Germain's letter wrought on Congress and procured that for them which the public virtue of this people could not obtain.

Difficulties of another character appeared in a different quarter while these transactions were occurring. The executive of Vermont was informed by one of the sheriffs in that part of New-Hampshire which had united with Vermont, that the government of the former state were about to compel the insurgents to submit to their laws and authority. The militia on the east side of the mountain were ordered out by the Governor, under the command of Lieutenant Governor Paine, to assist the sheriff in the execution of the laws, and to protect the citizens against any insults; and if an attack should be made with an armed force, to repel them by the same strength. A copy of the orders received were forwarded to the President of New-Hampshire, and Mr. Paine wrote that if New-Hampshire began hostilities, he should put his orders into execution, and did not doubt but that the enterprise would be sustained by the people, and that New-Hampshire must answer for all the consequences which might ensue.— Commissioners were sent to the general assembly of New-Hampshire, to effect a reconciliation of this alarming difficulty—the western union of Vermont was visited with troops, for the purpose of stopping the proceeding of those citizens who had united with this state. Gansevoort sent despatches to Colonel Walbridge, of Vermont, on the 13th of December, stating that in pursuance of a law of New-York, a body of troops had been ordered out to suppress an insurrection among some of the inhabitants; that he had come to assist the sheriff of the county in suppressing those who had revolted against the government, and was informed that a large body of the green mountain troops were on their march. He therefore desired to be informed what was the object of their movement into the interior parts of that state, and by what authority.

The commander of the Vermont force wrote that their object was to protect those of the inhabitants who professed allegiance to the State of Vermont; he desired that conciliatory measures might be employed, but declared that he would not be answerable for any injurious consequences which might ensue. Serious difficulties were anticipated, but hapily they had more discernment and wisdom than to proceed to hostilities.

The contest with Great-Britain which now engaged their attention, seemed to convince them that differences among themselves should not be suffered to produce a civil war. The danger apprehended from this controversy to the United States caused much anxiety in the mind of Washington. On the first day of January, 1782, he returned an answer to Governor Chittenden's letter, in these words: " It is not my business, neither do I think it necessary now to discuss the origin of the right of a number of inhabitants to that portion of country formerly distinguished by the name of the Now-Hampshire grants, and now by that of Vermont. I will take it for ganted that their right was good, because Congress by their resolve of the 7th of August, imply it, and by that of the 21st, are willing fully to confirm it, provided the new state is confined to certain described bounds. It appears, therefore, to me, that the dispute of boundary is the only one that exists, and that being removed, all other difficulties would be removed also, and the matter terminated to the satisfaction of all parties. You have nothing to do but withdraw your jurisdiction to the confines of your own limits, and obtain an acknowledgement of your independence and sovereignty, under the resolve of the 21st of August, for so much territory as does not interfere with the ancient established bounds of New-York, New-Hampshire and Massachusetts. In my private opinion, while it behooves the delegates to do ample justice to a body of people sufficiently respectable by their numbers, and entitled by other claims to be admitted into that confederation, it becomes them also to attend to the interests of their constituents, and see that under the appearance of justice to one, they do not materially injure the rights of others. I am apt to think this is the prevailing opinion of Congress." The prudent and successful management of Washington, in conducting the affairs of the war through scenes of hardship and danger, gave him a pre-eminence among the people, unattained before by any individual in America. His influence rested not merely upon the superior distinction of his generalship, but upon the steadiness of his integrity and virtue. While politicians were every where striving for popularity and power, the most honorable and important of all distinctions reserved for him was a pre-eminence in the dominion of reason, wisdom and virtue. This letter from the General was laid before the legislature of Vermont, then convened at Bennington, February, 1782, and it reconciled all the difficulties which before had operated as an impediment to their acceptance of the resolutions of Congress. The idea of extending the jurisdiction of Vermont beyond the bounds of the original grants from New-Hampshire was entirely given up by the legislature. They very judiciously determined that the resolutions of Congress which had been passed upon the subject of the admission of Vermont into the Union of the States, were equitable and proper. They therefore resolved, that the west banks of Connecticut river, and a line beginning at the north west corner of the State of Massachusetts, from thence northward twenty miles east of Hudson's river, as specified in the resolutions of Congress in August last, be considered as the east and west boundaries of this State. The legislative body also relinquished all claims and demands to and right of jurisdiction in and over any and every district of territory without said boundary lines. This union which had kept and preserved Vermont from dismemberment between New-Hampshire and New-York, was dissolved, but not without resentment from those members who had a seat in the legislature by the confederation, and which they supposed would be perpetual union of the state with those towns which were represented.

The resolutions were fully complied with, and four agents, Jonas Fay, Moses Robinson, Paul Spooner and Isaac Tichenor, Esqrs. were elected delegates to negotiate the admission of Vermont into the confederacy of the United States, and in case an agreement should be effected, to ratify the articles of union with the confederated States of America. The friends of Vermont now confidently anticipated an immediate termination of the controversy with New-York; and having complied with the conditions demanded by Congress, she expected to be immediately admitted into the Union. A law was enacted by the federal government, providing that if in one month from the time that it should be communicated to Thomas

Chittenden, the inhabitants should comply with the conditions of the resolves of Congress, passed Aug. 7th and 21st, 1781, then their admission into the Union should be immediate, but in case they refuse and continue to exercise jurisdiction over the lands guaranteed to New-Hampshire and New-York, Congress would consider such neglect a plain indication of hostility to the Union, and that all applications made by the inhabitants for admission into the Union would be fallacious and delusive, and that thereupon the forces of the United States should be employed against the inhabitants, and Congress would consider all the lands within the territory to the eastward of the ridge of mountains, as guaranteed to New-Hampshire, and all the lands to the westward of said line, as guaranteed to New-York; and that the public functionaries do, without further delay, carry it into full execution. After various attempts a vote could not be obtained in favor of adopting these resolutions.

A few days after these implacable feelings were expressed in Congress, the agent arrived, and on March 31st, the compliance of the legislature of Vermont with resolutions of Congress were officially laid before that body.

A committee of five, to whom was referred the proceedings of Vermont, reported "that in the sense of the committee, the people of said district by the last recited act have fully complied with the stipulations made and requested of them in the resolution of the 7th and 21st of August, as preliminary to a recognition of their sovereignty and independence and admission into the federal union of the states. And that the *conditional* promise of Congress of such recognition and admission is thereby become *absolute* and *necessary* to be performed."

Vermont was by report of the committee, recognized and acknowledged to be a free, sovereign and independent state. On the report being read in Congress, a motion was made for the consideration of the same on the first Tuesday of October, which by the vote taken was decided in the negative. The third Tuesday in June was also assigned for the transaction of this business, when a decision like the former was given. A motion was then introduced for considering the vote on the following Monday, and the vote was found in the negative for the third time.

The evasive policy formerly adopted by Congress towards Vermont, seemed now to be revived. Having no prospect of accomplishing any thing by their agency, the business was concluded by the delegates in addressing a communication to the President of Congress, representing that Vermont in consequence of the plighted faith of Congress had complied with their resolutions in the most ample manner. The delay of Congress in not executing on their part according to the meaning of the resolve, occasioned great disappointment. Vermont was now reduced to a critical situation, she was exposed to the principal force of the enemy in Canada, and destitute of the assistance of the United States, which occasioned a great solicitude among the inhabitants that an unnecessary delay might not deprive them of the advantages of the confederation.

The proceedings of Congress, after making every reasonable allowance for their imperfections, cannot be very favorably considered. Decisive measures were at this time demanded in their proceedings upon the petition of Vermont. The resolutions of Congress on the 7th and 21st of Aug. 1781, were construed as a conditional promise on the part of Congress, and the condition had been fully complied with on the part of the settlers. The faith of Congress and the honor of their distinguished and respected General demanded the most exact performance of what they had engaged, and induced the people of Vermont to confide in. Had the agents of Vermont expressed themselves in terms of the greatest indignation at the public trifling of those whose proceedings should have been marked with the strictest fidelity and the most delicate sense of honor, it would have been no more than just.

As soon as the resolutions of Congress were understood by the people of Vermont, a general opinion prevailed that they had been deceived, and there was no safety in trusting to public proceedings which could be changed by the intrigues and cabals of parties. Individuals and public bodies determined to maintain the independence of the state to the extent of their boundaries, and defend themselves by force against any body of men who should try to disturb or dissolve their government, and to solicit Congress no more on the subject of their union with the confederacy; but that no blame should be attached to them for their neglect, agents were appointed at their annual session in October, to procure the admission of Vermont into the Union of the States.

CHAPTER V.

A survey of the political affairs of Vermont from the year 1783, to her admission into the Union of the States.—Proceedings at Guilford.—Commotion in the southern part of the State.—Measures pursued by the New-York Legislature.—Resolutions of Congress.—Protest of the government of Vermont against them.—Cessation of hostilities with Great Britain.—Vermont averse to an union with the Federal Government.—New Constitution of the United States.—New-York proposes an adjustment of the controversy.—Settlement of the same.—Boundaries of the State established.—Vermont admitted into the Union.—Consequences of the controversy.

The civil commotions which agitated the external affairs of Vermont did not interrupt her domestic tranquillity and success. Various opinions were entertained of the utility and consequent effect of their assumption of the powers of government. Some were fearful that the undertaking could not be sustained, others were in principle attached to New-York, and another party were actuated by a lawless kind of feelings to be freed from all restraints of law and government.

Many of these sought protection and avowed allegiance to New-York, from whom they received civil and military commissions, and whose desires they endeavored to support to the great detriment of the government of Vermont. But with all these impediments, the government of this state became more efficient, not only from the exertions of those who were residents in the state, but by the accession of large numbers of emigrants from the other states who were generally in favor of the government, and added very much to its force, unanimity and numbers. These favorable occurrencies induced a degree of amicable feeling towards those who had opposed the government of the state. Accordingly the legislature of the state passed a general act of amnesty in February, 1781, in favor of those persons in the State who had previously opposed its authority.

In the Southern part of Vermont a considerable proportion of the settlers were, as before stated, prepossesed in favor of the government of New-York, and supported it and those commissioned under its authority, with zeal and fidelity. The town of Guilford, on the southern line of the State, was celebrated for parties, particularly those denominated tories, or the adherents of New-York and the British government. As early as 1776 they declared themselves in favor of their own State independence and that of the United States; and raised, paid and equiped nine soldiers for the continental army, which was done by a tax on the town. After this, in 1778, different sentiments prevailed.—A committee was chosen to defend the town against the pretended State of Vermont, and a selection of Yorkers was made to take particular care of the powder, lead and other stores. A further vote was given in 1780, upon the business of defending themselves against the insults of the pretended State of Vermont, and several other resolutions of a like character were also enacted.—These meetings were held annually, at which time a complete system of laws were passed for the government of the town. The town books having come into the possession of the opposition by a majority of votes, they excluded the other party from the ballot box by the force of arms. Armed forces frequently came from Brattleborough to stand sentry at their meetings, where hostile skirmishes ensued. Those attached to the State of Vermont kept up regular meetings, until their records were lost; and they in turn frequently sent scouting parties to the assistance of their friends in Brattleborough. The party in favor of the State of New-York having a disagreement with the government of Vermont, relative to the jurisdiction of the State, became so incensed at the other as to proceed to open hostilities. Captain Nathaniel Carpenter, of Guilford, commanding the Yorkers, commenced an attack upon the inn of Josiah Arms, of Brattleborough, the quarters of Farnsworth, the Commissary General, Major Boyden, Captain Waters, and Lieutenant Fisk, of the State troops, and demanded the immediate delivery of Captain Waters, concerning whom General Farnsworth expostulated with them in vain. The assailants became exasperated, and fired about thirty balls through the house, wounding Major Boyden and a traveller slightly. Resistance became unavailing; whereupon Captain Waters resigned himself up to the force who immediately carried him into Massschusetts; but a party from Vermont pursued and overtook them the next day at Northampton, and released Captain Waters. In the same year, 1783, Lieutenant Fisk, with about 40 men, marched to Guilford, and was fired upon by the Yorkers, when the Lieutenant and several others were wounded. On hearing of this affray, about 50 green mountain boys appeared and dispersed the insurgents.

Desperate and distressing was the situation of the inhabitants of Guilford, amounting at this time to 2,600 souls. They were so enraged at each other, that all went armed, to defend themselves against attacks. Connections and neighbors were opposed to each other, and the sick could not be visited by physicians, without a pass from the committee. Confusion had usurped the place of social order, when, fortunately, Colonel Ethan Allen arrived in town, with a force of one hundred Vermonters. He immediately issued a proclamation, declaring that unless the people of Guilford peaceably submit to the authority of Vermont, the same shall be made as desolate as Sodom and Gomorrah, by G—. The partizans of New-York, having fired on Allen's troops, he determined on humbling them. Martial law was proclaimed, and some of the people were made prisoners, and others put under bonds for good behaviour. Troops were quartered in town, under the command of S. R. Bradley and I. Allen, to bring the Yorkers to submission. Similar scenes revived in the winter of

1784, when Captain Knights, of Rockingham, was sent to quell the insurrection, who, after entering Guilford, on the 5th of March, drove the New-York party to Massachusetts, where a battle ensued, and one man was killed.

The town was soon after relieved from the martial law. During this period of confusion, the adherents of New-York had been so closely pursued by the civil and military authorities of Vermont, and their property so much confiscated, that they fled to New-York, and settled almost the whole township of Bainbridge, which was appropriated by that State to the New-York sufferers. While the supreme power was vested in the town meetings, refugees came from the neighboring states to this town; but when the civil law prevailed, they fled, and so great was the decrease of inhabitants, that where one farmer now possesses and occupies a tenement, there were formerly half a dozen log huts. Transactions of a similar character occurred in some of the adjoining towns, but this place appeared to be the seat and center for planning schemes of opposition and resistance to the government of Vermont, and quite a resort for those who espoused the cause of Great-Britain.

New-York now perceived that she could only support her jurisdiction in Vermont, by lenient measures; therefore, in April 14th, 1782, the assembly of that State passed an act, stating that divers persons in the northern part of Vermont, having denied the sovereignty of New-York, by their unlawful combinations, and being misled by artful and designing men, from their allegiance to this State, have professed repentance for their crimes, and desired the passage of an act of oblivion and pardon, whereupon it was resolved, that all capital, corporeal or pecuniary punishments, fines, forfeitures, judgements and executions, to which they were liable to in consequence of crimes and offences, are hereby remitted and discharged, and all such persons are fully restored to the same condition they were before the commission of the crimes; and that all charters of land, made by New-Hampshire, when a colony, or by the government of Vermont, prior to any granted by any other government, shall be ratified and confirmed unto their respective grantees; and all actual settlers, holding lands by possession, shall be confirmed in their possessions and improvements, and shall have a patent thereof from the government of the state, by paying the customary fees. But all persons convicted of adhering to the government of Great-Britain, shall not be restored in person or property, by virtue of any law in this State. These measures did not produce in the minds of the people, any different feelings towards the government of New-York. Exposed to an invasion from Canada, by the departure of the continental troops to the south, the government of Vermont found it necessary to order a draft of militia, for the purpose of defence. Some of them complied willingly, but others with extreme reluctance, particularly in the south-eastern part of the State, who by the encouragement derived from the Governor of New-York finally resisted the authority of the State. To some of these persons he gave civil and military commissions and a promise of support and protection. The exertions of those made insolent by the support derived from the government of New-York, proceded so high as to attempt the execution of the laws of that State upon the citizens of Vermont. Mild measures proved ineffectual: a military force was sent by the public authority of Vermont, to assist the sheriff of Windham county, and to protect the courts of Justice, against the violence and opposition of a mob. Five of the principal persons engaged in the opposition, were tried and sentenced by the Supreme Court to perpetual banishment, and others were amerced in pecuniary fines according to the usages of law. The authority of Vermont had so effectually checked the attempt at insurrection, that their only resort for protection and reward, was to the government of New-York. But that State was unable to afford them relief; they, therefore, made complaint to Congress, that their ordinances were publicly violated—a jurisdiction had been exercised over those persons who were the professed subjects of New-York. On the 14th of November, 1779, a committee in Congress reported that "the measures complained of were probably occasioned by the State of New-York having lately issued commissions both civil and military, to persons resident in the district called Vermont." It was further recommended to the State of New-York to revoke all the commissions which had been issued by that authority, since the first of May, and it was also recommended to Vermont to make restitution to those who had suffered damages. These resolutions, however beneficial they might have been to the people at that time, did not, after several attempts, receive the sanction of Congress.

When the business was taken up again, on the 5th of December, Congress, instead of proceeding to fulfil her engagements with Vermont, condemned them for punishing the insurgents; and in the miniatory language of authority, decreed "that the people inhabiting the district of country on the west side of Connecticut river, called the New-Hampshire grants, and claimed to be an independent State, in contempt of the authority of Congress, and in violation of its acts, did unlawfully proceed to exercise jurisdiction over those persons who profess allegiance to the State of New-York, having banished them, not to return on pain of death and confiscation of estate. These proceedings were pronounced dangerous to the government of the United States, and such as demand the immediate interposition of Congress, for the relief of such as have suffered by them and for preserving the peace until the controversy relative to the jurisdiction of the same shall be decided. They required of Vermont to make full restitution to those who were banished or had their property confiscated, and commanded them not to molest any one in person or property on their return to their habitations in said district. These injunctions Congress declared must be obeyed, or effectual measures would be taken to enforce compliance. These acts of Congress had a tendency to do away all the remaining attachment and respect which Vermont had for the proceedings of that body. The remonstrance of the Governor and Council, for severity of rebuke and strength of reasoning, is not inferior to the productions of the most eminent statesmen. The solemn engagements which Congress had entered into with the State, they informed them, had not been fulfilled. Their own articles of confederation precluded them from intermeddling with the internal government of any of the United States, much more with this, from whom not even a delegated power had been received. Upon principles of justice, this State has as good a right to independence as Congress, and has an equal right to pass resolutions prescribing rules to that body, as she has to order this State to receive those that were banished, and make restitution to them and other criminals, of the property taken from them by a due course of law, under the authority of the State. They were reminded that their conduct towards Vermont was the same which the British government pursued towards the Colonies: that their proceedings tended to make the liberty and rights of mankind a mere bawble and the sport of State politicians: that it was of no avail to establish one arbitrary power on the ruins of another: that they were free and should continue independent, notwithstanding all the power and artifice of New-York; and further, that they had no difficulty with the general government, complexly viewed, but were at all times able to vindicate their rights and liberties against the intrusions of New-York. In their answer, they enquire how the exercise of civil law in Vermont could very much endanger the strength of the United States or require the interposition of the general government to establish peace in the State? Laws and civil regulations, they declare, were established in Vermont before Congress passed their late resolutions, and what difficulties these could occasion time would unfold. It is a general opinion, that if Congress had carried their agreement with Vermont into effect, it would have had a more salutary influence in promoting the peace than their recent resolutions.

In that part of the communication relating to the banishment and confiscation of those who opposed the government of New-York, they observe, that Congress had been so mutable in their resolutions respecting Vermont, that it is impossible to calculate their designs or comprehend their meaning. At one time, a space is left by the limits of their guarantee to New-Hampshire and New-York, for the existence of Vermont; at another, Congress are within these limits, controlling the internal government of the State; again, the ratification of their preliminaries of confederation, when complied with on the part of the State, are unreasonably procrastinated. They finally close their appeal, in answer to the threats of Congress, in case they should refuse to comply with their resolutions, in this manner: That General Washington and most of the inhabitants of the contiguous States, were in favor of the independence of Vermont, and that if Congress had judicial authority to control the internal police of the State, the State had a right to be heard in its defence; that an *ex parte* decision of so important a matter, without any notice to the State, was unjustifiable on their own principles and contrary to the law of nature and nations. The remonstrance was concluded with a strong solicitation for Vermont to be immediately admitted into the confederacy of the States.

In the month of February, the assembly convened at Windsor, and sent forward a petition declaring in plain and decisive terms, that they were conscious of doing no act derogatory to the dignity or in contempt of the authority of Congress, or to disturb the peace of the confederacy; but solely with a view to the security of their just rights and the internal peace and tranquillity of the state. That they had from the commencement of the war braved every danger and hardship against the usurpation of Great-Britain, in common with the United States. As their inherent right of sovereignty and jurisdiction stand confessed upon the principles of the revolution and implied by the solemn transaction of Congress, they could not but be surprised at the resolution of that body, passed December 5th, and the manner in which the business was conducted.

The resolutions of Congress had an effect entirely different in Vermont from what had been anticipated. They considered them the result of their enemies' influence; a mere compound of contradictions and evasions, that deserved neither the faith nor respect of the people. A membership with the confederated states was no longer solicited, but was even viewed as detrimental to the prosperity of Vermont.

The hostile attitude of Great-Britain towards the United States, had been very distressing. But at the same time the union was more firmly cemented by the experience of such difficulties. The removal of the cause, however, produced a cessation of hostilities, and America was restored to a state of tranquillity and peace. The preliminary articles of peace were executed by the Ministers of the King of Great-Britain and the United States, January 20, A. D. 1783. This was the consummation of their wishes and the fruits of their toil. They were ranked by the concession of Great-Britain free, sovereign and independent states. This pacification relieved Congress from embarrassments and Vermont from the apprehension of danger. The state had now no enemies to oppose, or provisions for war to furnish: therefore, a connection with the union was no longer a matter of urgent or immediate necessity. Although the clouds of war had passed from the atmosphere of America, still, want and weakness encumbered the energies of the government.—Their currency had failed, their revenues were exhausted, and the public debt was unfunded, which occasioned great dissatisfaction in the army, and loud complaints among creditors. Congress had no power to raise money, but merely to make the requisitions upon the states. These were often disregarded, as no authority was given to enforce obedience. Thus the public affairs of the Union became more and more embarrassed with disorder and a want of credit and power. Neither did the articles of the confederation give them the power to regulate commerce: consequently treaties with foreign nations would not be obligatory upon the individual states. Unprotected by contracts, and unsupported by countervailing regulations, the American merchants were refused all participation in the commerce of the world, except on terms, at once troublesome and degrading. The commerce between the states, which were regarded as distinct and independent sovereignties, was also encumbered by numerous restrictions, occasioning frequent collisions, and diminishing the advantages which naturally flow from the unfettered enterprise and industry of man. Trade languished, and from the want of its vivifying influence, enterprise ceased, and the resources of the country lay dormant.

In this state of public affairs, it could be of no possible service, or importance, for Vermont to join the confederacy of the states. She was now free from the burthen of debts which lay on the United States, and undisturbed with the calls of Congress to raise necessary sums of money. The experience they had in the business of self-government operated very favorably upon their legislative and judicial proceedings. Their peculiar situation had prevented them from incurring large debts; therefore, they were under no necessity of raising great sums in taxes upon the people. The state having extensive tracts of uncultivated land, obtained a considerable revenue from the sale, to purchasers who were continually coming in from the different states in New-England. These settlers made large accessions annually to the numbers and wealth of the state. The public affairs of the United States or those of Vermont, offered no inducements for the people to join the confederation, if they could avoid the connection upon honorable terms.

The power invested in Congress was perceived by the first statesmen in this country, to be wholly inadequate to the purpose of administering and supporting the federal government. In September, 1786, on the proposition of Mr. Madison, of Virginia, a convention of commissioners from five of the middle states was held at Annapolis, for the purpose of planning and recommending to the states, a uniform system of commercial regulations. On deliberating upon the subject, the commissioners concluded that nothing short of a complete reform of the existing government should be attempted. By a resolution of Congress, a law was adopted recommending that a convention of delegates from all the states should be held at Philadelphia, for the purpose of forming a federal constitution, adequate to the exigencies of government, and the preservation of the Union. All the states complied with this recommendation, except Rhode-Island, when a new federal constitution was adopted by the people of the United States, and a new Congress met in the city of New-York, March 3d, 1789.

The fears which had been entertained by many, respecting the operation of the federal constitution, were dispelled, as they found that the government had been struggling to restore the public credit, and to establish a system of equal laws and justice. Measures so strongly marked with wisdom and justice, served to conciliate the public mind, and to bring the strength of the state to act with vigor and union in support of the federal system.

The ancient controversy with New-York was still unsettled. However, the idea of subduing Vermont by force or policy was abandoned by that state, and she well knew that Vermont was, and would remain, free and independent. The only matters of dispute now agitated were the title to certain tracts of land, which were granted by the governors to individuals. These lands, by means of the growing settlements and wealth of Vermont, had become very valuable. The legality of these grants had been uniformly denied, and all submission to the acts of the legislature of New-York, refused by the government of Vermont. The grantees of New-York kept complaining of the injustice done them, in not being allowed the possession of their property. Endeavors were made to compromise the difficulty, but without success. New-York considered themselves under no obligation to refund to individuals, that which the state had no hand in granting, but was simply the act of the crown, executed by the will of the royal governors, usually for the benefit of friends, or personal profit, but never for the advantage of the government or people.

Circumstances at length occurred which mitigated the asperity of feelings that New-York had so generally indulged toward Vermont. The permanent seat of the federal government was a very desirable acquisition for the rival cities, New-York and Philadelphia, which after repeated trials, was fixed by a small majority at the latter place. The exclusion of Vermont from a representation in Congress, operated very much to the disadvantage of New-York, in the removal of the seat of the general government. Interest in the case called loudly for some measure to be taken for uniting Vermont with the confederated States. Accordingly on the 13th of July, 1789, commissioners were appointed by New-York, with plenary powers to acknowledge the independence of Vermont and adjust all difficulties with the same. Vermont also, on the 23d of October, 1789, appointed commissioners to remove every obstruction to her connection with the United States. After much debate among the commissioners, relating to a compensation for the lands claimed by the citizens of New-York, which had been re-granted by the authority of Vermont, the matter was brought to a just and amicable settlement.

The commissioners for New-York, on the 7th of October, 1790, by virtue of the power granted to them, "declared the consent of the legislature of New-York that the state of Vermont be admitted into the Union of the United States of America, and that immediately all claims of jurisdiction of the state of New-York shall cease, and thenceforth the perpetual boundary line between the states of New-York and Vermont, shall be, as was then, and is now, holden by Vermont." The legislature of Vermont accepted the proposals of New-York, and paid them thirty thousand dollars on the 1st day of June, 1794, for their acquittance to all rights and titles of land in the state of Vermont. All the grants, charters, and patents of land, lying within the state of Vermont, made by and under the late colony of New-York, were declared null and void, those only excepted which had been made in confirmation of the grants of New-Hampshire.

In this amicable way the controversy between New-York and Vermont was settled, which had been agitated with great animosity for twenty-six years. The contest had become irksome to both parties, and fortunately for them the general state of American affairs was such as led to a wise and equitable adjustment of the controversy.

After the difficulties with New-York were removed, the assembly proceeded to call a convention of the people, to see if they would connect themselves with the federation. At a convention, holden at Bennington, the subject of the proposed union was discussed; when some of the members urged that it would be more for the interest and safety of the State, to defer the question for future consideration, but a large majority were of the opinion that the matter could not be suspended without prejudicing the prosperity of the State. On submitting the subject to the members, it was decided, by a majority of one hundred and five to two, in favor of the union. The general assembly met at Bennington on the tenth of January, and elected Nathaniel Chipman and Lewis R. Morris, commissioners to attend Congress and negotiate the admission of Vermont into the Union—Vermont was therefore by the unanimous act of Congress, admitted into union with the States, on the 18th of February, 1791. During the first part of the controversy, there was no settled form of government: the people transacted their business in town meetings, by leaders and officers and committees appointed or submitted to by general consent. The struggle with New-York constantly agitated the minds of the settlers, with the most violent and uncomfortable passions. However, but one instance of bloodshed occurred during the quarrel, and that took place at Westminster, the 13th of March, 1775—Mr. French was shot through the body in the court-house. A contrariety of claims at this period proved very detrimental to the progress of settling the country. Some cases of personal violence were offered, which presented a very serious aspect. A constable under the authority of Vermont, had arrested one of the inhabitants of Chesterfield, in New-Hampshire, who still adhered to the jurisdiction of that State. He denied his authority, and was assisted by an officer in New-Hampshire to resist the execution of his precept. This officer and his coadjutor were taken and imprisoned by the constable of Vermont. Orders were then given by the government of New-Hampshire, to call out the militia and liberate the imprisoned sheriff by force.— The executive of Vermont despatched three agents to Exeter, to settle the matter with the government of New-Hampshire. One of these was a sheriff of Vermont, whom by way of retaliation, they immediately imprisoned at Exeter. Alarmed at this approach of hostilities, the government of each state was obliged to interpose to prevent more violent measures, which threatened to burst into a civil commotion. In 1784, the secretary of Vermont was taken in the city of New-York, on account of political management in Vermont. The subject was brought before the legislature, and they resolved to make a reprisal of so much land belonging to the citizens of New-York, in the limits of Vermont, as would sell for money enough to make restitution to their secretary for all the losses which might be sustained on account of his arrest in New-York.

The people of America showed by their forbearance, a great unwillingness to proceed to the sad extremity of embroiling themselves in the horrors of civil war. On the contrary, amidst the greatest animosity and personal resentment, they united with the utmost vigor against the insolence and power of Great-Britain, to secure the independence of their country. They, however, ran into some very great errors and mistakes on other points. Had the government of New-York been contented with the exercise of jurisdictional authority over the territory of Vermont, without regranting their lands which they obtained from another power and improved with much hardship, there would have been no trouble or controversy between the states. But when she proceeded on this business, the proprietors would not acquiesce in their imperious demands. The settlers did right in opposing those acts of oppression, committed under the ostentatious authority of the king, the law, and the government of New-York.— They felt as though those rights which they held in common with all mankind, were of higher authority than the variable decisions of the British King, or the rapacious views of a provincial governor and council. The union with a part of New-Hampshire was ill-judged policy, and operated very much to the prejudice of Vermont. And the attempt of New-Hampshire and New-York, to divide Vermont between them, was a sufficient justification for such an act retributive of justice.

The royal decision, made in 1774, gave New-York jurisdiction over the whole territory of Vermont. The settlers acquiesced in this disposition of their rights, until they were dispossessed or ejected from their lands. They then applied themselves to the business of establishing a government and forming laws to regulate the whole affairs of the State. Ordinary perseverance, talents and enterprise could never have sustained them against the overpowering influence, numbers and wealth of their enemies. The claim of New-Hampshire to the whole state of Vermont, was very impolitic, having no color or shadow of title, they could not expect to establish an ownership to any part, upon rules of justice.

How far it was necessary or equitable for Congress to adopt an evasive policy, under the peculiar circumstances of the country, would be difficult for those unacquainted with public affairs at that time, to determine. It was one great object with the government to unite the States, and prevent contention, from disturbing the common cause.— All parties seemed to be rather displeased with the measures respecting the controversy of Vermont with New-York and New-Hampshire, than satisfied:—Such was their uncertainty, their contradictory and evasive measures, that when the dangers occasioned by the war, were removed, the people of Vermont had very little to desire, or inclination to be connected with Congress. It was not until more steadiness, vigor and ability appeared in the federal government, that the people were willing to be brought into the American union.

CHAPTER VI.

A Sketch of Politics from the year 1791 to the American Embargo in 1808.—Prosperity of Vermont on her union with the States.—Annual proceedings of the Legislature of the State.—Effect of the Revolution in France upon the policy of this country.—Resignation and death of Governor Chittenden.—Mr. Tichenor elected Governor.—His proceedings.—Civil affairs of the State, and measures pursued by the General Assembly at Vergennes, Windsor, Middlebury, Newbury, Burlington, Westminster, Windsor, Rutland, Danville, Middlebury, and Woodstock, embracing a period of eleven years from 1798 to 1808.—Outrage committed by the British ship Leopard upon the United States frigate Chesapeake.

A season of peace, when the rage of controversy and the calamities of war had passed from the council and fields of the nation, was very welcome and propitious to the pursuit of private business and the prosecution of public affairs. The federal and state government were both conducted by individuals in whose talents and virtues the people of Vermont had the utmost confidence and faith. Governor Chittenden, as a magistrate and as a man, had long been endeared to the affections of his acquaintances and the state; his manners were easy and familiar, and characteristics, such as a new state required. The only requisition for the security and advancement of the people, was the improvement of those natural and civil advantages, which were already in their possession. No subject of political consequence offered any great temptation to the people. The appointment of Councillors was not of sufficient importance to make it a matter of much emulation and strife. The only chance for ambition and intrigue was in the appointment of civil officers, which was generally decided in a short time without much electioneering or management. These matters were generally determined on the first week of the legislature; after that the greater portion of the time was occupied in granting new townships, laying out roads, authorizing a tax for annual expenses of government, and enacting such laws as the local circumstances or particular situation of individuals, or towns, or the state might require. About four weeks was generally spent in the business of legislation. While the Americans were enjoying under a government of their own choice, the blessings of independence and freedom, the French nation, by whose assistance these privileges had been obtained, were suffering all the miseries of anarchy. They, however, arose in the majesty of their physical strength, with a determination to be freed from those institutions which originated in times of ignorance and barbarism. Before the energetic exertions of the people, prompted by enthusiasm, and directed by fatal skill, their ancient government crumbled to the dust.— Passing from a state of slavery to one of entire liberty, their conduct was marked with the most shocking excesses. In the heat of their zeal to accomplish a revolution, they not only put down the monarch, the nobility and the church; but considered that perfection could be given to republicanism by destroying churches of public worship and matrimonial obligations. They praised the American discovery of true liberty, but boasted that it was reserved for them to carry freedom to a state of perfectibility. Its accomplishment, however, was based upon the destruction of all former attachments to the ancient customs and habits, and upon the absolute denial of the existence and perfections of Deity. Youthful ignorance and passions were enlisted in favor of the doctrine by treating the affection and chastity of the sexes as a matter of ridicule and folly, and the inclinations of the licentious were engaged to set aside at the option of either party, all the vows and obligations that had been connected with the institution and laws of marriage. "All that had acquired and claimed respect, on account of its antiquity, universality or supposed sanctity, was attempted to be destroyed, and reason, the perfectibility of man, and the clamors of the mob," were regarded and asserted to be the true and only divinity of Heaven.

Some of the principal causes which led to the French revolution were the progress of philosophy, the diffusion of general knowledge, and the freedom of examining subjects of government and religion. The views and feelings in favor of liberty elicited by the American revolution, and disseminated on the return of the French officers and troops from the United States, the despotism of the government, the discontent among the great mass of community on account of their oppressed condition, and the derangement of their finances were also among other causes which revolutionized the ancient government of France.

The people of the United States were, from principle, almost universally in favor of this overturn in their government, and most of them thought it would produce a more perfect system of government than that in America. But when the principles of virtue and common sense were deserted for impossibility and folly, the Americans became decided in their views and feelings. Some of them wished to adopt the French doctrines of freedom and perfectibility, but others were fearful of the experiment, and chose to remain within the limits of their own experience and government. The people of Vermont, and so through the United States, on embracing such views and sentiments, became separated into parties, one of which wished to increase and strengthen the powers of the federal Constitution, and the other desired that more weight of government should be placed at the disposal of the people.— Thus, parties of different principles arose, both wishing to alter the federal constitution, the one by adding, and the other by diminishing the powers assigned to the President and Senate of the United States.

The manner of conducting public business, at the General Assembly, had a great effect in checking the growth of faction and party spirit. No speech was made by Governor Chittenden at the opening of the legislature, of course there was no opportunity for intrigue and controversy, in furnishing a reply. After completing the appointments of civil officers, nothing more was necessary to be accomplished, than to proceed with the usual business of the State, which rarely presented matters of much interest to those ambitious of political distinction and power.

When peace and intelligence prevail, the opportunity is presented and often improved of accomplishing some wise and judicious undertaking. Such a season ensued, and the legislature of the State improved it in reducing the statutes of Vermont to a concise and well arranged code. The supervision of the work was refered to a committee appointed for that purpose, and a faithful and judicious system of laws were compiled for the internal regulation of the state. The laws of Vermont have been so altered, revised and repealed, that the code then established has almost passed from the statute book. The whole system was compiled and arranged in 1807; in 1816 the public acts up to that period, were compiled in a separate volume, and again in 1824, the statute was arranged, and such parts of it as was inoperative and obsolete were left out of the text. Law making has been a source of much perplexity to legislators, jurists, and the people; but for demagogues and partisans, it has furnished a fair opportunity for displaying their consequence and obtaining offices of power.

1797. This year was memorable for the resignation and death of Mr. Chittenden, the first Governor of Vermont, and one of the earliest settlers in the northern part of the State. Among those who, in the new and unorganized territory of Vermont, contributed to the establishment of American independence, the organization and ultimate acknowledgement of the privileges of this State, no one was more active than Governor Chittenden. He was a native of Guilford, Connecticut, but removed in early life to Salisbury, where he was elected to a seat in the legislative councils of that State, and also received other civil and military appointments. In the year 1773, he purchased a tract of land on Onion river, removed his family and commenced a settlement, when there was scarce a family or any roads in that part of the State. Soon after he began his settlement, the war of the American revolution commenced. The inhabitants of the infant settlements, ignorant of the measures which the Indians would pursue, and unable to protect their defenceless habitations, removed to the more settled parts of New-England. Mr. Chittenden left his farm and removed to Arlington. More acquainted with public business than most of the settlers, he became the principal conductor of their councils and debates. To the transactions of New-York, concerning the title of their lands, he was early and strenuously opposed, and become one of the most influential members of the convention. The American war, which distressed and endangered every portion of the country, convinced him that an opportunity would present itself for terminating their controversy, by declaring their independence and establishing a new State, in this disputed territory. Pursuing this firm and decisive plan of policy, he at length had the pleasure of seeing it embraced by the inhabitants and acknowledged by the federal government. His prudence and information secured him the highest delegations of power, which he always exercised to the advantage and satisfaction of the people. He was a firm and consistent friend of liberty. In difficulties, he did not hesitate, and in want, he failed not in the resources of contrivance.— The inhabitants of the New-Hampshire grants elected him with others, in 1775, to take the advice of Congress, upon the subject of the affairs. Two years after he was chosen President of the council of safety, the only species of government that was known in this district. This tribunal exercised the functions belonging to the three of powers which in the consternation of that period was almost unmanageable with perplexities and care. On the declaration of the independence of Vermont, Mr. Chittenden was called to the executive branch of the government, and so continued, for nineteen years, to fill by annual appointments, this important station, until he declined a re-election. From his acquaintance with the character of the people and his judgment matured by observation and experience, he appeared to be better qualified for a governor of this State, than one more skilled in theoretical knowledge, or possessed of more polite accomplishments. He died on the 25th of August, 1797, in the 68th year of his age. In life he was sincerely esteemed, and his death was universally lamented by his friends, acquaintances and the people of the State. Concerning his character, it may justly be said that he was intelligent, upright, and unostentatious, open hearted and liberal, the stranger and unfortunate had free access to his friendship and the bounties of his fortune.

On the demise of Governor Chittenden politicians found new motives, for their appearance and exertions, and still more so on the resignation of President Washington.— Mr. Adams, the successor to the Presidency, was openly opposed to the principles of the French revolution, which occasioned dissatisfaction among a large portion of community. Restraints incident to feelings of respect for the great and good had now somewhat abated in the public excitement. New parties, styled Federal and Republican, appeared, and each exerted themselves to secure the election of a governor of their political sentiments. The legislature met at Windsor, and no choice was made of a Governor by the people. Judge Tichenor had a plurality of votes, and was afterwards constitutionally elected by the legislature with a very large majority. The practice of making a speech at the opening of the legislature was adopted by the new Governor. He asserted that the state and federal constitutions were founded upon republican principles, and that Washington's administration justly merited the highest approbation. "The known experience, firmness and integrity of those who are placed at the head of its administration, he adds, ought to inspire us with a proper degree of confidence in future," alluding to those measures which Mr. Adams was pursuing.

An answer to the speech was returned, containing the following sentiment:—"We are not disposed to call in question the wisdom or integrity of those who have been concerned in the administration of the general government, nor to withhold our confidence where it ought to be inspired by your wisdom and energy in every measure which in our opinion will secure and promote national prosperity." A degree of decorum was kept up in conducting the public business.—The acrimony and fierceness of party spirit had not assumed a very formidable front, and the business proceeded on without the sarcasm and bitterness of faction. Abilities and moral virtue, rather than political opinions, seem to have been the standards for civil appointments. The federalists, though there was decidedly a majority in the house, still they appeared to be fearful about their numbers and anxious to preserve their popularity and power.

1798. Governor Tichenor was re-elected this year by a very large majority, and the session of the legislature was holden at Vergennes. The whole community was now agitated with the revolutionary excitements of the French—illuminated reason had in that government dispelled by its brilliancy all civil rights and moral obligations. The vilest depravity and guilt was concealed under the mask of liberty. Violent depredations had been committed upon the American commerce, our ambassadors were refused admission to the performance of their appointed services, and under the name of a loan the French government was demanding a tribute. These proceedings and claims of France received the decided disapprobation of the President, and a proper degree of resentment from the American people. The spirit of party appeared to be extinguished. "Millions for defence, not a cent for tribute," resounded through every part of the Union. Congress declared that the treaty of alliance with France was broken and no longer in force. Letters of *marque* and *reprisal* were granted for capturing the armed vessels of France. Provisions were made for raising a small force of regulars, and in case of necessity, for increasing the number. Additional duties and a direct tax were laid upon the domestic trade and permanent property of the people.

At the meeting of the legislature the conduct and demands of the French nation were elaborately described in the speech of the governor, while the strongest confidence and adherence was expressed towards the federal government. Such views taken upon the subject were very congenial to the feelings of the house, who in their answer to the governor, declared they could not close it, without expressing their entire approbation of his administration for the first year, and their sincere wishes that his usefulness might be continued to the country.

An address to the President of the United States was prepared, by a committee appointed for that purpose, and passed in the house by a vote of 129 to 23. The management of the French was treated upon with extreme severity, and if necessity required, their readiness to engage in a war with that nation, was announced in the most decisive terms. Mr. Adams' administration was highly commended in the following sentiment:—"Permit us to add assurances of our personal respect—while we honor you as our Chief Magistrate, we respect you as a man, and it is to your glory we can say, we regard John Adams because we love our country."

While an overwhelming majority of the Assembly were opposed to the partisans of democracy, and no fears entertained that the state would soon favor such doctrines, a kind of proscription was introduced in making out their civil appointments. Judges and other officers of the government were displaced for no other reason than the sin of admiring the principles of the French revolution. And they also meant to carry their proceedings so far, as to intimidate others from appearing in opposition to the state and federal governments.

After the flame of party feelings had subsided, the annual business of the state was taken up. An application from certain Indian Chiefs, living in Canada, come before the legislature, demanding a compensation for a large tract of land, claimed by them, and lying in the present limits of Vermont. Their petition on the subject was addressed to the Governor of the State, in the following style:—

Great Brother—"We the Chiefs and counsellors of the Seven Nations of Lower Canada, send our respect to you and your family, by five of our agents, whom we have sent to you to treat about our hunting lands that lie in your State. Beginning on the east side of Ticonderoga, from thence to Great Falls on Otter Creek, and continue on the same course to the height of land that divides the streams between lake Champlain, and the river Connecticut, from thence along the height of land that divides Missisque bay, and down that bay. This is the land belonging to the seven nations which we have sent to settle for, with you, as we have settled with New-York."— Twenty Chiefs of different nations signed this application on the 29th of September, 1798.

The committee appointed by the legislature to investigate the facts relative to the Indian claims, reported that they had a claim to the above described tract of land by an agreement entered into by other aboriginal nations of this country, and whether that claim had been extinguished by purchase, conquest, dereliction of occupancy, or in any other way, they cannot ascertain. And further, that whatever validity there may be to the claim, the authority to which they applied for an adjustment, have not the power to enter upon a negotiation of the kind, but it belongs exclusively to the United States. The committee advised the governor to obtain from New-York all the information he could, respecting a similar claim in that state, and that he would cause a present not exceeding one hundred dollars to be given them as a token of friendship from their brethren of Vermont.

The Indian Chiefs receiving one hundred dollars in such presents as were pleasing, and their maintenance, while they remained paid for by the state, departed well pleased with their reception, hoping that the game would prove still better another season.

A proposal for amending the federal constitution came forward from the state of Massachusetts, at this session of the legislature. The purport of which was that no person should be eligible for President or Vice President of the United States, except a natural born citizen, or one who had been a resident in the United States at the declaration of Independence and should have continued to reside in the same, or to be employed in its service from that period to the time of his election. This was so agreeable to the sentiment of the assembly, that the amendment was adopted by 152 against five. On examining the proceedings of the legislature, it is unpleasant to observe how soon the influence of irritated feelings prompt men to lay aside moral principles, and thus become misguided in their public and private conduct. Whenever a particular administration is taken as a standard for the necessary qualifications to civil office, the way is opened for intolerance, controversy, and dismission from office. If the party in power hesitated not to avow and justify proscriptive measures of policy, the same kind of proceeding is as right and proper whenever the administration falls into the hands of their opponents. "And thus a system of political oppression and persecution would commence, depending altogether upon a majority and the power of the prevailing faction, which is wholly at variance with moral principle or character, with justice and equity, the necessary qualification or the faithful discharge of the duties of office."

In reply to the address of the Vermont legislature, which was the first attempt of the kind ever made by the state, Mr. Adams remarked :—"Knowing as I do your origin, your progress, and the brave, hardy, industrious and temperate character of the people, the approbation of their representatives, their attachment to the constitutions, and determination to support the Administration, are the more to be esteemed."

1799. The government of the state was convened at Windsor in October, 1799. The feelings of the people were still highly incensed against the proceedings of the French. A check had been given to the rapacity of their privateers, by the energetic measures of Mr. Adams. The message of Governor Tichenor contained sentiments of the highest respect and attachment towards the chief executive of the Union, for the patriotic energy of the national administration. The measures and sentiments of the governor were highly applauded by the assembly. They declared their confidence in him increased as the wealth and prosperity of the state advanced. The people were now improving in their moral virtues, the science of government, habits of industry, and conciliation of feelings. In the appointment of civil officers, which is the most apt of any thing to agitate a popular assembly, those displaced in the preceding year were not re-elected, but more caution was used in selecting the sacrifices.

The affair concerning the death of one John Gregg, who had been arrested within the bounds of Canada, by individuals from Vermont, and was drowned in lake Champlain, while in their keeping, gave rise to a very serious difficulty. Indictments were found against them at the court of criminal jurisdiction in Montreal, and a demand was made by the executive of Canada upon the government, for the surrender of those indicted for the supposed murder. But happily for the credit of both countries, the matter was satisfactorily adjusted; and so high a sense was entertained of governor Tichenor's services on the occasion, that a resolution was passed, approving of his conduct, and requesting him to inform the governor of Canada that they entertained "a very high sense of the liberal, candid and delicate manner in which that unhappy affair had from its commencement to its termination been treated by his predecessor and himself. Their conduct, when our sense thereof is known to our fellow citizens, must tend to increase the general desire for the continuation of a mutual, a free and amicable intercourse with the country over which he presides."

The governor at this session communicated to the assembly the result of his enquiries relative to the Indian claims to lands in Vermont; which were as follows: The Indians now presenting their claim to lands in Vermont, anciently belonged to the confederacy of the Five Nations, which confederacy, or some tribe of them, might once have been the proprietors to the lands now claimed. On the breaking out of some former war between the French and English, while this country was under the government of Great-Britain, it appears that these Indians, called the Cog-nah-wag-has, separated from the confederacy, removed into Canada, placed themselves under the protection of the French, and united their fortunes with the king of France, in his war with the English. The subjugation of the French and their allies in this country, and in Canada, by the arms of the English, passed this territory into the hands of the latter, by right of conquest.— That when this country was invaded by the king of England, in 1775, these Indians were his allies, and thereby rendered themselves and their interest liable to its consequences. All the lands south of Canada line being ceded by treaty to the American government, the Indian claims were of course extinguished by this act. The committee raised by the legislature on this subject, coincided in opinion with the governor, that their claim, if it ever did exist, had long since been done away and become extinct, in consequence of the treaty of peace, in 1763, between the English and French sovereigns, and the treaty between Great-Britain and the United States, of which Vermont was a part, in 1783.

The passions of the assembly were most of all engaged and agitated about certain resolutions which had been passed by the legislatures of Virginia and Kentucky.— The government of the United States was highly alarmed at the great influx of emigrants, from France and other parts of Europe, uniting with the exertions of those citizens of the union whose political sentiments very much favored the principles and measures of the French, that they would involve the country in serious difficulties, and become dangerous and troublesome to the union. To guard against such evils, the President of the United States gave his signature to two acts, which were considered by those who were then called democrats, as dangerous to, if not subversive of the constitutional liberty of America. One of these, termed the alien law, empowered the President to direct aliens, whom he should judge dangerous to the peace and liberty of the country, to withdraw from the United States, on the pain of imprisonment. The other, the sedition law, defined the crime and punishment of reviling the Chief Magistrate, or other officers of the federal government, and imposed a heavy fine and imprisonment for years on those who should combine or conspire together, to oppose any measure of the government, and should write, print either or publish any false, scandalous and malicious writing, against any officer of the general government. Great use was made of these acts by those in the southern States, who were unfriendly to Mr. Adams' administration, and were wishing to prevent his re-election to the presidency. Nothing less can be said of their deserting a man so distinguished as Mr. Adams for his political experience, his talents, and the important services he had rendered to his country, in the revolutionary contest, than this, that the people discovered how jealous they were of the liberty they had obtained, and how resolutely determined they were to defend it from every possible danger. But, whatever might have been their object, the States of Virginia and Kentucky passed a number of uncommon resolutions, disapproving the proceedings of Congress, in the passage of the alien and sedition bills, and proceeding so far in opposition as to make the State authorities judges of the legality of the acts of Congress, and of the obligation any state was under, to obey them. On the reception of these resolutions, a majority of the members of the legislature considered them highly dangerous to the principles on which the general government of the States was first formed, and in their tendency, designed to lessen the powers of the federal, and increase those of the State governments. Such feelings and apprehensions invited discussion and opposition to the resolutions. Some of the most pointed parts in their answers were, that "the general assembly of Vermont do highly disapprove of the resolutions of the legislature of Virginia, as unconstitutional in their nature, and dangerous in their tendency, and that the power of deciding upon the constitutionality of the laws belonged exclusively to the United States courts, not to the State legislatures."— In answer to one of the resolutions from Kentucky, where it is asserted, "that confidence is every where the parent of despotism, free government is founded in jealousy and not in confidence": this, they declare, is a sentiment palpably erroneous, and hostile to the social nature of man.

The experience of ages evinces the reverse is true, and that jealousy is the meanest passion of narrow minds, and tends to despotism; and that honesty always begets confidence, while those who are dishonest themselves are most apt to suspect others.

A majority of one third of the members in the legislature of Vermont viewed these resolutions as highly arrogant in claim and prejudicial in their tendency to the federal government. The minority, however, were not contented or silent. They entered their protest upon the journals of the house, calculating by this to exhibit sentiments of stronger attachment to the principles of republicanism and the powers of the individual states, than the resolutions of the house had expressed.

An amendment to the federal constitution was proposed to the legislature, that the electors should in future distinguish in their votes which candidate was voted for as president, and which as vice president. This alteration of the constitution was considered at that time rather as a matter of expediency than of political principles, which afterwards became a subject of serious debate. A resolution was enacted, requesting the members of the senate and house of representatives in Congress to use their best endeavors that Congress should propose to the legislatures of the several states so to amend the Constitution of the United States that the electors of president and vice president shall respectively distinguish the person designed for president from the one for vice president, by annexing the appellation of office to the name voted for. 94 federalists voted in the affirmative, and those of the other 42 voted in the negative. The number of republican votes raised in opposition to these political measures, showed very considerable increase since their last session at Vergennes.

On the 14th of December, 1799, General Washington, the illustrious FATHER and benefactor of this country, expired, after an illness of one day only. Intelligence of this event produced deep, unaffected and spontaneous grief, every thought was absorbed in sorrow, and every feeling stung with anguish at this melancholy event.

In the year 1800, political irritation and resentment

seemed to have somewhat subsided, when the legislature convened at Middlebury. The usual topics of State affairs were urged upon the attention of the assembly, in the speech of the Governor, and the administration of the former presidents was approved as containing the measures of policy which ought to be pursued. An answer from the house was returned, expressive of the difficulties of legislation, the temptations of passion and interest, and the importance of honest and enlightened principles were rendered more important by the errors which had attended the violation of them in Europe. The sentiments expressed on this subject discover a devotion of the legislature to the doctrines of federalism. "Thankful to Heaven for the blessings we have enjoyed under the administration of a Washington and Adams, we devoutly implore the same wisdom, goodness and power to direct our elections and our governments, and to banish from us forever calumny and detraction." The violence of party spirit had descended from the practice of dictation to the mitigating work of re-appointing those to civil offices who were displaced at Vergennes, in 1798.

As the election of the President and Vice-President was soon to take place, the republicans obtained leave to bring in a bill for having the State divided into districts, and the choice of the electors given to the people—presuming that this method of electoral appointments, would prove more favorable to the interest of Mr. Jefferson, than an election by the general assembly. This question fully tested the strength and feelings of the parties, which was, after lengthy discussions, rejected by a majority of 22.— The proceedings of the federal government, in passing the stamp act, the land tax, the alien and sedition laws, and the expenditure of money for building a navy, and for other purposes, alledged to be impolitic or useless, had diminished the popularity of Mr. Adams' administration in the minds of many, and proved unfavorable to the advancement of federalism. The Indians were informed at this session, that the legislature had decided against the justice or equity of their claims, and that no more money would be given them for their right to any lands in Vermont, or to defray their expenses in attending any future legislature. Early attention was given by the assembly to the encouragement of education. A university was founded at Burlington, in 1791, but had not, according to expectation, gone into operation; and after much debate and reasoning upon the subject, a college was granted this year at Middlebury. A school, under very prosperous circumstances, had been established at Middlebury, which, by act of incorporation, was made the foundation of the collegiate institution. The opinion then advanced appears to have proved true, that the best way to encourage the cultivation of literature and the sciences in this State, was to favor those who would be at the expense and trouble of supporting such associations. The charter of incorporation for establishing Middlebury college, was sustained by a majority of sixty-six votes. The powers and privileges, excepting in one or more instances, are such as are usually incident to universities and colleges. The power of administering oaths not at variance with the constitution and laws of this State or of the United States, was granted to this institution. This was an unusual privilege for a corporation of this kind. No provision was inserted in the charter of Middlebury college, that it should not be under the direction of any one particular religious sect or denomination, nor was there a clause to prevent the president and fellows from establishing any doctrine, opinions or denomination they should think proper. They have a right to appropriate the learning and honors of the college exclusively in favor of any denomination whom they choose. A bill was afterwards introduced to prohibit the leasing of any more land by the corporation of the university of Vermont, which was dismissed by a majority of fifty-four votes.

1801. At this period, the election of a president again recurred. The republican party had been gradually increasing ever since the adoption of the constitution. A contest of unparalleled vigor had been maintained by the parties, now nearly equal. The federalists supported Mr. Adams and General Pinckney—the republicans supported Mr. Jefferson and Colonel Burr. A small majority of the electoral votes was received by the two latter; and as they received an equal number, the selection of one of them to be the president, devolved upon the house of representatives. After thirty-five ballotings, Mr. Jefferson was chosen. Colonel Burr, receiving the votes of the federalists, lost the confidence of his former friends; but by the provisions of the constitution, became vice-president of course. In taking upon himself the powers of government, Mr. Jefferson's message, delivered to the senate and house of representatives, presented a very conciliatory aspect. Disclaiming principles of political intolerance, and urging those of candor and magnanimity, he declared that a difference of political opinions was not a difference of principles; and although there was so great a difference of sentiment, with regard to the federal constitution and government, "We are (says he) all federalists—we are all republicans." As the federalists had been very boisterous in their declarations concerning the support and assistance which ought to be rendered to the federal government, they could not consistently do otherwise than support Mr. Jefferson, who was constitutionally placed at the head of the nation. The other party, so anxious for his election, could not fail of supporting him, the favorite of their wishes and choice. In this state of things, both parties were anxiously waiting for the measures of the new president, who soon removed their doubts, by displacing the marshal and attorney of the district of Vermont, and filling their places with those who had advocated different political sentiments. Changes of a similar kind were numerous in the other States, and with no other reason for such proceedings than an opposition or attachment to the former or present president. It was now thought that the political sentiments of the chief magistrate and his party would be considered the necessary qualifications to office.

In this state of public excitement, the legislature met at Newbury, in October, 1801. The manner in which the governor delivered his opinion upon the subject of appointments to civil offices, would lead to the conclusion that he had some doubts what measures to pursue, and what he had to expect from the tempers and feelings of the party which might prevail in the assembly. "It cannot (says he) be necessary nor expedient to make that which the constitution contemplates as a very serious and important duty, become a matter of party contention or private interest. Individuals the best qualified from their experience, honesty and information, should in all cases be prefered for offices of public trust." The majority of the assembly this year fell on the republican side. A committee of one federalist and two republicans was chosen to report a respectful address to his excellency. The composition of this article was unfortunately committed to a draughtsman but poorly qualified to write an address. In style, it was rough and incorrect; in compliments, awkward and disgusting; and in principle, it discovered an ostentatious affectation for republicanism. A motion was made to have some of the most exceptionable expressions erased; but the motion was lost, it being viewed as an attempt of the federalists to regain their influence and numbers. Nothing more could be expected by the federalists, from the violence of the measures pursued by them in 1798, than that the republicans would avail themselves of their majority to displace them from office. The appointments were made out according to the nomination of the particular counties, and the business of the State was attended to with diligence and tranquillity—without the appearance of partiality, discord, or the intrigues of faction. The custom introduced by the federalists of addressing the president, was considered nothing more than due respect to Mr. Jefferson, and much more on his introduction into office. An address therefore was prepared, containing professions of strong attachment to the constitution and administration of Mr. Jefferson, and expressive of a desire that "no one description of citizens might ever be favored at the expense of the other." Amendments were proposed to certain portions of the address, by the federalists, which put in motion all the different feelings and sentiments of the parties. Debates about improving upon certain words and phrases were protracted for the space of three days, and the votes were ten times taken by yeas and nays. Their feelings became so exasperated that no opportunity was left for discernment or considerate thoughts. A large party would hear no reasons for amendments, but immediately decided every proposition by votes, and their zeal and heat became so great by repeated votings, that when a federal member moved to strike out the word unanimous, 78 voted that they were unanimous, and 60 voted that they were not perfectly unanimous. At length the republicans, perceiving the folly which would attend their voting that they were unanimous, when their votes discovered the most violent contention and strife, moved the house to reconsider their decision on that question. After a reconsideration of the vote, the address was adopted, with some small corrections, by a majority of 27. "The proceedings of the house on this address, are a remarkable instance of the workings of resentment. How easily small objects may agitate the passions of a popular assembly, and when influenced by jealousy and intrigue, how incapable they are of commanding their reason, and amongst all other feelings to feel the passion of shame."

In the ambulatory method of holding the sessions of the legislature, Burlington was selected as the place of location for 1802. As no subject of high political dispute on matters of great interest were now before the public, a quiet session for this year, was anticipated. Mr. Tichenor still carried the election by a very considerable majority. The effects and change of party zeal, were mentioned by him, in his annual communication to the legislative body.

"One of the greatest misfortunes that attends a republican government is the progress and violence of party spirit. Our beloved Washington, with all his moderation, wisdom and virtues, was not able to repress this destructive spirit. We know that an independent love for his country, and a life devoted to its service, with the most upright intentions, did not shield him and his measures from its malignant effects. It existed in his day, and has progressed with time, and increased with violence until now."

An answer, designed as a description of the feelings and views of a majority of the legislature, towards the governor, and of their opinions and sentiments, respecting the characters of Washington, Adams, and Jefferson, was reported and put to the house for a passage. The increasing violence of party spirit was deplored, their wish to augment the strength and dignity of the United States; and their hopes that all their public acts would conduce to the advantage of the state, were expressed. A change of sentiment appeared to have prevailed, when the answer was presented to the house. On taking the votes for expunging some parts of the composition of this article, eight only were opposed to its amendment. Several members, considering the production dishonorable and disgraceful to the house, resolved not to be accountable for its passage. Whereupon fifty-nine of them entered their protest upon the journals of the legislature.

The contention and recrimination attending the business of making addresses, had become so great, that one of the members gravely introduced a motion, recommending in future, that the governor should not make a formal speech, and assigned for a reason, that an address and answer usually occupied a long time in useless debates, which delayed the more important business of legislation. But the honors of office, and the importance to be derived by this privilege, gave the vote of the majority against this motion.

Fortunately for the state, no other question was presented this session, calculated to enrage or disunite the feelings of the members. The elections to civil offices were mostly from the republican party. However, a general plan of intolerance and dismission from office, on account of political opinions, did not seem to be intended or pursued by the assembly. The customary business of the state was pursued with diligence, propriety, moderation, and wisdom, by the more judicious and useful members, who for several years past had chiefly obtained for the state, the substantial benefits of society and civil government.

In the succeeding year, 1803, the assembly met at Westminster. The whole country was now greatly agitated by the controversies of the two great political parties. An increasing majority was evidently in favor of Mr. Jefferson's administration.

The federalists, though least in numbers, were powerful in wealth and abilities, and had at their control most of the money and commerce of the country. Every opportunity was sought by each party to strengthen and favor their own cause; but their calculations were not confined to the progress of events in America. The variations of European politics was expected to produce a change, which would soon place the balance of power and popularity at the disposal of one of the contending parties.

The election of President and Vice President was a matter of more immediate consequence, and one which would occur within the course of a year; and though it was certain that Mr. Jefferson was in the favor of a majority of the people, yet the certainty of his election could by no means be calculated on. The votes being given without any designation, the highest number was taken for those of the President, which might in the event defeat the re-election of Mr. Jefferson to the Presidential chair. It was feared that the federal and republican electors would vote for Mr. Burr, the Vice President, and thus, obtain a majority of votes for President, contrary to the design of the republican electors. Two methods were suggested for preventing the occurrence of such an effect. The one was to destroy the popularity of Mr. Burr with the people, and thus prevent his election to either office, and the other was to have the constitution so altered that the name of the person voted for either as President or Vice President, should be expressed on the vote, which would prevent all manner of doubt or mistake. The principal republican members thought it best to avail themselves of both methods.

Congress was convened by Mr. Jefferson at an earlier period than usual, to determine on the purchase of Louisiana, and also to attend on the business, as was understood, of altering the federal constitution, before the Presidential election took place. The legislature of Vermont assembled, and the business of the session was entered upon with a speech from the governor of a very conciliatory character. An answer, which occasioned no debate, was returned. In this they affirm that the business of the present session is viewed with anxious solicitude, and they wished to discharge the several duties assigned to them with candor, ability and promptness, and that their suffrages might elevate to office some of the wisest and best citizens of the state, and that their deliberations might result in such measures as will promote the cause of piety and virtue among them, and secure the great objects of justice. Before the appointment of civil offices was taken up, party feelings and designs were not discoverable; but when these came on for selection and choice, it was evident that the republicans meant to employ their majority to weaken and discourage their opposers. One Judge of the supreme court, one sheriff, and several judges of the county courts, were displaced to make room for republicans. In the character and extent of the destruction and in the discovery and consequences of party zeal, this assembly manifestly exceeded the federal zeal and folly at Vergennes, in 1798. The object of the republicans was to intimidate and silence their opposers, and increase the number of their friends and supporters.

The suggested alteration of the constitution was brought forward. To test the strength of the parties, a resolution to that effect was made on the subject, which passed without any difficulty, and was adopted in the council.—With much impatience an order from Congress for altering the constitution was called for. To lengthen out their session to a longer period than usual, would diminish their popularity among their constituents; but to adjourn the assembly before the proposed alteration was adopted, would probably deprive them of the chance of accomplishing the business early enough to obtain the concurrence of the state of Vermont. Perplexed with delays, and out of business, a copy of the President's message was made the order of the day, and read during the forenoon. In the after part of the day a resolution was introduced for the purpose of congratulating the President on the present happy situation of the Union, as it respects foreign nations, and their own domestic felicity. Many members considered this attempt altogether improper for the legislature, and that it would be received in no other light than an answer by the legislative body to the President's message, of which no communication had been made to them by him. They, therefore, wished that so ludicrous a motion might be no further urged. An address was afterwards prepared and adopted, by a majority of 36 votes.

This was the first session, that the subject of establishing banks in Vermont, had come before the legislature.— All the adjacent States had established institutions of the kind, and most of the monies in circulation, were of this description. Petitions were sent from Burlington and Windsor, to obtain charters for establishing banks in these towns, upon the same regulations of those banks in the other States. Banking business was so little understood by the members of the house, and less by the council, that they were afraid of venturing upon the subject. After repeated proposals and resolutions, the subject was refered to the next session of the legislature. The customary period for adjourning the assembly had arrived, and no message from Congress had been received, announcing the proposed alteration of the federal constitution. In this critical situation, a motion for an adjourned session of the legislature, was made and determined in the affirmative, by a vote of 23, to be held at Windsor, on the last Thursday of January.

The time for the adjourned session at Windsor, arrived in January 1804. The answer of the President to their address of the preceding November, was presented by the speaker, and registered upon the journals of the house.— It contained expressions of friendship towards the inhabitants of the State, and remarks upon the general measures of the government, and the prosperous state of the country.

The much desired message from Congress, had now come, together with a copy of the proposed amendment of the constitution of the United States, concerning the election of the President and Vice-President. The substance of this amendment was, that the electors should name on their ballots, the person whom they voted for as President, or as Vice-President. The Congress of the United States had adopted this alteration, and if it should be ratified by three-fourths of the several State legislatures, it would become a part of the federal constitution. Some debates were had upon the mode of proceeding, after which it was adopted, and became a law of the State, by 93 votes in the affirmative, and 64 in the negative.

No political measure had ever occasioned more strife, or been pursued with a more fixed resolution than this.— Those who favored its passage considered such a measure was necessary to be taken, as the constitution of the United States, admitted of the possibility of a person's being seated in the executive chair contrary to the intention of its framers, and to the choice of the people. One instance had already occurred, which very much endangered the federal constitution, and probably it might again, and finally most of the States had expressed a wish for the alteration, and some, particularly Vermont, in the year 1799, had adopted the proposed alteration, and recommended it to the acceptance of the whole confederacy. Those who were opposed to the amendment, considered it done for the purpose of securing a doubtful election, that no other method could be devised for securing the re-election of Mr. Jefferson, than by altering the constitution.— If any alterations could be considered necessary, the favor and promotion of an individual ought not to be its object. Thus, opinions were as varient as the different topics of reasoning suggested on the subject. Which of the parties manifested the most consistency, is impossible to be determined, as both of them changed their votes in the course of four years. In 1799, the federalists were in favor, and the republicans against such an alteration in the constitution. In 1803, the order was entirely reversed —the republicans urged the measure, and the federalists opposed it.

The annual session of the legisture, in 1804, was holden at Rutland. Political proceedings had now taken a regular course, and it was known that the offices and emoluments of government, would not be bestowed upon the federalists. Among other things, which were presented for the attention of the legislature, was a proposition from the State of Massachusetts, for altering the constitution of the United States, so as to have the representatives apportioned among the States, according to the number of free white inhabitants, in exclusion of those elected, by the suffrages of slaves. Had this resolution taken effect, the influence of the slave-holding States, would have been very much diminished, and their number of representatives lessened. This attempt at abolishing and stripping slavery of all political consequence, was worthy of the representatives of a free people, who were accustomed to speak, in the highest terms, of freedom and the rights of man. The proposition, after being debated as usual, was decided by 106 for rejecting the proposal, and 76 for adopting it. The federal compact would undoubtedly have been endangered, had three fourths of the State legislatures adopted the Massachusetts amendment.

Complaints had been made for some time against the judges of the Supreme Court, for taking illegal fees, which were made the subject of enquiry in the latter part of the session. The matter was referred to a committee of three, to report the facts; and afterwards, a change was made in the committee, with the addition of such a delegation from the council. As the council were the proper board for trying cases of impeachment, which would be the case if the respondents were found guilty before a board of enquiry, they refused to join. Several reports were made; the last of which, stated that the fees were taken agreeable to the fee bill. This report was read and accepted, so far as related to the facts stated therein; but not as to the opinion given of the legality of the proceedings. The house adjourned the same day, and left the matter in a state of indecision, to conjecture, doubt or belief, as best agreed with their own desires or system of politics. To leave business of such consequence in this dubious situation, was not proceeding very respectfully towards the judges, prudently with regard to the people, and honorably in respect to themselves.

Danville was selected for the seat of government in 1805. The usual business which would engage the attention of the assembly, related to the internal affairs, the appointment of state and county officers, necessary improvements of the laws, and whatever business by legislative enactments, could enhance the general interest of agriculture, manufactures, and the public peace, were noticed in the Governor's communication to the legislative body. The custom of the preceeding legislatures, respecting an answer to the Governor's speech, was pursued at this session of the assembly. A concise and respectful communication was addressed to the chair, written without ostentation or a design of securing party emoluments and favor. The judges could not properly be elected until the complaints of their alledged corruption in taking illegal fees were removed. A resolution was therefore introduced, referring the matter to the committee of unfinished business, and empowering them to send for persons, papers and records, and to use proper means to enable them to report all the facts, that the house may form a correct decision on a subject so important to the honor and dignity of the state, and the persons implicated therein. The committee reported, that it had been the practice of the judges, to take the fees complained of, and numerous cases and actions that were mentioned. After reflecting upon the subject, the committee of the whole agreed to recommend to the house, to adopt the following resolution:—that the judges had conducted honestly, and, therefore, by law made the judges, of what is a reasonable and fair construction of the fee bill, and therefore, no further order ought to be taken relative to the said judges taking of fees, as aforesaid. The report was accepted by the house, with 100 in the affirmative and 82 in the negative.

The controversy thus terminated in favor of the honesty and propriety of the practice which the judges had pursued in taking fees. "Candor, therefore should not complain that the committee were inclined to believe that they were taken with upright views. But the reason which they assigned for the justification, that they were by law made the judges of what is a reasonable and fair construction of the bill, had more of the appearance of the subtle and evasive distinctions of the schools and Jesuits, than that of the language or decision of statesmen or men of business."

Proposals from Kentucky and North Carolina, for amending the constitution of the United States, were laid before the legislature. That from North Carolina was designed to prohibit the importation of slaves into the United States. The proposal was agreed to by Massachusetts, and unanimously adopted by the assembly of Vermont. The amendment proposed by Kentucky was designed to confine the judiciary power of the United States' courts to cases of law and equity arising under the constitution and laws of the Union and treaties which are or shall be made under their authority, and all matters affecting ambassadors or other public agents, cases of maritime jurisdiction, and controversies in which one or more states or the United States are a party. Pennsylvania had concurred in the resolution. Vermont, however, with much wisdom, thought it not proper to venture so material a change in the original compact. The subject was defered for consideration to the next session of the legislature. The northern boundary of the state became a subject for enquiry at this session of the legislature. By one of the acts of this body, the governor was empowered and requested to have the latitude of the north line of the state ascertained by proper observations on the bank of Connecticut river and lake Memphremagog. The future seat of the legislature, after the year 1808, was also fixed, by a law, at Montpelier. The proceedings of the legislature at this session discovered more moderation and wisdom than had appeared for several years before; and whether it arose from the absence of some former violent members, or to more sagacity and prudence than usual, or to the termination of disputable subjects, cannot be determined.

The legislature met this year (1806) at Middlebury.— Mr. Tichenor was again re-elected, by a considerable majority, although uncommon exertions had been employed to remove him from his office, and his opposers seem to have been confident of success. The disappointment of his opposers, constituting a majority of the legislature, appeared to cause much vexation, when they found that the votes of the people were still in his favor. They declared these sentiments, in their answer to the governor's speech. "We shall endeavor to avail ourselves of the advantages, by your excellency pointed out, to promote harmony in our councils, as far as is consistent with that spirit of enquiry which constitutes the basis of a republican government. But we cannot try to avoid those changes which are conformable to our constitution." The attention of the legislature was directed to the subject of the lands which belonged to Vermont, as ascertained by a recent observation of the latitude on the north line of the state, but which lay within the reputed bounds of Canada. It vexed them exceedingly that the result of the enquiry should favor the exertions and judgment of the governor, and tend to increase his influence and reputation. In order therefore to counteract every prospect of this kind, their zeal and folly proceeded so far as to give a political direction to a mathematical line. The remonstrants stated, as a formidable objection to the establishment of the northern boundary line of this state, made under the direction of the legislature of Vermont, that it can be legally accomplished only through the medium of the national government, and that it might so affect the interests of the state of New-York as to require her co-operation.— "Whether we would urge the enlargement of this state, at the risk of lessening the state of New-York, and perhaps of the United States, by transfering several settlements on the river St. Lawrence, is a question of the highest importance." No question could be made in theory or in fact, but only in the imagination of some intriguing politician, that could possibly concern the rights or privileges of New-York. Amidst such a spirit of intolerance, it was considered unreasonable for the federalists to complain, and an evidence of weakness in them to expect any civil appointments. The utmost that the assembly professed was to let those remain unmolested who were in their power and to protect those who exercise an honest diversity of opinion on speculative subjects.

The Kentucky resolutions, which were refered from the last session of the legislature, were now taken up with no fearfulness of apprehension, but with an increased desire that the federal constitution might be weakened in the name of liberty, and their own powers augmented under the appearance of joining a sister state in the cause of freedom. In a committee of the whole, the house adopted the Kentucky resolutions, by a vote of 148 in an affirmative, and 34 in the negative.

A motion was made and agreed to without opposition, to

make an address to the President of the United States.—This address was designed not merely for a complimentary article, but as a matter of interest and policy. In the opinion of many, Mr. Jefferson was, from his intimations, about to decline a re-election and retire to private life.—A large majority of the assembly desired to assure him that they highly approved of his public services, and should afford him their cordial support. These assurances and sentiments were expressed in their communicated address. "We venture to hope that the insinuation is unauthorized, and to express a wish that, in the full possession of faculty and talent, you will not refuse the citizens the benefits arising from long experience, and deprive them of a full opportunity of exercising their choice and judgment in selecting their President from the whole number of the people."

The subject of banks, which had for several years been discussed in the legislature, was now urged upon their attention with zeal and warmth, by petitions of that kind from many of the most respectable towns in the state. Institutions of this kind were probably desired by a majority of the members, but their views were so local and so much in favor of those particular places, where they expected to be benefitted, that it was found impossible to enter upon an agreement at what towns they should be established. A state bank, with the profits accruing to the state, was the only institution of the kind on which their minds would meet. Having made several trials, the legislature fixed on two respectable towns, Middlebury and Woodstock. In the former of these, a branch, and in the latter, the parent bank was founded. These banking institutions, with two branches at Burlington and Westminster, have run down with great loss to the state, which shows conclusively that legislative authority and influence in the direction of such establishments are not consistent with confidence, property and safety of individuals or the public.

In 1807 the general assembly of the state convened at Woodstock. The republican party had succeeded in elevating Israel Smith, the competitor of Governor Tichenor, to the gubernatorial chair. He was a great admirer of the principles and proceedings of the French revolution, and therefore expectations were very high that he would be very strongly devoted to the republican party. In his address to the legislature, reflections of party excitement were not expressed; but a degree of manly sentiment and useful suggestions were exhibited in the production. The attention of the legislature was particularly directed to a variation in the mode of punishment by the criminal code of Vermont; suggesting at the same time, that a substitution of confinement to hard labor, instead of corporeal punishment, was very desirable, as it respected the influence of the example and the conformation of the culprit to habits of useful industry. "By substituting the punishment proposed, the government may not only prevent the expense to which other modes of correction must be subject, but may make it a source of revenue to the state." The committee appointed for that purpose, reported an answer to the governor's speech, which was accepted by the house. This communication carried in its style evidence of transported feelings. Exertions which had long been displayed by the republicans, to remove the former governor from office, were now triumphant; and their congratulations upon the occasion assumed the tone of flattery.

The long services of Mr. Smith in the cause of his country, and the confidence which existed between the present executive of the state and that of the United States, were enumerated among those qualifications which rendered him highly acceptable to the people of Vermont.— Topics of law suggested by the governor, as necessary to be adopted or improved, they declared worthy of receiving that careful attention which the nature, importance and respect due to the governor's recommendation demanded, and in the language of the answer, "We most cordially reciprocate the sentiments of your excellency, that there are at the present day such degrees of light and information diffused among the people, in relation to the science of government, as will defeat if not totally prevent all future attempts upon their supposed ignorance and credulity."

In June, 1807, the attack of the British ship Leopard upon the frigate Chesapeake, while coasting upon the shores of the United States, and unsuspicious of danger, concentrated upon the British nation the whole weight of popular indignation. The American vessel being unprepared for action, struck her colors, and was then boarded by a detachment from the Leopard, when three of her men were killed, eighteen wounded, and four carried away under pretence that they were British deserters. The fire of the assailants was opened upon the Americans at a time when there was not the least suspicion of danger, and was continued for thirty minutes. Commodore Barron observed that he considered the Chesapeake a prize to the Leopard. The reply of the officer was, that he had obeyed his directions in seizing the men, and wanted nothing more of the vessel. On an investigation of the subject, it was ascertained that three of them were citizens of the United States, who had been impressed into the British service and afterwards made an escape.

This insolent attack upon a national ship—this wanton exercise of power, derogatory to national honor, aroused the spirit of the republic. The rancor of party spirit, which had so long embittered all the intercourse of social life, was extinguished in the desire for avenging the injury. All concurred in declaring their determination to support the government of their country in its efforts, whether by treaty or war, to obtain satisfaction for this insulting outrage. The president issued a proclamation prohibiting all British ships of war from continuing or entering within the harbors or waters of the United States. Instructions were sent to Mr. Monroe, the American minister at London, to demand reparation for the injury, and security against any future aggression. A special session of Congress was summoned to determine what further measures should be taken. The act of the officer was peremptorily disavowed by the British government; but, delaying to adjust the difficulty, and refusing to adopt adequate measures to prevent the continuance of aggression, the feelings of hostility, which had somewhat abated, were now aroused and inflamed.

The assembly of Vermont, co-operating in their views with the general sentiment of the American people, adopted a resolution, with but one dissenting vote, stating that they viewed with indignation and abhorrence the unjustifiable conduct of the British cruisers, in the impressment and murder of American citizens, and the plunder of their property upon the high seas and even in the very entrance of the harbors, and more especially in the late hostile attack made upon the American frigate Chesapeake by the British ship Leopard. They resolved, that "at this awful crisis, when our national honor and independence are insulted by a nation with whom we, forgetful of former injuries, have not only endeavored to cultivate harmony, by preserving a strict and perfect neutrality, but to conciliate their friendship by every act of benevolence, humanity and assistance compatible with the justice due to ourselves and others; it is a duty of every American to rally around the constituted authorities of his country and to support them with his life and fortune, in resisting any encroachments on our national and individual rights by any foreign power whatever; and in procuring redress for the many injuries we have sustained, and which our patient and friendly forbearance has suffered too long, injuries committed in a manner unusually barbarous, and calculated to fix an indelible stigma." And further, that the measures adopted by the president of the United States on this trying occasion merited their highest approbation, and that the most implicit confidence was placed in his wisdom, integrity and ability in directing the energies of the government so as to preserve the honor of the nation free from reproach and individual liberties secure from violation; and they further declared, that, fearless of the dangers to which they were exposed as a frontier state, they should ever be ready to obey the calls of the country, whenever it shall be necessary, either for the purposes of redress or vengeance. A copy of these resolutions was transmitted to the president of the United States.

A law, establishing a state penitentiary, was passed, and a tax of one cent per acre was granted for carrying the aforesaid act into effect. No enactment of the legislature, on the subject of punishment for crimes, ever had so salutary and useful a tendency as imprisonment and hard labor for certain periods of time. Punishment by whipping, cropping and branding, a relic of feudal barbarism, has been abolished since the establishment of the state's prison. The usual business of appointing civil officers and passing several acts of a public and private nature, was accomplished with an unusual degree of harmony and quietness. A very unpleasant circumstance to the public, and unfortunate for the individual, occurred. It was the case of Mr. Spencer, a member of the legislature, from Rutland. He was a gentleman of high standing as a lawyer and former speaker of the house of representatives; but was by a committee appointed for the purpose of investigating certain charges of a highly dishonorable character, prefered against him, found guilty of feloniously taking ninety-three dollars in bank bills, the property of Messrs. Oliver Gallup, William B. Marsh, and James Herrington, all members of the present session. A resolution, together with the minutes of the evidence, was taken before the house, when the question was tried by the votes, and he was unanimously expelled from his seat in the legislature.

CHAPTER VII.

A review of the legislative proceedings from the year 1803 *to* 1815.—*Embargo laid by Congress upon the vessels of the United States.*—*Disturbances under that law in* 1808.—*Flood in July,* 1811.—*John Henry's mission.*—*United States declaration of war against Great-Britain, June* 18*th,* 1812.—*Riotous proceedings at Georgia.*—*Correspondence between Governor Chittenden, James Monroe, Generals Strong, Newell and Macomb.*—*Hartford Convention.*

When Bonaparte announced his design of enforcing with rigor the Berlin decree, and the British government solemnly asserted the right of search and impressment, the President of the United States recommended to Congress the detention of the American seamen, ships and merchandise in port, to preserve them from the danger of cruisers, which was effected by the restrictions of an indefinite embargo. This was designed to coerce the belligerant powers to return to the observance of the laws of nations, by withholding from them the advantages of the American trade. Within a few days, information was received that neutrals, comprising almost every maritime nation of Europe, were compelled to pay tribute if they traded with France or her allies. This was immediately succeeded by the Milan decree, declaring that every neutral vessel which submitted to the British restrictions, should be confiscated if they were afterwards found in their ports, or taken by the French cruisers. Thus, orders and decrees were in existence at the time of the embargo, subjecting to capture almost every vessel sailing on the ocean.— The highly prosperous commerce of New-England was by these regulations almost annihilated. The federalists, bearing a greater proportion here to the whole population than in other parts of the Union, pronounced the regulation burthensome and unwise. These representations and the sufferings which the people endured, changed public sentiment so rapidly that a majority were soon opposed to the measures of the government.

In March, 1809, the non-intercourse act, prohibiting all intercourse with France or Great-Britain during one year, was substituted by Congress for the embargo. For the purpose of retaliation, the Rambouillet decree of Bonaparte, authorising the seizure and confiscation of American vessels, excepting those charged with despatches to the government, was issued. The non-intercourse law expired in May, 1810, and government made proposals to both belligerant powers, that if either would revoke its hostile edicts, this law should only be revived and enforced against the other nation. It had ever been the American policy to observe a perfect impartiality towards each belligerant, in concluding and managing the affairs of national intercourse. The authorities of France informed the American officer, Mr. Armstrong, that the Berlin and Milan decrees were revoked in August, and this revocation would take effect on the first day of November ensuing. Trusting to this assurance, a proclamation was issued November 2d prohibiting all intercourse with Great-Britain, and allowing an unrestrained commerce with France. Great-

Britain was called upon by the American envoy to fulfil her promise in revoking her orders, as the government of France had repealed their decrees. She objected to the validity of the transaction, as a letter from the minister of State was not a document of sufficient authority, for that purpose. This objection was refuted by proof derived from the French admiralty courts, that they considered them repealed, and that the American vessels having entered the ports of France, had not been subject to these prohibitions. Notwithstanding these proceedings, Great-Britain still persisted to enforce her orders. She established a kind of a blockading system, throughout the principal harbors of the United States. Vessels departing or returning, were boarded and searched, and some of them sent to British ports, as legal prizes. The Americans suffered greatly from these incursions. Their seamen were impressed, their vessels captured, and their property confiscated. No assurances were given by the government, that a satisfactory arrangement, on the subject of impressment, or the repeal of the orders in council, would be made. But these orders, on the contrary, continued to be enforced with rigor, and on the restoration of free commerce with France, a great number of American vessels, with valuable cargoes, destined to her ports, fell into the hands of the English cruisers. The situation of business was such, that the United States suffered the evils, while Great-Britain reaped the benefits of the war. Nine hundred American vessels had been taken by the English, since 1803.

After enduring such evils to the last extremity of patience and forbearance, Congress was called together, on the first of November, 1811. The situation of foreign affairs was laid before them, and it was recommended by the President that the republic should be placed in the attitude of defence. And the people expressed, by their representatives, their general wishes, in accordance with the views of the President.

1808. This year the legislature convened at Montpelier, the new capital of the state, which had two years previously been established, by an act of the legislature, as the permanent seat of government. Mr. Tichenor was elected in opposition to the incumbent for the last year.—His communication to the legislative body delineated upon matters of public interest as candidly as could be expected in such violent party times. Still, his views of the policy adopted by the general government evinced a direct opposition to the leading measures of the administration.—"While (says he) we regret the stain upon the character of a respectable class of our citizens, who have violated the law of the general government, suspending our commerce by an embargo without limitation, we sincerely regret that the law was not accompanied with that evidence of national necessity or utility which at once would have commanded obedience and respect." There was not at this crisis of our national affairs, according to the governor's observations, a fitness in the restrictive system. According to the answer of the house, as given in the reply, a majority were in favor of the measures of the administration and strongly incensed against the alledged cruelties and oppressions of the British nation. The subjects of the American government, though desirous of remaining neutral, were exposed to inconveniences and afflictive losses during the contest between Great-Britain and France. Enjoying an extensive commerce, as the carriers of the produce of France and other countries, they felt the ill effects of the clashing decrees of the belligerent powers. "We cannot (they observe) but consider the law alluded to as necessary; yet we feel a dignified pleasure that this, the only practicable measure which could have averted the danger and horrors of war with one or more of the contending nations of Europe, has been patiently submitted to by every well informed and well disposed citizen of the nation." The committee to whom the foreign affairs were referred, entered into all the feelings of the president. Having commented upon the right of the United States to the use of the ocean " for the purpose of transporting in their own vessels the produce of their own soil and acquisitions of their industry to a market in the ports of friendly nations, it was then alledged that the people could not remain passive under the accumulated injuries inflicted by Great-Britain. As an improper seizure of their ships and seamen was made, it was proper that the States should be put in the attitude of defence demanded by the crisis, and agreeing with the national spirit and expectations, measures for increasing the national force, though opposed by some, were sanctioned by the majority.

A transaction of a very fearful and alarming character ensued upon Onion river, between the party cruising upon the lake and river, under the employ of the federal government, for the purpose of suppressing the violations of trade and intercourse between the American and British governments, and a smuggling vessel, called the Black Snake. During the contest, two men were killed by the smugglers, whereupon these aggressors were arrested, and a special session of the court was holden at Burlington, for their trial. Day, one of the party, was discharged by the States' Attorney; another, by the name of Dean, was executed, and the remainder were sentenced to the state's prison. The perturbation and excitement raised among the people, by this transaction, checked for a time the illicit trade between this state and the British provinces.

1809. Mr. Galusha, one of the former judges of the Supreme Court of Vermont, was chosen governor of the state. His election was supported by the republican party, which had managed so adroitly as to secure a majority over the old governor, who for years had served the state with fidelity and applause. The passions incident to the feelings of the parties discovered themselves in the public transactions and private intercourse of the people—criminations were thrown upon one another—French and British influence were the imputed errors of partizan zeal.

The Governor's message to the assembly evinced sentiments of decision upon the subject of our foreign relations with two of the most powerful nations of Europe, who, regardless of neutral rights and the laws of nations, have interdicted the commerce of the United States by embarrassing it with exactions hitherto unheard of, which if submitted to by the general government, would lead to the surrender of our nautical rights, and virtually the independence of the country. Although measures had been pursued to remove the embarrassments, without resorting to arms, says the communication, yet they proved unavailing. "With these views, the adoption of such measures as will have the most direct tendency to conciliate the affections of the people, and unite them in their great national interest, cannot be too strongly recommended. But while it is recommended to you cheerfully to submit, and as a member of the Union, to carry into effect such measures as have been or may be adopted by the United States for the preservation of our national rights, at the same time it becomes you, as the guardians of those rights and powers that are not delegated by the constitution of the United States, but are reserved to the respective states, or the people, to observe and defend their proper use and continuance." The attention of the legislature was also directed to make such further regulations and provisions as were necessary for arming and disciplining the militia in case of their services being wanted in times of danger. The sentiments of a majority of the legislature were, from the style of their answer, exactly similar to those presented in the speech of the Governor. The following paragraph will exhibit the strife of feeling which was cultivated by the party. "We have seen with just alarm that spirit of discord which has prevailed, weakening the bonds of the general government, and rendering abortive salutary measures by them adopted, to maintain our commercial rights, and our national honor and independence; but this alarm is greatly diminished by the marks of returning patriotism and a renewed attachment to the interest and happiness of our country and to the administration of our general government; and we hope ere long to realize that union of sentiment among the citizens of this State and the United States, with regard to our political interest, which will awe the powers of Europe into a practical sense of national justice, and prove the surest palladium of our liberties and independence." As a literary production it is very inelegant and absurd, and the sentiments egotistic and inflated.

Those in power congratulated themselves and the citizens of the state upon a happy and prosperous situation of affairs, so long as they continued in office, and reprobated the practices of those previously in power. This answer were a general response to arguments advanced in the speech.

A committee, appointed for the purpose of addressing Mr. Madison, furnished a communication replete with matters of complaint, against the proceedings and commercial aggression of the European powers. The vivifying touch of republican resentment, arrayed in all the horrors of inhuman vengeance, was detailed in the relation they gave of the European blockades, and unlawful violations and restrictions of the American commerce. As the spirit of the times can best be learned from the acts and declarations of legislative bodies, no declaration could better answer for a description of their feelings, than the following: "The people of Vermont, though mostly devoted to agricultural pursuits, have, during the late and present embarrassments, felt an uncommon interest with her sister States, and have long and anxiously waited in hopes that a strict and impartial neutrality maintained by the general government towards all nations, the just and reasonable offers of accommodation it has repeatedly made, would have before this brought the offending nations to a sense of justice, and created a disposition to restore to us the peaceable enjoyment of our national rights; but in this they have been disappointed, and with extreme concern behold the most friendly, just and pacific overtures treated with silent contempt by one nation, and by another met with what is still worse, fruitless and delusive propositions and arrangements, calculated solely to weaken the bonds of government, and to defeat those wise precautionary means adopted to obtain a redress of our wrongs." In consequence of the American embargo, laid in pursuance of the restrictive system of France and England, adopted in 1806, 7 and 8, the commerce of Vermont had diminished very much. The Canada trade, formerly very lucrative, was at this time kept up only by the illicit transactions of smugglers. The embargo withholding the merchant from a career in which he imagined that he might still be favored of fortune, occasioned discontent and clamor. In the New-England States, except Vermont, a majority became federalists, and opposed all the measures of the government.

A proposition from the legislature of Virginia, for amending the constitution of the United States, was brought forward for the consideration of the legislature. The design of the resolution was to have the law so altered that Senators in Congress might be removed from office by a majority of the whole members of the respective state legislatures, by which they have been or may be appointed. But the suggested amendment was regarded by a majority of the house as an unwise encroachment upon the constitution, which ought to be preserved inviolate, without some more palpable reason than the present was urged in favor of an alteration.

The election of the chief magistrate for the State terminated in 1810 in favor of the governor for the past year, and all the officers chosen by the general ticket were of the republican party. The critical attitude which the federal government bore in relation the the powers of Europe, appeared at this time to furnish the principal grounds of difference between the two political parties of the government. After noticing the unjust restrictions of some of the European sovereigns, governor Galusha observed "that these rival powers had determined on the destruction of each other, and each, unable to encounter his opponent with success, have employed a mode of warfare substantially affecting all neutral rights, and every commercial state has experienced the cruel effect of this unrighteous policy. All the nations of Europe have, by flattery or the sword, been obliged to take part with one or the other of these powers in their warfare." The utmost stretch of power was also alleged to have been exerted by France and England to draw the United States from their neutral position; yet the wisdom of Congress had resisted their temptations and eluded their strength. And further, that if every American was sufficiently barred against foreign influence and attached to his own government, the strength of Europe might be set at defiance. But notwithstanding the aggressions from abroad, and dissensions at home, the civil and religious liberties of this country, bestowed by heaven and guaranteed by a republican government, remain unimpaired. The subject of education, which had often received the attention and patronage of the legislature, was finally declared to be the great suppressor of vice and hand-maid of virtue, and the grand pillar of our Independence.

The answer to the governor's speech was composed in a style rather conciliatory for the zeal of the times. "After buffeting the storms of faction and discontent, we have arrived at a period distinguished by such evident traces of patriotism, as almost precludes the idea that we are or can be a divided people." It had been the business of the legislature, ever since the first organization of the government, to sustain petitions for new trials, for the liberation of poor debtors from imprisonment, and re-judging cases which had received a final trial before the highest judicial tribunal in the state. Such an exercise of power over the judgments and opinions of the supreme court, was, in the minds of the more intelligent part of the legislative body, considered unconstitutional, and a direct violation of its privileges; a union of two distinct powers in one branch of government, which were in the most expressive language of that instrument, declared to be separate and distinct.

Proceedings of this character destroyed the confidence of the people in the courts, which, together with their annual appointments, rendered them, so far as human nature is swayed by motives which tend to their own preservation and power, subservient to the will and management of the legislative body. Numerous suspensions for poor debtors, freeing their bodies from arrest and imprisonment for a certain number of years, were annually granted by the general assembly. This stretch of power favored so strongly the wild misrule of despotism that the practice was but slightly followed for a number of years anterior to its final disuse. The Supreme Court have decided, in several cases, that the bonds were valid and collectible of the bail, where the principal had been authorised, by an act of suspension from the legislature, to leave the liberties of the jail. The acts granting such suspensions were declared unconstitutional and all proceedings had under them void.

The bills of the Vermont state bank were, by an act of the state, made a lawful tender in payment of all land taxes granted at that session of the legislature. Kentucky subsequently undertook to validate their state bills and make them a tender in discharge of any contract entered into by the citizens of that state. But measures of this kind directly contradicted that part of the federal constitution which declares that no state shall "make any thing but gold and silver coin a tender in payment of debts.— Whatever pecuniary embarrassments were intended to be removed by such legislative enactments, ruin has ensued wherever the experiment has been attempted. Bank bills, as a representative of wealth, are of no more value than so much weight in paper rags, if no funds are deposited for their redemption.

Mr. Israel Smith, the fourth governor of Vermont, died at Rutland the present year. He settled in Vermont at an early period, in the practice of law, and soon rose to distinction in his profession and usefulness in the public affairs of the state.

In 1797 he was elected Chief Justice of the Supreme Court of Vermont, and afterwards was successively chosen a member of the house of representatives and the senate in the Congress of the United States; and finally elevated to the highest office in the gift of the people. Concerning his character it may justly be said, that he was a man of the purest morals, stern integrity, undeviating justice, and discharged the duty of his public appointments with honor to himself and advantage to the public.

1811. This year was distinguished for a very remarkable fall of rain on the 22d of July. So large a quantity had never been known to descend at one time since the settlement of the state, as there did at this period. From twelve to fifteen inches was the estimated quantity that fell upon a level. The wind blew in a direction from the south-west to the north-east, bringing with it a darkened envelope of clouds. Commencing at lake George and extending to Connecticut river, every rivulet and stream was swollen to full banks, with foaming cataracts of water: mills, bridges, fences, and in many instances houses and barns, were swept in the vortex and embosomed in the wide waste of water. Scarcely a mill or machine propelled by water remained within the limits of this devastating storm. The internal lands bordering upon the rivers and streams were in many places cut up and the soil carried away to the depth of several feet, and in other places flood-wood, trees, rocks and sand-buried the surface of the soil many feet below. So complete a work of destruction can be but imperfectly described. Some lives were lost, and others had but a hair's breadth escape from a watery grave. Twenty-two towns, embracing the whole width of the state, from Fair-Haven, Castleton and Poultney to Hartland, Hartford and Windsor, experienced the exterminating ravages of the flood; but its violence was the most severe on the west side of the mountain. Appearances of its desolating force are visible to this day. Where the smooth lawn skirted along the meandering river a barren surface of pebbles only remains. The legislature assembled in the fall of this year, and the executive power was again placed in the hands of Mr. Galusha, who, after addressing them upon those subjects which demanded their attention, received the customary answer from the house.

A resolution, passed by the Congress of the United States, proposing an amendment to the federal constitution, was brought before the house. The spirit of the resolution accorded well with the feelings, habits, and views of the hardy yeomanry of the green mountains.— Unacquainted with the titles, honors and equipage of imperial courts, the republican occupant of the hard hills and frosty mountains of Vermont spurned those distinctions of rank unknown to his own republican institutions. The amendment enacted by Congress and concurred in by the legislature of Vermont, was, that any citizen of the United States, who shall accept, claim, receive or retain any title of nobility or honor, or shall, without the consent of Congress, accept or retain any present pension office or emolument from any sovereign or foreign power, such person shall cease to be a citizen of the United States, and shall be incapable of holding any office of profit or trust under them or either of them.

The people of Vermont were this season very much afflicted and alarmed on account of the prevalence of the spotted fever, which had spread its ravages the two preceding years. The attacks and progress of the disease were generally sudden. Children would awake in the morning in a comatose and distressed state, with a very quick pulse, and in a few hours die. Cases have frequently occurred of people possessing every appearance of the most firm and athletic habits being prostrated by it in a few days, and sometimes in a few hours, without apparent symptoms of dissolution. From weakness or abberation of intellect, they were incapable of describing their feelings and commonly died in a state of stupidity. This disease has now entirely disappeared.

1812. This year was an eventful period in the history of the American States. Faction and its concomitant evils had disordered the union of society—war and its devastating consequences destroyed the subjects and resources of the government—commerce was driven from the ocean, and peace from the hallowed sanctuary of freedom. Rulers were distrusted by the people, and the people in return were charged with infidelity to the government.—Silence was construed into disaffection and loyalty into oppression. The very name of parties was enough to produce the appellation of an enemy.

Early in the year, John Henry, a former resident in Canada, had passed through Vermont to Boston, as early as 1809. He stopped at Burlington and Windsor, to confer with those citizens who were disaffected with the government, upon the subject of making a separation of the New-England States from the rest of the Union, and their forming a political connection with Great-Britain. He exhibited documents in support of his disclosures, which he was led to make, by the neglect of his employers to reward him for his services. It did not, however, appear that he had succeeded in corrupting the fidelity of any individual, but the undertaking, in a time of peace, and in the midst of the most devoted friendship, not only continued in full force, but extended the previous irritation. This failure Henry attributed entirely to the willingness Mr. Madison had manifested to accept the conciliating propositions of Mr. Erskine, which deprived him of the opportunity of raising an opposition to the administration, on the representation to them that he was engaged in the interest of France. After the British government refused him a remuneration for his services, the authority of the United States rewarded him for disclosing the object and proceedings of his mission with the sum of fifty thousand dollars, and sent him out in an American ship of war to France.

In April 3d Congress laid an embargo for ninety days on all the vessels within the jurisdiction of the United States. Although the government continued to be engaged in making preparations for war, a hope was still indulged that some change of policy in Europe would render the commencement of hostilities unnecessary. Despatches were received from London at the same time, by the ship Hornet, containing the information that no prospect existed of a favorable change. The message of the president contained these as the principal reasons for declaring war— "the impressment of American seamen by the British—the blockade of her enemies' ports, in consequence of which the American commerce had been plundered in every sea, and the British orders in council," which were submitted to Congress, whether they would endure them any longer or resort to arms. On the 18th of June an act was passed in the house of representatives, by a vote of 79 in the affirmative and 49 in the negative, and in the senate by a majority of 19 to 13, declaring war against Great-Britain. A considerable portion of the citizens of the United States were decidedly opposed to this measure. Exercising the undoubted rights of freemen, they examined with the severest scrutiny the measures and motives of the government. The war they asserted to be unnecessary, partial and unwise; that it was unnecessary, because in their opinion a satisfactory adjustment of all disputes might have been effected by farther negotiation; that it was partial, because France had given greater provocation, in proportion to her means of annoyance, than Great-Britain; that it was unwise, because the nation was not prepared for war; and further, by declaring it against almost the only remaining enemy of France, the United States indirectly but powerfully aided the Emperor of France in his attempts at the subjugation of the world; and finally, the advantages sought to be obtained would be more than counterbalanced by the expense and sufferings of the nation.—

The bounds of temperate and candid discussion were exceeded by a virulence of invective which no government should be the subject of that is not manifestly corrupt.

Soon after the declaration of war rendezvous for enlisting soldiers were opened in Vermont, and a cantonment for the northern army was fixed at Burlington. The quota of militia demanded by the president of the United States were called upon to march by orders from the governor; subject however to service only within the United States. Nothing of importance transpired this year in the army within the territorial bounds of this state.

In October, 1812, the legislature assembled at Montpelier, and Mr. Galusha was again elected to preside over the state. His zeal for supporting the administration of the general government was very forcibly expressed in his speech to the legislature. After representing the injuries and injustice done to the federal government by the British nation, and their submission to the cruel edicts and arbitrary power of that kingdom, he remarks: Although some doubt the propriety of the measures adopted, yet war being declared by the constituted authorities of our country, it ought no longer to remain a question of policy, but it has become a duty of the state governments, and of every individual, with promptitude to espouse the sacred cause of our injured country—to second the measures of our general government—provide for the defence and safety of our citizens, and with zeal pursue such measures as will tend to procure an acknowledgment of our national rights—a release of our impressed seamen—remove the encroachments on the grand highway of nations—put a final period to the calamities of war, and establish a permanent and honorable peace. "Is it possible to conceive that any citizen, living under such a mild government, can be so destitute of a principle of patriotism, and so lost to their own interest, as, through a fond passion for a foreign power, the violence of party zeal or a sordid spirit of avarice, to betray the just cause of their suffering country, prolong the horrors of war, invoke the vengeance of Heaven, and be guilty of the blood of thousands by devoting their talents and yielding their support to a nation whose pledged faith has been so often violated, and whose tender mercies have by experience proved to consist in cruelty." Party resentment was wrought up to the highest pitch of irritation. They denounced each other as enemies to their common country, and under the influence and domination of foreign powers.

The answer to the governor's speech was kindled to a blaze of resentment against the federal party, as the transcribed sentiments plainly indicate. "We hope, when the blinding influence of the present black electioneering whirlwind shall have passed away, the returning good sense and candor of a large portion of our disappointed citizens will lead them to see clearly, consider carefully and pursue vigorously the great cause you have recommended to our attention." The party in power entered so engagedly upon the measures of the general government as to exceed the bounds of prudence in some of their proceedings.

A majority of the general assembly of Vermont, thinking that the difficulties of the times required their sentiments to be known among the other states, adopted a resolution that the constituted authorities of our country having declared war between the United States and Great Britain and her dependencies, it is our duty as citizens to support the measure; otherwise we should identify ourselves with the enemy, with no other difference than that of locality. "We therefore pledge ourselves to each other and to our government, that with our individual exertions, our example and influence, we will support our government and country in the present contest, and rely on the great Arbiter of events for a favorable result.—This resolution was adopted by 128 in the affirmative and 79 in the negative. Those members who voted in the negative drew up a protest and entered it upon the journals of the house, with the following reasons for their dissent:—
"Although we feel ourselves under the most sacred obligation to yield a prompt and faithful obedience to every law of the general government and to support with our lives all that is dear to freemen, the independence of our country, yet it is no less our duty as men and as guardians of the public good, to express our decided disapprobation of any law or measure of the government, which, on a candid

examination and due consideration, we are compelled to believe impolitic and injurious to the public; and by all lawful means, we will endeavor to remove the evil by effecting a change in the measures of the administration or by changing the administration itself. We verily believe that the resolution is calculated to confirm and establish a doctrine incompatible with and subversive of the true principle of a republican government, inasmuch as it assumes the principle that because "war is declared, we are bound as citizens not only to yield prompt obedience to all the requisitions of government, but also to use our individual influence in support of its measures; otherwise we should identify ourselves with the enemy;"—conceiving it utterly impossible that in the fair, open and honest exercise of our duties as citizens, we can consistently use our influence in favor of a measure of which we ourselves disapprove." These dissenting members unequivocally expressed their disapprobation of the declaration of war, by pronouncing it premature, inexpedient and likely to be extremely injurious to the people. Such were the extreme points to which almost every act of the legislature was pressed, that scarcely any quarter of the Union discovered more zeal and preparation for carrying forward the measures of the general government. By one act all the intercourse between the citizens of this state and the province of Lower Canada was prohibited, without a permit from the governor, under a penalty of one thousand dollars and imprisonment to hard labor in the state's penitentiary for the term of seven years. All trade between the subjects of the same governments was also forbidden. States attornies and grand jurors were empowered to enter a complaint before any magistrate in the state. Justices of the peace were privileged with the power of inspecting trunks or the papers and letters of any person travelling to or from the province of Canada without a warrant, and could call to their assistance the citizens of the state, to carry into effect the provisions of the law. By another act, the body or property of any officer or soldier belonging to this state, while in actual service, on whom a writ of summons or attchment may have been served, should not be holden nor should a judgement be rendered thereon or any writ of execution be issued after the passage of this act against such officer or soldier on any judgment then already obtained.

Several other laws were passed during this session of the legislature, worthy of a passing notice. A tax of one cent on each acre of land was granted, in addition to the usual assessment on the grand list, for the support of government, and another law regulating the method of detaching the militia and increasing the pay of the officers and soldiers drafted in compliance with the directions of the President of the United States, to the sum of three dollars and 34 cents per month, received the sanction of the legislative councils of the state. The expenditures of the government of Vermont for the present year exceeded those of any former one by a very large amount. The occasion of this was the defensive operations of the government in arming and supporting the militia to defend the frontiers. The effect of these legislative regulations aroused the indignation and resentment of the people to such a degree that there began to be a re-action of feeling. Numbers took part with those opposed to the measures of administration, and so great was the depression of business, arising from the restrictions upon commerce, that the measures of the general government become offensive to many of its former supporters. Nothing was left undone, whether true or false, to render the proceedings of the state or federal government odious to the people; the war was declared unjust and destitute of all advantage to any excepting Bonaparte and the French government; the restraints on commerce, calculated to increase crimes rather than starve the enemy, and the difficulties between the United States and the sovereigns of Europe, were removed in fact by their amicable propositions and willingness to make every reparation that justice could demand. These and the representations of the opposition, operated so powerfully as to give a majority on the part of the federalists and place the government of the state in their power.

1813. Political controversies this year exceeded in violence any thing of the kind that had ever occurred since the first settlement of the State. Electioneering plans were pursued by the most unfair and reproachful measures. Misrepresentation and abuse were the prominent instruments employed in their proceedings. Secret societies were organized for the avowed purpose of doing acts of benevolence and cultivating a taste for literary pursuits, but in fact for the object of political ascendency. The party opposed to the war strengthened their cause and increased their numbers by the general concert effected through the agency of these societies. So odious had the restrictive system become to the people accustomed to free trade, and so direful was the turmoil of war, when compared to a situation of independence and peace, that the federalists increased in numbers very rapidly.

No choice of a governor being made by the people, the election of course devolved upon the house. The parties arrayed themselves in the strength of their numbers, which upon trial, were found to be equally divided. Effort at persuasion were perfectly unavailing; conciliation could not be expected between parties so exasperated in their feelings. Great feats at maneuvering were attempted, and plans devised to obtain a conquest, but their numbers continued equal. The election of Mr. Chittenden, the federal candidate, was at last carried, by a very small majority, and another gentleman of his political tenets for lieutenant governor. Much was said and done about the improper means employed by certain members and other gentlemen, in trying to influence the vote of one Carpus Clark, a member from Worcester, or hire him to leave the State before an opportunity for giving his vote for the governor, occurred. Mr. Clark, who was tampered with to vote for the federal candidate, was a republican, and gave his suffrages for the administration party. In the progress of their management, attempts were made to hire him at an extravagant price, to convey a load from Vermont to Boston: the property to be transported consisted of such articles as were necessary to be there by a certain time, let the expenses or difficulties be what they would. They next concerted the plan of buying his real estate, which was situated in Worcester, and place him under a contract to remove immediately from this to the western country. Several offers were made by the agents of different parties in this disgraceful proceeding to sway his feeble or at least his tempted understanding from the course of duty and his oath. One did it with a view of being benefited by his vote, and the other, the federalists, for having less strength against them by his absence. On account of his guilt, arising from an improper course of conduct in suffering himself to be trifled with, and setting up his elective franchises for sale to the highest bidder, a committee was appointed to enquire into conduct so discreditable and derogatory to the dignity of the house.— This delegation reported a resolution that Carpus Clark, for dishonorable conduct, ought to be expelled from the legislative body. Afterwards, by an act of the legislature, he was ejected from the privileges of a representative.— These proceedings were protested against by 34 of the members, who voted in the minority on the expulsion of Mr. Clark, and the proceedings were entered upon the journals.

A remonstrance against the election of Mr. Chittenden to the office of governor of this state, was laid before the council and representatives in joint committee, which provided that in case the facts set forth in said memorial should be supported, that they proceed by joint ballot of both houses to elect a gov. of the state for the year ensuing. After a lengthy debate, the governor elect appeared in the house, accompanied by the lieutenant governor and council, and after the necessary qualifications, he, among other matters of business, expressed his views upon the subject of the militia in this manner:—"I have always considered this force peculiarly adapted and exclusively assigned for the service and protection of the respective states, excepting in the cases provided for by the national constitution, to wit, to execute the laws of the Union, suppress insurrection, and repel invasion. It never could have been contemplated by the wise framers of our excellent constitution, who, it appears, in the most cautious manner, guarded the sovereignty of the states, or was guarded by the states which adopted it, that the whole body of the militia could not, by any kind of magic, at once be transformed into a regular army for the purpose of foreign conquest; and it is to be regretted that a construction should ever have been given to the constitution so peculiarly burdensome and oppressive to that important class of our fellow citizens."

At this season of war and the call for large detachments of militia, no subject presented for legislative consideration could have aroused the exertions and sensibilities of the people more than this. It called forth public indignation to be obliged to contribute men and money in support of a war which they considered unprovoked, unnecessary and unwise. Various constructions were given to this clause of the constitution, which declares the president empowered in certain cases to call the militia into actual service.—Those who opposed the measures of the government disputed the power of the federal executive to call the militia at any event into a war of invasion or out of the limits of the state, for any other causes than those above mentioned. The sentiments of the federal party upon this subject are fully expressed in this paragraph of their answer to the message:—"When we candidly view our political and commercial relations, our diplomatic intercourse with France and Great-Britain, and the injuries received from both, we are compelled to doubt the necessity, expediency and justice of the present war. Its continuence is still more unnecessary, as the orders in council, the principal alledged causes, were removed before the declaration of war was known in Great-Britain, and within a reasonable time after the promulgation of the repeal of the Berlin and Milan decrees; inexpedient, as Great-Britain never claimed a right to impress American seamen, and their practice of impressment was never considered a sufficient or justifiable cause of war by the former administrations, but a subject of amicable negotiation. We regret that the treaty made by Messrs. Munroe and Pinckney, in 1806, and the provisions for a final adjustment of all differences which were considered by them to be perfectly safe and honorable to our country, had never been laid before the Senate of the United States, and adopted, which would have prevented all the restrictive measures of the general government and the calamities and demoralizing effects of an expensive war. The conquest of the Canadas will be an inadequate compensation for the blood and treasure which must be lost. And we have yet to learn that an offensive war upon the Canadas will defend and secure the rights of our seamen upon the ocean." Seventy-nine members, who voted in the negative on the reported answer to his excellency's speech, entered upon the journals some of their reasons for so doing. They believed that an improper attempt was made to excite the sympathies of the people in favor of a corrupt government of the old world, and that the militia in the present case had not been called into actual service or for any other purpose than that contemplated in the constitution. And further, that no safe and honorable terms had been offered by the belligerant nations of Europe to the American republic; that their commerce had been dispoiled, their ports blockaded and their citizens impressed on board of the English navy, and that all the offers of our government at a reconciliation had been answered with insults. An appeal to arms they considered the only way to vindicate the suffering honor of their country; and, since this alternative was resorted to, they considered themselves in duty bound to sustain and encourage it with their honor, possessions and lives. Feelings so spirited could not easily be checked. They declared that they could not recommend an acquiescence in the assumed right of Great-Britain to revive her orders in council at pleasure nor sanction the monstrous principle of British impressment.

After the choice of the civil officers for the year ensuing was made out, several acts were passed in direct opposition to some of the last session. The militia called into actual service were by the present law rendered amenable in person and property to a civil process. The statute prohibiting all intercourse between the British government and Vermont, was repealed; and a provision for the militia drafted out into the service of this state, was derived from a tax of one cent upon the dollar on the grand list. Three new judges of the supreme court were elected from those who were opposed to the war and general measures of the administration, and other changes were effected among the lower grades of appointments. So great was the zeal between the parties, that they denominated each other tories, traitors and enemies to the country and the general interests of the land.

The liberties taken by the deputies of the custom house departments, and the authority given to justices of peace to stop and search the premises of any person they chose, without a warrant from the civil authority, caused great personal conflicts and a constant irruption of the peace of society. In charging the grand jury, the supreme court directed them to make inquiry and present all cases where people were searched for property without a warrant, and on trials parties were not justified in molesting people and taking their property by virtue of a commission only.— The frontier towns upon Canada line were subject to great disturbances and strife by reason of the smuggling transactions. Resistance had in no instance proceeded to more fearful extremities than in the north-east part of the state. Sometime about the commencement of the year 1813, Mr. Samuel Beach, of Canaan, received a permit from the governor to go into Canada for the purpose of repairing a saw mill. Having sent forward his workmen and teams, he proceeded on afterwards, when his team was taken by John Dennet and others, and drove back to Canaan; but Beach, in attempting to regain his team, was fired upon by Dennet and killed. Dennet and his associates were taken and committed to jail, from which the former escaped in January following into the adjoining wilderness, where he continued until August, when he was re-taken, but not until he was mortally wounded by his pursuers. Dennet resisted, and it appears while he was attempting to kill one Morgan, he was shot by Sperry, one of the pursuers, in 1814. The business of smuggling, thus attended with blood-shed, violence and rapine, was kept up, although the perpetrators of such offences were indicted in the courts of the State as well as the United States.

On the 23d of July, of the present year, a party of smugglers proceeded from Missisque bay to St. Albans.— On their way they increased their numbers to about eighty and were all armed with pistols and other weapons. Mr. Hathaway, of Swanton, who was riding by unconscious of danger, was rushed upon by them and forced from his horse into a house, and there beaten in a most shocking manner. A grand juror from St. Albans made one of this riotous company. This mob declared their determination to give Georgia a scouring and root out the high-way robbers, as they called the custom house officers. After appointing one of their company to the command, they took a Mr. Anthony along with them as a prisoner. Halting on the way at Mr. Blodget's, of Georgia, they awoke him from sleep and gave him information that the smugglers had come, and they wanted his assistance in capturing them. Mr. Blodget and his sons had no sooner arrived at the place of their collection, than he was levelled to the ground by their clubs. One of his arms was broken, his head and body were wounded in various places. The windows of his house were broken in and a Mr. Conger was taken a prisoner. Proceeding on their way to the south part of Georgia, they called on a Mrs. Hubbell, in the absence of her husband, to leave her house, declaring that on their return they should destroy it. An officer of the custom house department, supposing they had smuggled goods, requested them to stop, when suddenly they surrounded Messrs. Dee, Barker and Robinson, took them and tied their arms behind with cords, and rode off three miles with their prisoners to Mrs. Hyde's, in Georgia.—Here a large number of citizens soon after collected to oppose them with arms. When, discovering their danger, they immediately dispersed.

Governor Moses Robinson, one of the principal men in the early settlement and organization of a government in Vermont, died this year. He was possessed of a vigorous and discriminating mind, cool and deliberate judgment, and of free and independent principles. The public were long and faithfully served by him, in the various capacities of judge, senator in Congress, and governor of the State.

The general assembly convened in October of the present year, 1814; but there was no choice made of a governor by the people. Pains or trouble had not been spared in electioneering for the respective candidates for governor, but all their exertion, trouble and industry proved ineffectual and unavailing, as the votes returned stood nearly equal. The election was again taken before the house, and Mr. Chittenden was chosen to preside over the state: the lieutenant governor, the secretary of state, and the executive council, were re-elected, all of whom professed principles of federalism: the latter were appointed by the suffrages of the people.

Concerning the achievements within or near the jurisdictional boundaries of Vermont, it was well observed by governor Chittenden, in his speech to the legislature, that these glorious deeds are not surpassed in the records of naval or military warfare. New lustre is added to the national character. Having commented upon the brilliant achievements, the brave and patriotic conduct of the officers and soldiers at the battle of Plattsburgh, he has these observations on the subject of the war in which our country was unfortunately engaged:—"I feel disposed at this critical period to say as little as may be consistent with my duty," about the causes and origin of the war. "But I consider it due to myself, and more especially to my constituents, explicitly to state that the events of the war have in no instance altered my opinion of its origin or progress. I have conscientiously and uniformly disapproved of it, as unnecessary, unwise and hopeless in all its offensive operations. And notwithstanding the few brilliant successes we have met with in our operations of defence, I can see very little in its general complexion which affords the least consolation. Many very considerable places on our sea-board are now in the possession of the enemy.— The capital of our country, that proud monument of better times, has been possessed and destroyed by the enemy—a humiliating reflection to every real American."— An answer was returned by the house, which contained sentiments honorable to the enlightened body from which it eminated. For manner of expression and favorable sentiments entertained concerning those brave and skilful defenders of the northern frontiers, the production is a distinguished effort at conciliation between the parties.

The minority against the passage of the vote for answering governor Chittenden's speech, entered their protest upon the journals of the house, in these words: that they could not join in the declaration that good order and peace had prevailed throughout the state during the past year more generally than in former years; but, on the contrary; for the whole year past the laws of the United States have been entirely disregarded and boldly set at defiance, in the prosecution of a continued and almost uninterrupted illicit intercourse between this state and the British provinces of Lower Canada, is a truth which it is in vain for this house to endeavor to suppress or contradict. In addition, every other kind of unlawful commerce, contrary to the most fundamental principles of law and justice, has constantly been and still is continually carried on among us, furnishing provisions and other necessaries of war, for the support of those very armies and fleets against which we are contending, and which are destined for our destruction. And it is with the deepest regret we are compelled to state that from the sanction and encouragement which have been afforded to these treasonable practices by a portion of our citizens, it has been utterly impossible to prevent or to put an end to their commission.

The correspondence between governor Chittenden, James Monroe, then secretary of the United States, generals Strong, Newell and Macomb, was called up by a resolution in the house of representatives. The communications commence with a request from general Macomb to governor Chittenden for a detachment of Vermont militia to assist him at Plattsburgh, as the enemy were fast advancing towards that place. Fearful apprehensions were entertained for the safety of the town, and aid was actually wanted, as the garrison was small and the enemy in considerable force. The answer of the executive to this request was replete with assurances that the most effectual measures should be taken to furnish such a number of volunteers as may be induced to turn out for the assistance of the general. A letter was transmitted by his excellency to general Newell, recommending him to take the most effectual measures to procure as many volunteers as could be collected from the immediate vicinity, for the assistance of general Macomb. General Newell, in reply, stated that whenever he was called upon to order out his brigade, he should hold himself in readiness to obey; but from what was stated in his excellency's letter, he could do no more than to request the voluntary services of the militia over whom he had the command, which might be followed or not, just as they chose to act with regard to the subject. In a further call and explanation of Mr. Chittenden, he said he had no constitutional power to order the Vermont militia out of the state. He therefore earnestly requested that forces should volunteer, and represented it as his opinion that such measures would have more effect than an attempt to assume an unauthorized power, on all such as were willing to turn out for the defence of their country. A request was then made by colonel Fassett, on the governor, for a quantity of ammunition, which was subject to his order at Vergennes. Permission was given to the colonel to take the same, if there was any, at the place above mentioned. About this time, the governor's military aid, A. W. Barnum, Esq. and Samuel Swift, Esq. secretary to the governor and council, were sent to confer with general Macomb, at Plattsburgh, and obtain his opinion upon their undertakings to furnish assistance. A large number of volunteers from Franklin, Chittenden, Addison, Rutland, and Grand-Isle counties had crossed over the lake and placed themselves under the command of major-general Samuel Strong, with a determination to defend the honor and independence of their country, at the risk of all that was valuable to them, their lives and possessions.

From the encampment at Plattsburgh, General Strong addressed letters to his friends in Vermont, dated the 10th and 11th of September, stating that the British had arrived with an army of 8 or 9000 men, and the volunteers, who had then joined them at the encampment, from Vermont, amounted to 1812, and 700 of the same grade of forces had assembled from the adjoining parts of New-York, and that general Mooers was immediately expected with two thousand of militia more : these, together with 2000 regulars, constituted the whole force to meet and contest the field with the veteran forces of Europe. It was also stated that 2500 volunteers from Vermont, had encamped on the south bank of the Saranac, opposite to the enemy's right wing, commanded by general Brisbrane. Governor Chittenden was informed in a letter from general Strong, dated the 11th of September, from the same place, that they had the satisfaction of seeing the British fleet strike to the brave commodore McDonough. Attempts were made at several places, to cross over the river, but were foiled, except at Pike's encampment. Skirmishings had been kept up during the day, when twenty or thirty of the enemy were taken prisoners, but the number killed was unknown. In his last correspondence with Mr. Chittenden, written at Vergennes, on the 16th of the same month, he mentioned their success in repelling the enemy, and his mortification on learning that the citizens of a government like ours, where all officers are limited in their official powers, urging the propriety of that power, being exceeded in an unconstitutional and arbitrary manner.

Dispatches were also addressed to the governor of Vermont, by James Monroe, Secretary of the United States, requesting a force of 2000 militia to assist general Macomb in defending Plattsburgh and the northern frontiers.

To meritorious deeds nothing is more pleasing than testimonials of gratitude. It recompenses the sufferings of war and the privations of distress. The government of the United States have very carefully attributed those honors to the heroic achievments of their citizens, which their conduct and bravery deserve. The thanks of the general government were given to the brave and patriotic citizens of Vermont, for their prompt succor and gallant conduct in the late critical state of the northern frontier. The legislature of this state also resolved that their thanks be presented to general Macomb and his compatriots in arms—to general Strong and the patriotic volunteers of Vermont, and likewise to commodore McDonough, lieutenants Cassin, Smith and Budd, and the subordinate officers and crew of his squadron, in testimony of the high sense entertained by the legislature of their distinguished bravery and good conduct on the memorable 11th of September, 1814, which ended in the repulse of the land forces and capture of the British squadron on lake Champlain. The legislature passed an act directing and empowering the treasurer of the state to make out, or cause to be made out a good and sufficient deed to captain McDonough, of a "certain tract of land belonging to this state, lying near Cumberland Head, in the state of New-

York, in full view of the splendid naval engagement fought under his command, on the ever memorable 11th of September, 1814, to be presented by the governor to captain McDonough, in testimony of the high veneration entertained by this legislature for his distinguished services."

During this session of the legislature a communication was received from the president of the senate and speaker of the house of representatives of the state of Massachusetts, accompanied with a resolution from that body inviting the legislature of Vermont to appoint delegates, if they should deem it expedient, to meet and confer with such delegates as may be appointed by the other New-England states. Massachusetts, Rhode-Island and Connecticut elected delegates, but New-Hampshire neglected to send; and Vermont, by a vote of the legislature, unanimously refused to appoint any. On the 15th of December, these delegates, together with two appointed by counties in New-Hampshire, and one similarly elected in Vermont, convened at the city of Hartford, in Connecticut. They held a secret session of near three weeks, and proceeded to suggest several alterations in the federal constitution, with a view to their adoption by the several states in the Union. Upon their adjournment, they published an address to the people, in which, with bold and forcible language, they enumerated the measures of the national government supposed to be particularly destructive to the interests of New-England and those engaged in commerce, and proposed such amendments to the constitution as would hereafter prevent the adoption of similar measures. Seven articles of amendment were suggested: first, that representatives and direct taxes shall be aportioned to the number of free persons: secondly, that no new state shall be admitted into the Union without the concurrence of two thirds of both houses: . thirdly, that Congress shall not have power to lay an embargo for more than sixty days: fourthly, that Congress shall not interdict commercial intercourse, without the concurrence of both houses: fifthly, that war shall not be declared without the concurrence of a similar majority: sixthly, that no person unnaturalized shall be eligible as a member of the senate and house of representatives, or hold any civil office under the authority of the United States: and seventhly, that no person shall be elected twice to the presidency, nor the president be elected from the same state two terms in succession.

In defence of the convention, it was urged that the situation of the country was such as occasioned serious grounds of alarm, to reflecting men. The operations of the war had been singularly disastrous; the recruiting service languished; the national treasury was almost pennyless; the national credit was shaken, and loans were effected at a ruinous discount. The New-England seaboard was left exposed to the enemy, and instead of securing the confidence of the people in the eastern States, by filling the civil and military posts, under the general government, with known talents and character, the administration committed the interests of the nation, at a critical period, to men contemned by a vast majority of the people in the States. They further considered the calling of a convention, which, from the earliest history of New-England, had been customary to be done in times of danger, as a very judicious and proper measure. The opposition of the federal party to the measures of the general government, sunk very rapidly, both in numbers and popularity. A war of defence had now united the feelings of the people, and the glorious achievements obtained by the northern army, rendered their construction about constitutional powers and privileges, quite unpopular with a majority of the public. They began to consider it would be right for the governor to comply with the requisitions of the president, or at least, it would be a piece of good policy had the militia been ordered to the assistance of their brethren in arms, at the invasion of Plattsburgh.

To every action in bodies, there is a corresponding reaction, and so it is with respect to the evolutions of thought in political affairs and the government of a country. The federalists of this State perceived their numbers receding to a minority among the whole body of the people. Their ambition was directed to measures for sustaining their situation, rather than for opposing the views and inclinations of the other party. Conciliations were attempted in their deliberations and by their votes, but it was all to no purpose: federalism had found its grave in the returning peace of the country. Numerous bills of a local and private nature were passed this session. Amongst which, were several incorporating manufacturing companies.—This branch of industry had received considerable attention, since the irruptions which the war had occasioned to the country.

CHAPTER VIII,

Condition of the United States at the commencement of hostilities with Great-Britain in 1812.—General Dearborn appointed commander-in-chief.—Northern campaign for 1812.—Expedition against Canada, under the command of general Hull.—Surrender of his Army.—Attack upon Queenstown by general Van Rensselaer.—Disorderly conduct of the militia.—Capture of the American forces.—Exploits of Captain Wool.—Proceedings of general Smythe.—Abandonment of his enterprise against the British provinces.—Military operations at Champlain.—Overtures for peace by the American government.—Termination of the campaign for 1812.

We shall now revert to the commencement of hostilities between the United States and Great-Britain, as a detail of civil and military events concurring at the same period of time could not be given without a great interruption of each particular subject. The order of time was considered, therefore, of much less importance than a distinct view on subjects of separate interest. It will now be necessary to leave the political history of the state, at the termination of the year 1814, and take up one of more imposing and momentous concern, beginning with the summer of

1812. The people of the United States proudly recollected the patriotism and bravery displayed by their forces in the revolutionary war, and a majority of them calculated that the operations of the present war would be such

as to secure to them a speedy victory over the enemy.—
They did not reflect that peace had enervated the military
energies of the republic, while their enemies, by continual exercise in arms, had accumulated not only additional
strength, but greater skill to use and apply it. A selection was made from those veteran officers who had acquired honor for their bravery in the former conflict, to fill
the principal posts in the new army. Henry Dearborn,
one of the survivors of the revolutionary war, was appointed major-general and commander-in-chief of the army
in the United States. He was present at the memorable
battle of Bunker-Hill, and served as a captain under Arnold, in the expedition against Quebec. After a series of
distinguished transactions, he was before the close of the
war promoted to the rank of colonel, and afterwards discharged the duties of secretary of war with exemplary industry and skill. Thomas Pinckney, of South-Carolina,
was also appointed to an equal grade of commission.—
And Wilkinson, Hull, Hampton and Bloomfield, received
commissions of brigadier generals.

The head quarters of the commander-in-chief were fixed
at Greenbush, opposite to Albany, and the forces acting
under his direction, composed principally of the New-York
militia, were stationed at Plattsburgh and the Niagara
frontiers. Those at the latter place acted under the command of generals Porter and Hall, and the forces at Detroit were directed by brigadier-general Hull.

It may be proper, by way of digression, to observe that
in giving an account of the late war, with reference to the
history of the state, a brief survey of the whole proceedings upon the northern frontier will be taken, some of
which may not come within the immediate scope of our
narrative of the state.

The military establishment of the United States, upon
the declaration of war, was in a very defective condition.
Congress had voted to enlist twenty-five thousand volunteers, and to call out one hundred thousand militia, for the
purpose of defending the frontiers and the sea-coast. But
the want of good and experienced officers was severely
felt. Government now contemplated, and gave orders to
have Canada invaded from the different posts upon the

17

lines, as soon as sufficient forces for this purpose could be obtained. About one month after the declaration, 2000 regulars and volunteers, under the command of general Hull, invaded the British provinces. At the same time, he issued a pompous proclamation to the Canadian settlers, offering them the great blessing of civil and religious liberty, and declaring in a tone of dictation "that his force was sufficient to break down all opposition," and that a much greater one was soon to arrive. His calculations were probably to capture Malden, and then proceed to Montreal. Useless delays and ill-timed resolutions destroyed all the confidence of the Canadians, and the zeal and ambition of the troops. The reinforcement at Malden and the surrender of Detroit to the British and Indians, who were marching down the river in numbers far surpassing the American forces, so affrighted general Hull that he immediately commenced a retreat back to Detroit. He was pursued with a large force of militia and Indians, under the command of general Brock. The American fortifications were effectually cannonaded on the 15th of August, from the batteries erected by the British, opposite to Detroit. On the next day, the enemy passed the river and encamped about three miles above the city. General Brock resolved to march precipitately and attack the fort, as the American forces were then absent, and from his past experience concluded that he should meet with no obstacle or resistance on the way. On receiving intelligence of the enemy's approach, the troops under the command of general Hull, anticipating an easy conquest, manifested a brave and deliberate course of conduct. But to their surprise, Hull directed them to proceed immediately to the fort.

The troops became insubordinate and crowded into the fort without any order from the general, depositing their arms upon the ground. The army becoming so tumultuous and the belief that myriads of Indians were without ready to fall upon the inhabitants, operated so powerfully upon the mind of the commander that he hung out a white flag from the fort, demanding protection from the British. A capitulation was concluded without provision for his army or the safety of his Canadian allies. Public property was given up—the regular troops surrendered as prisoners of war; and the militia returned home, not to serve again during the war, unless exchanged. The belief generally prevailed that Hull was either a coward or a traitor. So disgraceful a transaction originating at a place where success was confidently anticipated, caused in every part of the republic feelings of shame and astonishment. Disappointed at the failure of this expedition, general Hull's conduct was universally censured. Probably his greatest fault was a want of that decision and energy which were the characteristics of his youthful strength, talents and ambition.

The number of effective men at the surrender of Detroit did not probably exceed 800, while those of general Brock's amounted to more than 1,300.

This occurrence so alarmed the people in some of the western states, that nearly ten thousand tendered their services, and a part of them, placed under the command of general Harrison, marched for the territory of Michigan. But the insubordination of the volunteers to the restraints of necessary dicipline and the approach of winter. placed many obstacles in the way of accomplishing much in the important enterprise. Incursions were frequently made into the country of the Indians, who, instigated by the British agents and the celebrated Indian prophet, and commanded by the valiant Tecumseh, had become very hostile and dangerous to the inhabitants of the western states.

In one of these expeditions several hundred Indian warriors attacked fort Harrison, garrisoned with only fifteen effective men, and they were repelled with great intrepidity by guards, having many of their numbers killed or wounded. In return for the defeat, the Indians surprised and massacred a settlement containing twenty-one persons, at the mouth of White river. Similar excursions were conducted by general Hopkins, colonels Russell and Campbell, against the prophet's town and Kickapoo village, and the Indian towns Pimertams and Mississenema, which were destroyed and the inhabitants either killed or taken prisoners.

With the design of invading Canada in another quarter, an army of regulars and militia were collected on the northern boundaries of New-York. This force was, however, far less numerous than the government anticipated.

The poorest class of American citizens was in so comfortable a condition that few could be induced to enlist as soldiers. Massachusetts, Connecticut and Rhode-Island maintained the plausible doctrine that the officers of the general government have not power over the militia, until called out into the service and consigned to their authority by the state executive, and that even then they cannot be compelled to march beyond the boundary of the republic; and their governors refused to furnish detachments officially called for by the President, which diminished a species of force that was very much relied on by the government.

The operations upon the New-York frontier were, as has been before stated, under the direction of general Dearborn, whose head-quarters were still continued at Greenbush. The fort at Plattsburgh was commanded by brigadier-general Bloomfield, and that at Buffalo by general Smythe. The militia from the state of New-York, then in the service of the United States, which was called the army of the center, were under the command of general Van Rensselaer. These, amounting to about 5000 men, were principally stationed on the Niagara frontier.— Bodies of regulars and militia were also encamped at Black Rock, Sackett's Harbor and Ogdensburgh. General Van Rensselaer had his head-quarters at Lewiston, on the Niagara river, and on the opposite side was Queenstown, a fortified British post. The militia were much engaged to be led against the enemy, and the general determined to gratify their desire by crossing over to Queenstown.— On the 11th of October, the tempestuous state of the weather detered them from passing the river. The force in the American garrison was reinforced on the 12th with 300 regulars, under the command of colonel Christie.— On the morning of the 13th a party, led by colonel Solomon Van Rensselaer, effected a landing about 4 o'clock, although opposed by a British force stationed on the bank of the river. Soon after embarking, the troops were arranged under the command of colonel Van Rensselaer, with a design of storming the heights at Queenstown.—

The Americans were attacked by the enemy, before they received orders for ascending the heights. A spirited opposition, however, obliged the assailants to retire, but their continual fire enfiladed the ranks of the Americans, of whom a considerable number were killed and wounded. The colonel was severely wounded, but the troops under captains Wool and Oglevie advanced to storm the fort.— Wool, the chief in command, on being wounded, proceeded to Van Rensselaer, and represented to him the critical situation of the troops. The colonel directed, as the only effectual measure, the one first proposed, which was to storm the British battery upon the heights. The execution of this adventure being undertaken by the voluntary services of captain Wool, who silently and circuitously conducted his forces by the battery and ascended an eminence which commanded it. At the approach of the Americans, the British retreated down the heights to Queenstown. At the moment of their success, general Brock arrived from fort George with a reinforcement of six hundred men. A white flag, the customary signal of surrender, was raised by an officer, but indignantly pulled down by Wool. To keep the enemy back until he could arrange his troops, a detachment of sixty men were despatched, who advanced and returned without firing a gun. They pursued on and drove the Americans to the brink of the precipice. Wool, being ably seconded by his officers, rallied and led on his forces to the attack. The British, in their turn, gave way and retreated down the hill. Upon this, the conflict was renewed, when general Brock, and his aid, captain McDonald, fell almost at the same moment. After a severe engagement, the British fled in confusion.

General Van Rensselaer, colonel Christie, and lieutenant Totten, an able engineer, now crossed over for the purpose of fortifying the heights preparatory to another attack, should the enemy be reinforced. They joined their forces to those under the command of the gallant captain Wool, who, faint with the loss of blood, was, with the prisoners, conveyed over the river. However, the fortune of the day was not yet decided. A body of about one thousand British and Indians, under general Sheaffe, from fort George, arrived at 3 o'clock in the afternoon, and joined the garrison. The enemy again attacked the Americans, and were a third time repulsed. General Van Rensselaer, perceiving the army on the opposite shore embark very slowly, quickly recrossed the river to hasten their advance. But those who had expressed so much anxiety in the morning to share the consequences of a battle, having witnessed the distress and sufferings of their wounded companions who had been brought over, now became entirely regardless of the general's commands, and refused to go to the relief of their countrymen. More than twelve hundred of the militia positively refused to embark. The sight of the engagement had cooled that ardor which, before the attack, the commander-in-chief could hardly restrain. While the contest for victory was pressed on by their countrymen, they could quietly remain spectators of the scene. The entreaties and commands of their brave and intrepid commander availed nothing. They now concluded it would be unconstitutional and wrong for them to pass the national boundary for carrying on an offensive war. The Americans continued for a while to struggle against the force of the British, but were finally overpowered by their superior numbers, and surrendered themselves prisoners of war. About sixty of the Americans were killed and one hundred wounded. Those that surrendered themselves, including the wounded, were about seven hundred. Of the one thousand men who crossed into Canada, but few made their escape.

On the retirement of general Van Rensselaer from the service, general Alexander Smythe, of Virginia, succeeded to the command. In an inflated address to the "men of New-York," he declared that in a few days the American standard should be planted in Canada, and invited them to "come on" and share in the dangers and glory of the enterprise. A considerable number volunteered, more probably from their confidence in general Porter, who was to be associated with him and have the exclusive command of the volunteers than from the effect of the general's turgid appeal. His force was now augmented to 4,500 men. General Smythe sent out two detachments, one commanded by colonel Bœrstler and the other by captain King, who was attended by lieutenant Angus of the navy, with a small party of marines, to make preparations for crossing the river. Bœrstler with his force proceeded down the river several miles, dispersed the enemy captured several of them and returned. King was directed to attack the batteries opposite Black Rock, which he effected in the most gallant manner. His party sustained a loss of nine naval officers and nearly one half of the seamen, who were either killed or wounded. By their exertions the enemy were dispersed, their artillery dismantled, and suitable preparations were made for safely landing the army at the time appointed, which, however, from unforeseen delays, did not embark until noon. But afterwards, disembarking for necessary refreshments, general Smythe ascertained that the boats prepared could not carry over three thousand men at once, which was the orders of the secretary of war. He therefore concluded to delay the contemplated invasion to a future period. Most of those who crossed with captain King succeeded in returning. The morning of the 30th of November was again assigned as the time for crossing; and that for the purpose of fulfilling the declaration of planting the American standard on the Canadian shores. But their first disappointment visably checked their resolution. They did not embark as early as was expected, and, when ready, but 1500 men were found willing to go over. A council of war unanimously decided against the expediency of proceeding, and the troops were again ordered to embark. The enterprise which he so exultingly promised to fulfil was shamefully abandoned without an effort. The failure of the undertaking was attributed by the soldiers to their commander, and so highly were they exasperated that for several days his life was in danger from their fury.

The northern army entered upon no further operations of importance during the whole of this campaign. In September, a party of the enemy moving down the St. Lawrence, were defeated by a detachment of militia from Ogdensburgh. These being reinforced, compelled the militia to retire. On account of this proceeding, the destruction of Ogdensburgh was attempted by the enemy on the 2d of October, but they were vanquished by the brave commander, general Brown.

The army stationed at Plattsburgh, on the 11th of November, marched to Champlain, under the command of general Dearborn. When, immediately after, colonel Pike, at the head of his regiment, made an incursion into the territory of the enemy, surprised a party of British and Indians, and destroyed a considerable quantity of public stores.

The causes of military movements among nations engaged in the turmoil and ravages of warfare, may be traced to their civil and political transactions. Immediately after the United States had declared war against Great-Britain, Mr. Russell, the American minister at London, was instructed by the American government to notify the British nation that whenever the wrongs which America justly complained of were redressed, she was ready to make peace. Authority was given to Mr. Russell to negotiate an armistice by land and sea as soon as the British government would repeal their orders in council, discontinue their practice of impressment, and restore those Americans who were already in their service. A rejection of these propositions was communicated by Lord Castlereigh to Mr. Russell, who at the same time informed him that measures had been taken to authorize Sir John B. Warren, a British admiral on the American station, to propose a cessation of hostilities, and in that event to assure them that full effect should be given to the provisions for repealing the orders in council. The British government were now ready, he said, to receive any proposition which would have a tendency to check the abuse of the practice, but they could not consent to suspend the exercise of a right on which the naval strength of the empire essentially depended, until they were convinced other means would be devised for securing the object without resorting to impressment. On the 30th September, Sir J. B. Warren, then at the Halifax station, informed Mr. Monroe of the revocation of the orders in council, proposing a cessation of hostilities, and threatening, in case of a refusal, that the orders should be revived. Mr. Monroe, on being informed of the failure of Mr. Russell's negotiation, stated among other things in his answer to Sir J. B. Warren, that the practice of impressment by the British was to take their subjects from whatever vessels they chose, which frequently terminated in the seizure of American citizens. But further, that he was willing Great-Britain should be secured against the evils of which she complains; but he should demand on the other hand "that the citizens of the United States should be protected against a practice which, while it degrades the nation, deprives them of their rights as freemen, takes them by force from their families and country into a foreign service to fight the battles of a foreign power, perhaps against their own country and kindred." The negotiation was concluded without effecting any adjustment of the difficulties alleged or producing any degree of conciliatory feelings between the belligerant powers. The rejection of these propositions was approved of by Congress, who, instead of relinquishing the undertaking, pursued more effectual measures for carrying on the war. The soldiers' bounty and wages were increased. A law was passed authorizing the president to raise twenty additional regiments, to issue treasury notes, and to borrow money. The building of four ships of the line, six frigates, and as many other vessels as the exigencies of the times require, was also provided for.

In the campaign of 1812, some instances of unusual gallantry had been displayed, yet nothing decisive was effected, and the losses sustained were numerous and great. Those who were in favor of the declaration of war, felt disappointed, chagrined and cast down. The calamitous progress of the controversy was attributed by them to the conduct of the federalists, whom they accused of endeavoring to prevent enlistments into the army and of dissuading the militia from entering upon the service of the country. The federalists, on the contrary, declared these failures attributable to the imbecility of the administration and to the injudicious selection of military officers. But the transactions upon the ocean somewhat redeemed the misfortunes on the land. The honor of the American flag was well supported by the determined bravery of the republican officers and seamen.

CHAPTER IX.

Northern Campaign for 1813.—Battle and Massacre at Frenchtown.—Seige at fort Meigs.—Surrender of York.—Death of general Pike.—Fort George taken.—Capture of generals Chandler and Winder.—Proceedings at Sacketts Harbor.—Repulse of the British at Fort Stephenson.—Perry's Victory on lake Erie.—Battle at the Thames.—Defeat of the British Army.—Commodore Chauncey captures the British Squadron on lake Ontario.—Willkison takes the command of the center Army.—Engagement at Williamsburg.—Affair at Chateaugay.—Americans defeated at Black Rock.

The scene of military operations for 1813, embraced the whole northern frontier of the United States. At the commencement of the campaign, the western army, under general Harrison, was stationed near the head of lake Erie, and the army of the center, under general Dearborn, while general Hampton was destined to the command of the army in the north, and stationed upon the shores of lake Champlain. The American troops still contemplated invading Canada, which was comparatively destitute of regular troops.

The army at the northwest, under the command of general Winchester, encamped at Frenchtown, was surprised by a combined force of British and Indians, commanded by colonel Proctor, and the Indian chiefs, Roundhead and Splitlog. A portion of the American force that was stationed in the open field, were immediately thrown into disorder. Many of them, unable to escape, were killed by the Indians, while general Winchester and colonel Lewis were taken prisoners. The contest was sustained with vigor by the American troops, until orders were given by general Winchester for their surrender. Colonel Proctor had assured him that if the Americans would surrender, they should be protected; otherwise, he would not be responsible for the conduct of the Indians. The faith which had been plighted by the enemy was violated by a cruel and barbarous scalping and murdering of the prisoners, and a conflagration of the town. The American loss in killed and wounded amounted to 500, and an equal number were taken prisoners. These were, for the most part volunteers from some of the most respectable families of Kentucky.

General Harrison had now marched his forces to fort Meigs, on the Miami. On the 15th of May, the garrison was besieged by General Proctor, with a force of 1000 regulars and militia, and 1200 Indians. The commanding position of the American fort enabled them to resist effectually the attacks of the besieging army. Their anxiety about the dangers of their situation, were now relieved by the arrival of general Clay with a force of 1200 Kentuckians: separating his men into several divisions, and making an impetuous attack, he drove the besiegers from their works, and took a number of prisoners. His troops, thinking the victory complete, and disregarding the orders of their commander, were drawn into an ambush prepared for them by the Indian warrior, Tecumseh. All but 150 of the party were cut off. Colonel Dudley, who commanded a detachment of 800 men, strove in vain to rescue his troops. About the same time, Colonel Miller entered upon an engagement with the enemy, and entirely defeated them. In these encounters, two or three hundred of the Americans escaped into the fort, something like three hundred were killed or made prisoners, and the rest fled to the nearest settlement. The defence of the fort was still continued, but the Indians, unacquainted with sieges, became weary and discontented. Notwithstanding the entreaties of their chief, Tecumseh, they deserted their allies on the 8th of May. Thus situated, Proctor raised the siege on the day following, and retreated to Malden.

General Dearborn having assembled a large body of troops at Sackets Harbor, where great exertions had been made by commodore Chauncey to prepare a flotilla for aiding in the operations of the ensuing year, embarked on the 25th day of April, with 1700 men, to the attack of York, the capital of Upper Canada. The force of the enemy at this place consisted of 700 regulars and militia, and 100 Indians, under the command of general Sheaffe.

General Pike pressed on his forces and landed, although opposed at the water's edge by a superior force. After a severe contest of half an hour, the enemy were driven to their fortifications. The remainder of the troops having landed, they advanced forward, destroyed the first battery, and were moving towards the main works, when a tremendous explosion of the enemy's magazine at 600 feet distance, hurled upon the advancing columns vast quantities of stones and fragments of wood, which caused great havoc among them. Many were killed and wounded, and among the latter was the gallant Pike. The British commandant finding resistance unavailing, retreated with the regulars towards Kingston, leaving the commanding officer of the militia to make the most favorable negotiation in his power. The terms of the capitulation were agreed on, and the Americans took possession of the town.— The brave and lamented Pike survived his wounds but a few hours; but before his death the flag which waved over the fortress his valor had conquered was at his request placed under his head, when, with a smile of triumph, he calmly expired amidst the shouts of victory. The loss on the part of the Americans was three hundred and twenty in killed and wounded, and mostly by the explosion of the magazine. One hundred of the British were killed, about three hundred wounded, and as many made prisoners. The capital of Upper Canada was evacuated by the American commander, who crossed the lake to leave the wounded at Sacketts Harbor, and again sailed and landed his troops at Niagara. The reinforcements of the enemy induced general Dearborn to change the place of attack. Accordingly he re-embarked at fort George on the 27th of May.

After a warm engagement the enemy abandoned and the Americans entered the fort. The fugitives retreated to the heights at the head of Burlington bay. Three hundred of the British were killed in the defence of the fort and seventeen only, of the Americans were killed and forty-five wounded. Fort Erie immediately followed the same fate: lieutenant-colonel Preston took possession of it on the 28th, it having been previously abandoned. The British on their retreat being joined by a detachment from fort Erie and Chippeway, were pursued by two brigades under generals Chandler and Winder. Colonel St. Vincent having ascertained their position settled his plan of attack. He came in the security of darkness upon the American station, and with the roar of his cannon and yell of the savages, spread a most dreadful scene of confusion and carnage around. The darkness was such that a distinction could not be made between friends and enemies.— General Chandler designing to place himself at the head of his artillery, rushed into the midst of a British party, and, in a few minutes after, the fortune of general Winder, by a like mistake, was the same. Satisfied with the capture of these officers and some other prisoners, they made a precipitate retreat. The Americans, after a loss of two or three hundred in killed and wounded, made a retreat under colonel Burns from Stoney Creek, the place of action, to Forty mile Creek, the former position of this force. This misfortune was soon followed by the unfortunate transaction at Beaver Dams. Lieutenant-colonel Bœrstler had been ordered to march from fort George and disperse a body of the enemy collected at that place.— An attack was made on the Americans within a short distance of the Beaver Dams, and after contesting the battle ground, colonel Bœrstler's ammunition failing, he was obliged to surrender his whole detachment, which consisted of 570 men. Commodore Chauncey, in conjunction with colonel Scott, learning that the British had a quantity of stores at Burlington bay, proceeded with 200 men to destroy them. On arriving at the place, they found a force double of their own, strongly intrenched and defended by eight pieces of cannon; whereupon the enterprise was abandoned. Five pieces of cannon, eleven boats, and a few prisoners were taken away.

The British sought the opportunity, while the Americans were employed in the provinces, to make an attack upon the important post of Sacketts Harbor. The squadron hove in sight of the town on the 27th of May, when the inhabitants of the adjacent country immediately assembled. General Brown, of the New-York militia, had the command of 1000 men, for the purpose of defending the town. A temporary breast work was quickly thrown up at the only place where the enemy could effect a landing, and this was employed for sheltering the militia and regulars stationed here under colonel Backus. On the morning of the 23d, the British landed one thousand troops from their vessels and advanced toward the fortifications. The militia affrightened fled in the utmost confusion, and colonel Mills, in attempting to rally them, was mortally wounded. The regulars, unable to sustain the force and superiority of the enemy, gave way and retreated toward the town, taking shelter in the houses upon the road.— From these coverts they poured so destructive a fire upon the advanced party of the British, that it halted and returned back. This slight check was, by the contrivance of general Brown, turned into a hasty retreat. Having collected the panic struck militia, he marched them along the road which, while it conducted from the village, appeared to the commander of the British to lead to the place of landing. Seeing them marching with precipitation, he concluded their design was to cut off his retreat, and re-embarked so hastily as to leave most of the wounded behind. The adroitness displayed by this management of general Brown, and the importance of his services, gained for him the appointment of brigadier-general in the regular army.

On the 20th of July, Proctor having again collected about 500 of his Indian allies, with nearly as many regulars, marched to the attack of fort Stephenson, on the Sandusky river. He soon after invested it and demanded its surrender. But by the gallantry and resolution of major Croghan and 160 men, the full complement of the garrison, they determined on defending the fort to the last extremity, notwithstanding the threat which in former instances had been found so powerful, the Indians could not be restrained after the commencement of the contest.

An account of the naval transactions performed by the American forces upon the ocean, has, from our prescribed limits and the local descriptions suitable for a history of the State of Vermont, been necessarily omitted; but the lakes, upon which those scenes of naval valor, now rising to the grandeur of victory, have no longer to remain in obscurity and unimportance. Nothing of general magnitude had previously to September, 1813, transpired upon the lakes. The most that had been done was in fitting out fleets and conveying the land forces from their different places of rendezvous. Captain Elliot, in October, 1812, with 100 men, embarked on board of two boats, crossed the Niagara from Black Rock, and took two of the enemy's brigs from under the guns of fort Erie, on whom the garrison poured a tremendous and incessant fire. One of them was burned and the other was connected with the naval force of the United States. During the summer of 1813, commodore Perry was engaged in preparing an American squadron for service on lake Erie. It consisted of nine vessels, the largest of which carried twenty guns, and the whole mounting fifty-four. The enemy's fleet was built and equiped under the superintendance of commodore Barclay, an experienced officer from the British navy. It consisted of six vessels, mounting sixty-three guns in the whole. The American squadron, under the command of commodore Perry, sailed out and offered battle to their adversary. On the 10th of September, the British commodore having a favorable wind, left the harbor of Malden to accept the offer. The firing commenced on both sides a few minutes before twelve o'clock.— The British, at the commencement of the action, bore so heavy upon the Americans, that the commodore's vessel, the St. Lawrence, became entirely unmanageable, having her guns rendered useless, and the greater part of the crew either killed or wounded. No hopes of success remained but in the execution of the attempt now undertaken by the American commodore. He quitted the St. Lawrence in an open boat, and when passing along no less than three broadsides were fired at him from the British vessels when he escaped. The wind now shifted quarters, giving the Americans the advantage; but the Lawrence was so disabled, having only eight men fit for duty, that she lowered her colors. Possession, however, not being taken of her by the British, they again hoisted her flag. At forty-five minutes past two, a signal was given for close action. As the Niagara was but very little injured, commodore Perry resolved to pass through the enemy's lines with her, which he did with great skill and bravery. Captain Elliot had the direction of the smaller vessels, which, with the Niagara, were now brought into close combat. In a short time, one of the British vessels surrendered, and soon after another; and the remainder of the American fleet now joining in the action, the victory was rendered decisive and complete. The American loss was 27 killed and 96 wounded—the whole loss of the British in killed and wounded was estimated at 160.— The number of prisoners amounted to six hundred, which was more than all the Americans engaged in the action.— In three hours from the commencement of the action, the commodore of the victorious force was enabled to announce to general Harrison the capture of the whole British squadron, in the following expressive style:—"We have met the enemy and they are ours." The news of this victory diffused universal joy throughout the Union, because it was achieved against a superior force, and was the first they had ever gained over a whole squadron.— These circumstances threw every other victory into the shade, and cast the brightest lustre upon the characters of the heroes who had gained it. This victory opened a passage to the region which had been surrendered by general Hull, and general Harrison was immediately conveyed in transports, with a large body of Kentucky militia, to Malden.

This movement being understood by the British commander, he abandoned that place, and on the 28th of September it was occupied without opposition by the American army. General Harrison pursued the retreating party through Detroit, up the river Thames, to the Moravian village, on the 5th October. Proctor's force consisted of 2000 men, of whom more than half were Indians. The British army were strongly posted; their left, resting on the Thames, was defended by their artillery; the right reached to a swamp that run parallel to the river, and was supported by Tecumseh and his warriors, who were stationed in a thick wood which skirted the morass. Colonel Johnson's regiment being much relied on by the general, was ordered to charge the enemy's center, with the design of breaking their lines and getting in the rear. The

Kentuckians advanced boldly to the charge and succeeded so far as to throw the enemy into confusion, but failed in penetrating their lines. The army now moved and attacked the right and left flanks of the enemy with great effect. The celebrated Tecumseh led on his Indian warriors against colonel Johnson and his battalion. These heroes now met each other in a contest which, from the character of both, must terminate the life of one. The Indian commander raising his tomahawk to despatch colonel Johnson, received a pistol shot from his intended victim, and fell dead at his feet. The defeat of this savage warrior was the overthrow of the army. Since the defeat of Harmer, Tecumseh had been in almost every engagement which the whites had had with his race, within or on the boundaries of the United States. He visited the various tribes at the commencement of the war, and his eloquence and influence engaged his countrymen to bear arms against the United States. About two hundred of the British, with the commander Proctor, escaped, and the remainder surrendered themselves prisoners of war. Nineteen regulars were killed, fifty wounded, and six hundred taken prisoners. The loss of the Indians was one hundred and twenty. Fifty of the Americans were killed and wounded. The fall of Detroit brought the Indian war to a close, and gave security to the frontiers. It also put them in possession of what was lost by the surrender of general Hull. Various skirmishes having succeeded on lake Ontario, since hostilities commenced between America and Great-Britain, yet nothing of a decisive character occurred until the 5th of October, when commodore Chauncey, after repeatedly chasing the British fleet, and failing to bring them into action, encountered a squadron of seven sail, which was bound for Kingston with troops and provisions. He captured five of these, one was burned, and the other effected an escape. The number of prisoners taken amounted to two hundred and sixty-four. General Wilkinson was appointed to the command of the army of the center, in consequence of the removal of general Dearborn. The first object of his instructions was to make an attack upon Kingston, and after that, close his campaign by the reduction of Montreal. The force designed for this service was an army of 5000 at fort George, 2000 under general Lewis at Sackett's Harbor, and the army of general Harrison, whom general Wilkinson expected would join with his army and proceed with him down the St. Lawrence. The command of the northern army, which was to proceed to Canada by the way of Champlain, and form a junction upon the St. Lawrence, was given to general Hampton.

The secretary of war proceeded from Washington to Sacketts Harbor for the purpose of assisting in the enterprise. His orders were awaited by the commanding officer, which were to proceed direct to Montreal, rather than in pursuance of his former orders to make an attack upon Kingston. The forces were ordered to descend the St. Lawrence, but such were the difficulties in collecting them and such the want of vigilance in the commander, that they did not sail until the 5th of November. On their way down the river, they were impeded by constant attacks from the enemy posted at convenient distances along the Canadian shore. These annoyances were so troublesome that general Brown ordered his troops to disembark and proceed in advance of the boats. The movements of the invading army were closely watched by a corps of observation from the governor of Canada, to follow in their rear and annoy them at every opportunity. General Boyd disembarked his troops on arriving at the rapids, and marched down the river as general Brown was doing at some distance in advance of them. On the 11th of November a battle was fought at Chrystler's fields, near Williamsburgh, between the combined force of general Boyd's, Brown's and Swartwout's brigades, and a party of the British, under the command of lieutenant-colonel Morrison. The action was supported than two hours with unyielding resolution, when a body of the Americans, who had been left to cover their retreat, were routed by the British, which gave them the possession of the field. Both parties, however, claimed the victory; the British retreating to their encampment, and the Americans to their boats. Three hundred and thirty-nine in killed and wounded was the ascertained loss on the side of the Americans; but that of the British is unknown.—

Among those wounded, of the Americans, was general Covington, who died soon after. The army arrived at St. Regis the next day, where general Hampton, who had the command of Plattsburgh, had been ordered to meet them. But here general Wilkinson, to his great amazement and confusion, was informed by general Hampton that his situation was such that he could not join him there, but intimated that he might do so lower down the river. By the determination of a council of war, that was called on the occasion, the attack upon Montreal was abandoned, and the army under general Wilkinson took up winter quarters at the French Mills. Orders were sent to general Hampton to invade Canada by the way of Champlain, at which place he rendezvoused on the 25th of September, but was afterwards directed to march to Chateaugay, and proceed to Montreal by the direction of Chateaugay river. On the 21st of October, he left his encampment at Chateaugay four corners, crossed into Canada, and moved as far down the river as Ormstown. Having ascertained that the British had a force of six hundred men a few miles below on the way to Montreal, he despatched colonel Purdy with 2000 of his troops on the night of the 25th, for the purpose of destroying it.— The next morning the two divisions of the army under colonel Purdy and general Hampton, came within one mile of the enemy, on opposite sides of the river. General Izard took the command of the army, with orders from Hampton to attack the enemy immediately, which he did, but so unsuccessfully as to be obliged to retire from the field. The detachment under colonel Purdy being disabled by the fatigues of their march, did not join general Izard's troops. The enemy observing them, and supposing their number inconsiderable, passed unperceived within a short distance of their rear, and began an attack, when the Americans made a disorderly flight to the river. The army then returned to the encampment at Chateaugay, and the expedition to Montreal being abandoned, they marched to Plattsburgh for winter quarters.— On the 24th of October general Harrison arrived at Buffalo and proceeded directly to Sacketts Harbor, by which means the Niagara frontier was left unguarded, except by a few militia at fort George. The British, in their turn, thought to invade the United States. Accordingly they sent on a force to Niagara, when general McClure, intimidated at their approach and misunderstanding the orders he received from government, reduced the village of Newark to ashes. Colonel Murray crossed at Niagara, captured the sentries, and immediately took the fort.— On the surrender of the fortress, consisting of three hundred men, the greater part of them were cruelly and wantonly put to death.

The forces of the enemy being increased, they marched to Lewistown, where they were opposed by Major Young, who was soon compelled to retreat. The villages of Lewistown, Manchester and Tuscarora were destroyed by the enemy. Black Rock was the next place of their attack. General Hall commanding a force there, repelled them for some time, yet they with considerable difficulty effected a landing and drove the Americans from their batteries to Buffalo. All hopes of withstanding them here were entirely vain, as only six hundred out of two thousand militia were willing to risk an engagement. Buffalo and Black Rock were consigned to the incendiaries' torch, as was the country for several miles along the river.— The last scenes of this year's campaign were more like the exterminating ravages of the barbarous Indians than the contests of civilized nations or the more improved method of modern warfare. Plundering, burning and indiscriminate slaughter were practised by the invaders upon the innocent and defenceless inhabitants.

A body of the Vermont militia, which had been drafted into the service of the United States and marched to Plattsburgh, in New-York, were, by a proclamation from governor Chittenden, discharged from public service, upon the ground that it was unconstitutional for them to be taken beyond the limits of the state, and that in a war of invasion the President of the federal government had not the authority by the constitution to call upon the militia without permission from the state executive. This was a principle established by the supreme court of Massachusetts, and adhered to by most of the states in New-England. Those officers who were zealous for the war objected to this order from governor Chittenden, and drew up a protest signed by twenty-two commissioned officers, stating their views upon the controverted subject and their unwillingness to concede to the requisitions of his excellency. However, the militia returned before their term of service had expired, and the subject was no further agitated before the public.

In the progress of our narrative, an event which happened upon lake Champlain has been omitted, in the order of time, but may as properly be described after the closing scenes of the campaign have been recited as at the period when it occurred. The Growler and the Eagle, commanded by lieutenant Smith, sailed from Plattsburgh on the 2d of June, in pursuit of some British gun-boats, then in the waters of the states. On the morning of the third day they discovered three gun-boats, to which they immediately gave chase. The channel being narrow and the wind blowing briskly from the south, ran them so far into it that there was no possibility of a return. One of the vessels became unmanageable, and sunk in shoal water; the other fought for more than four hours, until obliged to yield to superior force. The enemy had the advantage in another respect: the narrowness of the lake afforded an opportunity for the soldiers upon its banks to do considerable execution. Another squadron sailed up the lake on the first of August, consisting of two large sloops, three gun-boats and about forty batteaux, filled with troops.— They landed at Plattsburgh, destroyed all the government property, and then retreated. A short time afterwards commodore Macdonough sailed out of Burlington bay and offered battle to the British, which they refused and retired to St. Johns.

The result of the campaign for this year was not so favorable to the country as the administration party had anticipated: yet it had been filled with incidents highly honorable to the American arms. If the war had increased the interruptions of commerce, it had cherished and multiplied manufactures: if it had given an opportunity for spoliations on the ocean and for predatory excursions on land, it had developed the best means of retarding the former and providing protection against the latter, and the result promised greater respect on the part of foreign nations for the rights of the republic, and a longer duration of future peace, than could be expected without the signal proofs which have been exhibited of the national spirit and resources.

CHAPTER X.

Proffered mediation of Russia declined by the British government.—Opinions of Great-Britain on the prosecution of the War.—Unsuccessful attempt at La Colle.—Oswego attacked by the British.—Battle of Chippewa.—Engagement at Bridgewater.—The British repulsed in their attack upon fort Erie.—Successful sortie of general Porter against the British garrison near fort Erie.—Capitulation of the eastern part of Maine to the enemy.—Sir George Prevost marches his army into the States.—Invasion of Plattsburgh.—McDonough's Victory over the British squadron, September 11th, 1814.—Retreat of the English army.—Sequel to the history of the war with Great-Britain.—A general treaty of peace concluded at Ghent.

An offer was made by the Emperor of Russia, with a view of arresting the desolating ravages of war, to assist the governments of Great-Britain and the United States in settling by negociation the unhappy controversy in which the respective governments were involved. The offer was promptly accepted by the United States, when John Quincy Adams, James A. Bayard and Albert Gallatin were appointed commissioners to negotiate a treaty of peace at St. Petersburg; for which, the British on their part appointed Lord Gambier, Henry Golbourn and William Adams; but they declined to treat under the mediation of Russia, but proposed a negotiation at London or Gottenburgh. The American government accepted this proposition, and chose Gottenburgh, for which Ghent was afterwards substituted. Henry Clay and Jonathan Russel were united with the commissioners already in

Europe. After the troubles in Europe had terminated, the English nation contemplated dictating peace to America from the capital of the republic, or at least the splendor of their triumphs and the burthens of American embarrassments would induce the New-England States to form a distinct government. Two distinct modes of carrying on the war were decided on by the British ministry; first to invade the coast of the United States, and in the next, after the protection of Canada had been secured, to conquer so much of the territory of the United States as would guard them against any future danger. To effect these purposes, fourteen thousand troops that fought under Wellington, were embarked from France to Canada, and a naval armament, with an adequate number of seamen, for invading the different ports of the American coast at the same time. The changes recently occurring in Europe restored peace between England and France, and the reason why America had continued her restrictions was, by acting in concert with France, the commerce of England might be very much deranged. This cause being now removed, it was judged expedient to repeal the embargo and nonimportation act, which was accordingly done in the month of April.

Soon after Congress assembled, the situation of the army received their attention. A bounty of one hundred and twenty-four dollars was provided for any one who should enlist for five years, and eight dollars for any person who should procure such recruits. Additional appropriations were also made for increasing the force of the country. The army under general Wilkinson continued at the French Mills, until he received orders from the Secretary of War, when he sent a force of 2000 troops, under general Brown, to the Niagara frontier, and having destroyed the public buildings, he marched to Plattsburgh. On the 21st of February, the enemy proceeded as far into the states as Malone, and destroyed the public property kept there, which had been removed from the encampment at the French Mills. By these movements the British concluded that the Americans were about to invade Canada; therefore, 2000 men fortified themselves at La Colle Mill, near the river Sorel. For the purpose of dislodging them general Wilkinson advanced with but slight opposition from skirmishing parties to La Colle, and there disposed his forces in such order as to cut off the retreat of the enemy. An attempt was made by the occupants of the Mill to retire, but they were repulsed. The invading army undertook to batter down the Mill with their cannon, but the stone of which it was built was so thick as to resist all attempts of the kind; whereupon a retreat was ordered, having lost one hundred in killed and wounded. The forces in Canada were marched from the St. Lawrence and stationed at St. Johns, for the purpose of securing the entrance of their fleet into lake Champlain. Great exertions had been made by commodore M'Donough to prepare a fleet that would compete with the enemy upon lake Champlain. It was necessary for the British to destroy the shipping at Vergennes, before it should make its appearance upon the lake. Their designs being understood by the commodore, a battery was erected at the mouth of Otter Creek. On the tenth of May, 1814, the enemy's flotilla, consisting of a brig, three armed sloops and thirteen gallies, proceeded up the lake and scoured the shores with their light boats as they passed along. Having gone as far south as the mouth of Otter Creek, they commenced firing upon the battery, who, after exchanging one hundred shots and being unsuccessful in gaining the rear of the battery, on account of a detachment of Vermont militia, which galled them so severely that they were obliged to retreat down the lake, effecting nothing by their adventure but a discovery of the military prowess of the Green Mountain Boys, in their able defence of fort Cassin.

The new brig that was afterwards commanded by M'Donough, at the battle of Plattsburgh, was launched about this time. The events of peace in Europe, by the dethronement and exile of Bonaparte and the restoration of Louis XVIII. gave Great Britain, now at peace with the whole world, except the United States, an opportunity to employ all that immense force which she had used in crushing her rival, against the American republic.

These prospects were duly estimated by the American people;—a severer conflict, attended with greater sacrifices and sufferings, was calculated upon by those in favor of the administration; but its opposers made great efforts to wrest the power from those they thought had shown themselves incompetent, which in no small degree lessened the strength of the government. Preparations were making by the British and Americans to gain the supremacy upon lake Ontario; but as yet the British had the control, which they employed in destroying unfinished vessels and stores along the United States shore.— General Drummond, with 1500 troops on board of several transports, attempted to effect a landing at Oswego— a deposit of naval stores then garrisoned by 500 men under the command of colonel Mitchell, in a fort which had only five guns. On the enemy's second attempt to effect a landing, the American commander, finding himself unable to sustain his position, retired and moved the public stores about twelve miles to Oswego falls. The enemy being interrupted in their progress by the destruction of a bridge, evacuated the town and returned to Kingston.— The military stores at Oswego were shortly after ordered to be removed to Sacketts Harbor, and on their passage, near Sand Creek, were attacked by the enemy's boats, as they entered the stream. Having formed an ambuscade, they completely surprised their pursuers, who yielded after a short encounter. The British had encamped 300 or more men upon the river Thames, whom captain Holmes, with 180 troops, was sent out to dislodge. He retreated to a favorable position, and then sent forward a body of rangers to ascertain their strength, who were pursued by the enemy. They attempted by a feigned attack and retreat to draw captain Holmes from his position, and by this manœuver succeeded. Various other proceedings were entered upon by the enemy to bring on an engagement, which at last occurred. The Americans fought gallantly for more than an hour, who were nearly surrounded at the time the enemy retreated. The loss of the Americans was only six killed and wounded, but their opponents sustained a destruction of sixty-nine of their numbers. In the beginning of July, general Brown marched his army to Buffalo, where the addition of Towson's artillery and a body of volunteers, under general Porter, augmented the number of his forces to something more than 3,000 men: with these he crossed the Niagara, and took possession without opposition of Fort Erie. The British, amounting to three thousand, under the command of general Riall, occupied a strong position at the mouth of the Chippewa. Small parties of the enemy continually annoyed the American camp, on account of which general Porter with about nine hundred volunteers, Indians and regulars, was sent out by general Brown along the creek, where he attacked a body of Indians about two miles from the American camp. The noise of the firing brought on a large reinforcement of Indians, which, after a warm engagement, obliged general Porter to retire.

Both armies were now under motion, advancing towards the destined field of battle. General Scott's brigade was in the advance, hastening to receive the charge, from those who had fought upon the ensanguined fields of Europe, and subdued the conqueror whose ambition had strove for and almost attained universal dominion; and whose energies raised him from obscurity to the highest destination of wealth, of grandeur and of power. The British outnumbered the Americans by more than one third, and arrayed in all the panoply of experience and power, boldly advanced to open combat. The heroism of general Scott equalled the best and purest exertions of human nature. The British gave way in the bloody contest, and Scott pursued and defeated them on all sides, until their retreat became perfectly disordered, and they sought shelter from their intrenchments. The enemy were totally repulsed by the decisive movements of general Scott, before general Ripley's brigade arrived. General Brown marched back his forces to the camp, without attempting any thing upon the fortifications of the enemy.— The British sustained a loss in killed, wounded and prisoners of 514; but the destruction on the part of the Americans did not equal this number by 186 men. This decisive victory, gained after so many reverses, was regarded as an omen of future success. Immediately afterwards, general Riall, leaving his works, marched to Burlington heights. Lieutenant-general Drummond, collecting all his forces at Burlington and York, took them under his command and marched back with his army towards the American camp, to fort George. The force of the British, collected for the purpose of opposing general Brown, including fifteen hundred Indians and militia, amounted to five thousand; but these constantly diminished by the desertion of the Indians.

On the morning of the 25th, intelligence was communicated to the American commander, by general Swift, that a detachment of the enemy from Queenstown threatened his stores at Scholsser. A movement under the direction of general Scott, upon the Queenstown road, was commenced late in the afternoon. The design of this was to make an attack upon the enemy, and divert their attention from his public stores. Proceeding but a short distance from the falls, information was communicated that a force of the British lay encamped behind the woods, and that they intended to attack the Americans the following day. This intelligence was hastily transmitted to the commander, and the forces under Scott proceeded rapidly through the wood, where he perceived the British strongly posted on an eminence defended by nine pieces of artillery. Near Lundy's lane, in front of the British position, he arranged his men in the order of battle. The thunder of the artillery gave the signal for attack. The Americans commenced and maintained the contest with a force not more than one seventh as large as that of the enemy. Had the British commander been apprised of their real situation, he might have captured the Americans with scarce the loss of a man.

It was night when the engagement commenced and darkness began to veil the earth in obscurity. The battle still continued and no reinforcement appeared. More than one fourth were now killed or wounded, which was a fulfilment of the rule for retreating. But at this difficult period, when many of their best officers and soldiers were killed or wounded, general Ripley led on his brigade to their assistance. The advancing general placing his brigade to the right of general Scott, found his position unfavorable for annoying the enemy, and assumed the responsibility of proceeding nearer to them before he formed. Suffering severely from this movement, Ripley then settled in his mind the bold adventure of storming the fort. "Will you attempt the reduction of that fortress," said general Ripley to colonel Miller. "I'll try," was his heroic answer. At the word of command, his men steadily ascending the hill, advanced to the mouths of their cannon, bayoneted the men while firing, drove the remainder before them, and took away their cannon. The arrangement of the American lines was now as follows: General Ripley's brigade was formed on the left—general Porter, with his volunteers, on the right, and the artillery of Towson in the center. The enemy rallied with all their vigor to regain their artillery, but their approach could not be distinctly ascertained. The moon now risen shone occasionally through the flitting clouds which enveloped the heavens. The roar of the cataract of Niagara was at times silenced by the thunder of the cannon and the din of arms, but was distinctly heard during the pauses of the fight.— In this situation the American troops were ordered to wait till the enemy's bayonet touched their own, and to take aim by the light from the discharge of their muskets.— The deadly fire of the Americans proved destructive to the British. The enemy recovering from their confusion, pressed on with their bayonets, and the assault was met by the Americans with firmness. The contest continued for more than twenty minutes, when the enemy retreated in disorder. Three times in the course of the night the same scene was repeated. The valor of America four times met and repulsed the enemy. After this the firing ceased, and the British were withdrawn, and the Americans left in the undisturbed possession of the field. Although the burden of the battle happened on the heights, yet efforts were made in other parts. General Scott's brigade forming anew, charged through an opening in Ripley's line, which in the confusion and darkness of the scene, proceeded between the fires of the combatants, and afterwards engaged in the battle by taking his position on the left of general Ripley. In another part colonel Jessup, with two hundred men, advanced against the enemy, brought them to action, drove them from the ground, and captured general Riall, with other officers and soldiers to an amount equal to his own. In this important contest the British lost eight hundred and eighty in killed, wounded and prisoners. Among the wounded were generals Drummond and Riall. The American number was reduced to eight hundred and sixty. Generals Scott and Brown, towards the close of the battle, were wounded, whilst major M'Farland and captain Ritchie were killed, with many other excellent officers.

The command now devolving upon general Ripley, he found his force so much reduced that he considered it expedient to abandon the captured artillery and return to fort Erie. The American army, now reduced to 1600, proceeded to erect fortifications at this place. They were besieged on the 4th of August by a British force consisting of 5000 men. The day following, general Gaines, from Sacketts Harbor, arrived and took the command of the Americans. Preparations were now hastily made in expectation of an attack.

The center column, under Drummond, succeeded in scaling the walls, and took possession of the bastion, while those of cols. Fischer and Scott made repeated attempts, but were repulsed. Almost as soon as the enemy gained possession of the works, a quantity of powder exploded and blew up with a terrible crash the whole party into the air. Those of the enemy who survived fled in confusion. The fortune of the day was peculiarly destructive to the British, 57 of their number being killed, 319 wounded, and 539 missing. To the Americans the battle had been less destructive: their total loss was 84. An army of 5000 men was now ordered on from Plattsburgh, for the relief of the bold defenders of the Niagara frontier. Constant reinforcements were received upon the British works, which general Brown determined to cut off, and thus destroy their batteries.

On September the 17th general Porter was ordered to march his detachment through the woods and attack the enemy. At the same time general Miller was directed to advance a short distance and secrete his men in a ravine between the fort and the British camp, until an attack should be commenced by general Porter. A reserve corps was commanded by general Ripley. The dangerous way proscribed for general Porter and his men was traversed and the enemy were completely surprised. Half an hour completed the capture of the garrison. The magazine, block house and part of the fort, and also the death of colonels Gibson and Wood, all succeeded. General Miller was warned by the firing that Porter had met the enemy and arrived at the time of the explosion. His division and general Ripley's corps of reserve approached in time to share the dangers and glory of this well conducted enterprise. By this successful adventure the British lost their works, a large quantity of ammunition, artillery, and one thousand men in killed, wounded and prisoners. The forces were conducted back to the fort by general Miller, in perfect order. The number of killed, wounded and missing amounted to about six hundred.

On the 21st of September, forty-nine days after the seige commenced, general Drummond withdrew his forces, relieving the garrison from their toils, which had been incessant, and from their danger, which had been encountered without fear. Troops have rarely deserved higher praise of their country. The arrival of general Izard with a reinforcement from Plattsburgh, happened on the 9th of October. Being the seignor officer, he took the command, and marched with his whole force on the 18th of October, in pursuit of the enemy, whom he found at Chippewa, securely stationed in a fortified camp. Several attempts proving unavailing to draw the enemy out into the field, therefore he evacuated Canada, and stationed his troops in winter quarters at Buffalo, Black Rock and Batavia.

An expedition was fitted out on lake Huron, under the command of commodore Sinclair, by water, and major Croghan, by land. Their design was to take Mackinaw, which was entirely frustrated by the forces of the enemy.

Eight ships and 2000 men, under the command of commodore Hardy, made a descent upon the coast of Maine, on the 11th of July, and captured Eastport and the country on the west of Passamaquoddy bay. An incursion was soon after made into the eastern part of Maine, by the governor of New-Brunswick, aided by admiral Griffith. They proceeded up the river Penobscot, as far as

Hampden, where the frigate John Adams was left for preservation. The guard placed here for its defence fled on their approach, after they had blown up the vessel. Possession was taken of the country east of the Penobscot river, in the name of the king of Great-Britain, and a proclamation issued by the council of New-Brunswick, confirming the validity of the proceeding, and for opening a communication with Canada and this capitulated territory.

Several thousand troops sailed from England early in the spring of 1814, and landed in Canada. With these, governor Prevost resolved to carry war into the United States, by the way of lake Champlain. His project, for enthusiasm and sanguine expectations of success, appeared like the imaginary calculations of general Burgoyne. Presuming on a defection among the inhabitants, he brought with him arms and clothing for those he expected would rally round his standard; and these ideas were confirmed by the American smugglers, who were wishing to secure the favor of the British. This plan further resembled that of Burgoyne's, as he contemplated marching his army by way of the lake and Hudson river to New-York. The departure of the troops from Plattsburgh, under general Izard, having left that post almost defenceless, the enemy employed the opportunity to make the contemplated invasion. On the 3d of September the governor-general of Canada, with an army of 14000 men, many of whom had been familiar with the European wars, proceeded into the territory of the United States. He issued a proclamation at Champlain, giving the citizens of the States the strongest assurance that his military efforts should be made only against the government and those who supported it, while the peaceful and unoffending should receive no injury.

This invasion of the American republic aroused the feelings of patriotism and called into action the brave sons of the green mountains. A large number of volunteers from Vermont hastened toward the scene of action. Distinctions of party were laid aside in the great cause of defending the possession and liberties of the country. General Strong, from Vermont, on his arrival at Plattsburgh, was elected to the command of the volunteers who, by his brave and skilful conduct, did honor to himself and the state. A difference of opinion, as was stated in the legislative proceedings for 1814, existed in the minds of the people of Vermont as to the right which the constitution conferred upon the president, or through him to any of the officers in the regular army, to call the militia into the service of the United States, and also the power which a governor of a state has under the constitution of the federal government to send his forces out of the state upon the emergency of repelling an invader. The governor and council were decided federalists and opposed from the beginning to the measures pursued by the prevailing power of the country, and to the rejection of the propositions made for an amicable settlement by the offending nations and to the declaration and management of the war. They could not from principle countenance the proceedings of the government and its agents so long as they had protested against the policy that brought about such a situation of affairs. Two thousand of Mr. Chittenden's constituents, who voted for him when elected to that Congress which declared war, petitioned against the enactment of such a law. Their feelings were embittered by the collisions of party resentment; but so far as the documents called up by a resolution of the legislature of Vermont, they show that governor Chittenden expressed himself favorably to the cause and encouraged volunteers to pass over the lake to the assistance of general Macomb. However, he did not order the militia out, for reasons that constitutional power was not given him, as he thought, to send the militia out of the jurisdictional boundaries of the state.

Fourteen thousand troops, under the command of governor Prevost, marched in two columns to Plattsburgh.— Their baggage and artillery were conveyed by a column upon the lake road, whilst another marched under the command of general Brisbane, by the way of Beekmantown. Colonel Appling, with his rifle corps, being stationed on the lake road, retired as far as Dead Creek, blocking up the road in such a manner as to impede the advance of the enemy as much as possible. On the 6th, the British, under general Powers, attacked a force of seven hundred militia under the command of general Mooers and major Wool, about seven miles from Plattsburgh. The militia, at the first fire, became intimidated and fled in every direction. Some, however, maintained their ground, and with the troops under major Wool, fought bravely against the superior numbers of the enemy, until they arrived within a mile of the town, where, being reinforced by captain Leonard with some artillery, they stopped for a while the progress of the enemy. On being compelled to retire, they contested every inch of ground, until they arrived at Saranac. Here, in attempting to ford the river, the enemy were repulsed. The loss of the British in this skirmish was about one hundred and six in killed and wounded, while that of the Americans did not exceed twenty-five.

The British took possession of the village north of the Saranac about eleven o'clock; but they were compelled to retire before night beyond the reach of the American artillery. Towards the close of the day their heavy artillery and baggage on the lake road crossed the beach, where a considerable loss was sustained from the fire of the American row gallies.

In this conflict lieutenant Duncan was severely wounded by a rocket, and four men were killed by the British artillery. There was a continual skirmishing from the sixth to the eleventh between the enemy's pickets and the militia, and both armies during the period were constantly employed—the Americans in strengthening their forts, and the British in erecting batteries, transporting heavy ordnance, and making other preparations for attacking their opposers. Captain Noadie, on the morning of the seventh, with a party, attempted to cross the upper bridge, seven miles from Plattsburgh, where they were met by captain Vaughan with twenty-five men, and compelled to retire with two killed and seven wounded.

Difficult indeed was the situation of general Macomb, whose force did not exceed 2000 men, and his fortifications a mere show of defence. If the British had pursued major Wool across the Saranac on the morning of the sixth, the American fortifications might have been secured without any difficulty. This delay proved very injurious to the British commander, by giving his opponents time to increase their forces. He erected several batteries, and contented himself to wait until the supremacy of the lake was decided.

General Prevost arranged his forces in two columns preparatory to the commencement of the action. One of the columns was stationed over the Saranac, and the other in the village, ready to move whenever circumstances should demand. After this manner were things disposed of by the British at the time their fleet sailed into Plattsburgh bay. This naval armament was commanded by commodore Downie, and consisted of four vessels and thirteen gun-boats, mounting in the whole 95 guns, and manned by 1050 officers and seamen. The frigate Confiance carried thirty-nine guns, brig Linnet sixteen—the two sloops, Growler and Eagle, seven each, and 13 boats with one each. The squadron under the American commander was anchored in the bay. It mounted eighty-six guns, having eight hundred and twenty men, and consisted of the Saratoga, carrying twenty-six guns, the Eagle of twenty, the Ticonderoga seventeen, Preble seven, and ten gun boats carrying sixteen.

At nine o'clock the enemy anchored in a line ahead, about three hundred yards distance from the American line, having the choice of position. In the arrangement of the squadrons the Confiance combatted the Saratoga, the Linnet the Eagle, the galleys, the shooner, sloops, and a division of the American galleys. The remaining American galleys fought against the Saratoga and Eagle. The wind had lulled away and the surface of the lake lay smooth and unruffled—reflecting on its clear waters the grandeur of the surrounding scenery. For a short time all was silent—not a motion or voice proceeded from the vast multitude that encamped near the battle-ground.— The Saratoga and the Confiance commenced the action by pouring in upon each other a most destructive fire, and the smaller vessels immediately followed their example. commodore M'Donough's situation became very dangerous on being exposed to a heavy fire from the enemy's brig, when the Eagle cut her cable and passed between the Saratoga and the Confiance. By a skilful manœuvre in winding up his ship (which the British Commodore was unsuccessful in doing) M'Donough brought a fresh broad-side to bear upon the Confiance, when she immediately surrendered. The brig Linnet receiving a fresh broadside, surrendered after a contest of fifteen minutes. A previous surrender was made by the sloop opposed to the Eagle and the galleys. Three of the galleys sunk and the rest escaped in a very shattered condition. The victors took one frigate, one brig and two sloops. The engagement terminated after two hours and twenty minutes. A loss of eighty-four killed, among whom was commodore Downie, and one hundred and ten wounded, was sustained by the British. Fifty-two Americans were killed and fifty-eight wounded.

The British opened their batteries by land as soon as the engagement between the fleets commenced. Several hundred shells and rockets were discharged, which occasioned but very little injury. The main body of the British lines attempted to cross the river in rear of the fort near Pike's cantonment, which after a brave resistance from three hundred and fifty of the New-York and Vermont volunteers, was effected, but on the arrival of lieutenant Sumpter's artillery, they commenced a precipitate retreat. The rear of the retreating party were attacked by the Vermont volunteers, who succeeded in capturing three officers and several privates of the enemy. Their hasty retreat was the only means of saving the detachment. Five of the Americans were killed and eight wounded. When the shouts of victory at half past eleven resounded through the American lines of the result of the battle on the lake, the efforts of the enemy became weaker. In the afternoon their intrenchments were deserted, and in the night succeeding, the whole enemy commenced a retreat to Canada. They were pursued some distance by the Americans, and several were taken prisoners; but the heavy and incessant rain compelled the pursuers to return.

The British lost of their land forces more than two thousand men in killed, wounded, prisoners and deserters, and a large quantity of ammunition and military stores; while the aggregate loss of the Americans did not exceed one hundred and fifty men.

Nothing further of importance occurred on the northern

frontier during the continuance of the war. The conflict in this quarter had been severe—troops never contested more bravely for the honors of conquest; but the exertions of the Americans were generally during this campaign crowned with success and the honors of victory. In most parts of the United States, upon the frontiers and the seaboard, the distresses of war and the horrors of battle had been experienced; yet no farther description has been given of the progress of hostilities between this country and Great-Britain than what related to the northern campaign. A recapitulation of the most celebrated and general engagements may serve as an illustration of many subjects embraced in the description of this state. Those instances of bravery and heroism displayed on the ocean and frontiers of the United States, can never fade from the recollection of those who are friendly to the cause of American liberty.

The campaign of 1812 was distinguished for naval engagements, in which the commanders of the United States frigates Constitution, Wasp, United States, and Constitution, commanded by commodores Hull, Jones, Decatur, and Bainbridge, captured the British ships of war Guerrier, Frolick, Macedonian, and Java, commanded by captains Dacres, Whinyates, Carden and Lambert. In January, 1813, the British, under general Procter, gained a cruel and blood-stained victory over general Winchester of the United States army.

Upon the ocean, captain Broke, of the frigate Shannon, conquered the American vessel Chesapeake, under the command of captain Lawrence. The British vessel Argus, sailed by captain Maples, took an American vessel commanded by lieutenant Allen. The Enterprize, lieutenant Burrows commander, took the British brig Boxer, sailed by captain Blythe. During the progress of the campaign for 1814, the American frigate Essex, commanded by commodore Porter, surrendered to a British fleet, under commodore Hillyar. The Frolic, commanded by commodore Bainbridge, was taken by the British vessel Orpheus. An English squadron captured commodore Decatur, with the frigate President. The British vessels Cayene and Levant were captured by commodore Stewart, of the American ship Constitution. The American vessels Peacock, Wasp, and Hornet successfully attacked and made prizes of the British vessels Epervier, Reindeer, and Penguin, commanded by captains Wales, Manners, and Nelson. The English forces at Baltimore, under general Ross, were signally repulsed by the Americans, commanded by general Stricker. Generals Packenham and Gibbs, with their European myrmidons at New-Orleans, were repelled with great loss by general Jackson.

The battles upon the northern frontier having been described in the work, it appeared proper to separate from them those before mentioned. In 1812, the British prevailed at the battle of Queenstown, owing to the defection of the New-York militia under the command of general Van Rensselaer. In the campaign of the following year, generals Dearborn and Pike conquered the British army at York, and took the capitol of Upper Canada. General Harrison of the American army gained a signal victory over the British and the celebrated Indian, Tecumseh, at Detroit. Generals Brown, Scott, Gaines and Ripley gloriously defeated the British veterans, under the command of generals Drummond and Riall, at the deadly battles of Chippewa, Bridgewater and fort Erie. Upon lake Erie commodore Perry, with the American squadron, captured the English fleet under commodore Barclay. In the campaign of 1814, the squadron under commodore McDonough, on lake Champlain, captured the British fleet commanded by commodore Downie. Sir George Prevost, governor-general of Canada, was repulsed by general Macomb, at the siege of Plattsburgh.

On the 17th of February, while the victory at New-Orleans was animating the feelings of the Americans, the welcome tidings of a treaty of peace, executed at Ghent on the 24th of December, 1814, was brought to America and ratified at the same time by the president and senate. The treaty now entered upon was silent on the subject for which the war had been professedly declared. It contained no express stipulation against those maratime outrages committed by Great-Britain, which had been the principal causes of the difficulties. Provisions were only made in it for the suspension of hostilities—the change of prisoners—the restoration of territories and possessions acquired by the contending powers during hostilities—the determination of unsettled boundaries, and for a united effort to abolish the trafic in slaves. The orders in council being repealed, and the termination of the war in Europe removing all the motives for impressment, the causes for which the war was declared did in fact no longer exist, although America had failed, as the combined neutrality of Europe formerly did, in compelling England to make a formal relinquishment of the principles on which her exhorbitant claims were founded.

The tumults of war had now subsided, and peace again revivified the drooping energies of the country. All classes of community rejoiced in the returning prosperity of the public and individual concerns of the Union.

CHAPTER XI.

A Narrative of the Legislative Proceedings from the year 1814 to 1824.—Unusual cold Summer in 1816.—President Monroe's Tour through the State.—Governor Galusha's resignation in 1819.—Mr. Skinner elected governor in 1820.—Resolutions upon the question of admitting Missouri into the Union.—Election of judge Van Ness governor of Vermont in 1823.—General La Fayette's visit to Vermont.—His reception among the people.

1815. Mr. Galusha, the former governor of the state, was placed at the head of the government, after two years magistracy of Mr. Chittenden. The asperity of party feelings was mitigated by the pleasures of social intercourse, and systematic opposition discovered itself only in the occasional paralysis of subsiding passions. The people discovered that their true interest consisted in the cultivation of friendly sentiments and the pursuit of peaceful occupations. Those portions of the state, which the improvements and changing condition of the people made some alteration or addition necessary, were noticed in the governor's communication to the legislative body.

Certain resolutions, proposing amendments to the federal constitution, from the legislature of Massachusetts, were submitted at this session for the consideration of the legislature of Vermont. Under these propositions of amendment, a convention had been called by three of the New-England states, at Hartford, the year preceding, at which time and place the people of this state were requested to send delegates; but their representatives, then at the annual session of the legislature, refused to join them or sanction their proceedings. The legislature now resolved that it was inexpedient to concur with Massachusetts in the amendments proposed. A copy of the resolution was ordered to be transmitted to each member of Congress from the state and to the governors of each state in the Union. Among the acts passed at this session of the assembly, one granting the exclusive privilege of navigating lake Champlain by steam, for the term of twenty-three years, to a certain company, was enacted.— Every other person under penalty of five hundred dollars, was forbid making or encroaching upon this privilege.— Such a monopolizing privilege, so clearly opposed to the constitution of this state and the United States, raised considerable opposition in the house. However, the company were secured in the exercise of these partial immunities until the judicial authority of the federal government decided such grants void, in the case of the steamboat company upon North river.

The case of Godfrey, who was sentenced to be executed at Woodstock, was brought before the legislature for commutation of punishment, or a reprieve. A delay for a few months was granted, but he was afterwards executed, which was the second punishment of the kind that ever took place under the government of the state.

The wanton and inhuman murder of sixty-three American prisoners, who were confined at Dartmoor prison, by captain Shutland and the garrison, occasioned a great excitement through the country. The matter was, however, so explained as to free the government from all implications in the transaction.

1816. In consequence of the embarrassments to which

the American commerce had been subject for several years previous and during the late war, large capitals were vested in manufactories of various kinds of goods.—But on the return of peace, the English, by the facilities and improvements in mechanism, were enabled to undersell the American manufacturers. This gave a severe shock, and many extensive establishments entirely failed. Petitions for protecting establishments of this kind, were laid before the general government, and additional duties strongly recommended by a committee on manufactures, appointed by Congress. A new tariff law was enacted, imposing small additional duties upon the importation of certain articles of foreign growth or fabrication. The commercial interest and planters of cotton in the southern states opposed this measure so strenuously that nothing effectual was accomplished towards the encouragement of this useful branch of industry.

Mr. Galusha was again elected governor of the state, and after the organization of the house, he requested their attention very particularly to the encouragement of manufactures; the importance of which to the commercial prosperity has been very ably advocated and urged by the principal heads of the government. They represented the manufacture of such raw materials as are the product or growth of the soil of Vermont, the only means by which commercial exchange can be supported. The raw materials must be manufactured into various fabrics and wares, by the inhabitants of the state, in order to compete with importations from foreign countries. The extensive variety and amount of merchandise which the taste and improvements of the age have put in requisition, find an inadequate resource for payment in the produce from the soil. Manufactures must be relied on to make up the deficiency.

In the spring and summer of this year, the weather was remarkably cold. Snow fell in almost every part of the state, and in many places to the depth of a foot and a half. Dry, cold weather succeeded in the fall. The clouds returned without moisture, and the air was filled with dust upon the slightest agitation of the wind. Such were the apprehensions of a general famine from the uncommon failure of crops, that the governor, in his speech to the legislature, recommended a prudent expenditure of the most scanty provisions, to avoid the evils and calamities of want. The annual complimentary answer was returned, after a long and spirited debate in the house, to the governor's speech. The sentiments contained in it exhibited certain degrees of party irritability, and in one instance the harshness of personal resentment was expressed against the federal party, when they "declared the withdrawal of confidence from those delegates in Congress of the United States, who have unnecessarily increased the public expenditures in a time of embarrassment, affords a pleasing proof that the citizens of the state look well to the men whom they place in authority, and that they are determined to detect and repel even the slightest encroachment upon their rights." The salary of the representatives of Congress had been increased the last session, contrary to the wishes of the freemen of Vermont, who by their suffrages this year changed every member of the delegation. This was the termination of a practice which had occasioned the most violent contentions and consumed much time and money, during the whole period from the first election of governor Tichenor, in 1797. No single topic introduced amongst the business of legislation had given rise to such impassioned feelings and useless altercation. To be freed from such a needless custom was very favorable to the accomplishment of public business in the general assembly.

1817. The internal affairs of the state assumed a more prosperous condition—a bountiful harvest supplied the wants of the people—returning peace brought tranquillity to its borders, and business became generally more fixed and certain.

The emancipation of the South American colonists was very particularly noticed by the governor, and strongly desired by the public in general. "Should the emancipation of the southern continent take place, we may rationally hope ere long to see arts and sciences, agriculture, commerce and manufactures flourishing throughout that vast, populous and fertile region, and every rank of its inhabitants, in the full fruition of all the blessings of civil and religious liberty, unshackled by superstition and unincumbered by the edicts of kings." But no one could foresee or predict such important revolutions in the moral and political condition of the people, as their recent transactions have effected. Several states have arisen to the blessings of free constitutions, and the subjects thereof emancipated from the bonds of slavery. Whether the people of these new governments are sufficiently acquainted with such useful and necessary information as to be capable of self-government, remains to be determined by their future proceedings."

Private acts were passed remunerating certain individuals for losses sustained in consequence of their proceedings in cases provided by the acts of the legislature, in 1812. By one, colonel Fifield, detached from the militia of Vermont, was granted the sum of 1112 dollars, to remunerate him for losses sustained in consequence of an order and subsequent attempt to carry into effect the Vermont non-intercourse act, in the year above mentioned. This law, by a decision of the supreme court of the state, was declared unconstitutional and all proceedings under it void. Claims of a similar character have frequently been brought forward for legislative remuneration, but their presentation has been quite unsuccessful. These originating from proceedings had under the established laws of the state, and declared illegal by the judiciary of the state, ought in justice and equity to be remunerated by the power which created them. In the course of this year an arrangement was concluded with the British government for the reduction of the naval force of Great-Britain and the United States upon the lakes, by providing that neither should keep in service on the lakes Ontario or Champlain more than one armed vessel and that to have only one gun.

During this year, Mr. Monroe, president of the United States, visited the eastern and middle states, for the purpose of examining the situation of public works, such as navy yards, arsenals and forts, and for viewing the general circumstances of the citizens through this portion of the Republic. He was received with demonstrations of gratitude and affection wherever he appeared. On entering Vermont, arrangements were made at the villages upon his route from Connecticut river on the east to lake Champlain on the west, for tendering the hospitalities and expressing the joy of the people, on their being favored with an interview from the venerable president of the Union.

1818. This year no changes were made in the heads of the government, and nothing of political excitement appeared before the councils of the state. The governor's speech, upon the subject of agriculture, contains observations of a practical and useful nature, and such as are and will continue (if practiced upon) to be the great sources of national subsistence and freedom. "Many useful improvements (says he) have been made in the state, while no considerable attempts have been commenced to improve the condition of agriculture." Although as much reliance as possible is placed upon home manufactures for the consumption of the state, yet it must be confessed that the main source of wealth and subsistence of every class of citizens must depend on the cultivation of the soil.— "When our farms were new and unimpaired by tillage, it was profitable to extend our labors and cast our seed over a large portion of the soil; but as our lands become less productive by the frequency of crops, it is necessary that new modes of husbandry should be resorted to, in order to keep them in a fertile state, and that the different qualities of the soil be improved to the best advantage for tillage or grazing, which in all probability will require more labor and expense in cultivating an equal quantity of land, and of course prevent the too frequent emigration of the laboring class of our citizens." It was further suggested, that something useful might be accomplished by authorizing enterprizing individuals to form societies invested with corporate powers, for the useful purposes of advancing the agricultural interest, encouraging manufactures, and improving breeds of domestic animals throughout the several counties of the state.

The business of legislation was transacted harmoniously, and many important public acts were enacted during the session. But in times of the greatest tranquillity, like the present, there is much need of care and perseverance, which are indispensible to the preservation of the rights and privileges of a free people. Republics have in all ages of the world been overthrown by the decay of virtue and intelligence among the people, rather than from a combination of potentates or armies.

The Congress of the United States repealed the law imposing internal duties upon imports into this country.— They also passed an act granting to every indigent officer and soldier of the revolutionary army, whose property did not exceed one hundred dollars, a pension of twenty dollars a month to each officer and eight dollars a month to every private who had served the term of nine months in the army.

A medical academy was instituted at Castleton by an act of the legislature of this session, for the purpose of instructing in the science of physic, surgery, chymistry, and all the various branches connected with the healing art. This institution has been connected with Middlebury college, and is in a very flourishing condition.

1819. The legislature assembled this fall for the last time under the administration of governor Galusha; who informed the members of the assembly and the public of his determination to spend the residue of his life in domestic retirement; and recommended to the freemen of the state to unite on some other person to perform the duties of chief-magistrate after his term of public service had expired: Adding that his zeal for the public good would never cease but with his reason or his life. Mr. Galusha had served in various public capacities almost from his first settlement in the state, in 1775. At the battle of Bennington, he fought at the head of a company belonging to Shaftsbury, over whom he had previously been appointed a captain. Two years, ending with the political year 1808, he was elected one of the three judges constituting the supreme court of the state, and afterwards received nine elections for governor of the state.— If it was a great and glorious act for Camillus or Washington, after having freed their country, to retire to a cottage, rather than to reign in a capitol, surely a resignation of the highest honors of office in Vermont discovers no less the humility of the individual and the patriotism of the statesman.

An address was adopted by the house and communicated to the governor, on his retirement from office, from which the following is an extract:—"On a review of the events of the memorable struggle of our fathers for independence, we find you in early life on the banks of the Walloomsack, with your patriotic band, teaching them boldly to defend their country. In discharging the duties of councillor, judge, and governor, you have ever merited and received the approbation of your fellow citizens."

The attention of the legislative assembly was requested upon the subject of freeing the body of debtors from arrest and imprisonment on debts of small amount. The following paragraph exhibits the views that were then entertained upon this much agitated subject. "I am of opinion that more property is spent in collecting small debts by law, especially where the body is taken in execution, than the amount of the debts saved by such collection. I also believe that it would discourage credit where it ought not be given, and produce punctuality in those who obtain it. Yet the only safe remedy against embarrassment or poverty is a retrenchment of family expenses and lessening the consumption of articles of foreign growth and manufacture."

The usual business of the legislature was accomplished with much unanimity of feelings. Among their proceedings, a resolution was adopted approving in the highest terms the laudable and humane exertions of many individuals in different sections of the country, in forming a society for the purpose of establishing a colony of free people of color on the western coast of Africa, and resolving that the senators and representatives in Congress from this state, be requested to exert their influence for the adoption of such measures as will most effectually promote the great and benevolent views and objects of the society— that the unfortunate Africans might enjoy the privileges asserted in our constitution, "that all men are born equally free and independent, and have certain and unalienable rights, among which are the enjoying and defending of life and liberty, possessing and protecting property, and obtaining happiness and safety." This subject has received considerable attention from some of the most influential men in the country.

1320. Mr. Skinner, the former chief justice of the state, was elected governor. His speech, delivered before the council and house of representatives, contained plain and comprehensive views of the laws and regulations of the state, and among the various topics to which the attention of the legislature were directed, that of making frequent alterations in the public statutes, was mentioned as a great evil. The best evidence which the representatives of the people can give of their faithfulness and intelligence, is a reluctant and careful approach at innovation.

The delays and expense which are incident to the administration of justice, are represented to exceed all that is required to sustain every department of the government; and when this practice is opposed to the bill of rights, which declares that every person ought to obtain right and justice freely, without being obliged to purchase it, completely and without denial, promptly and without delay.— This was referred to in the message of the governor, as a subject of the deepest interest. Trials in some cases of but a few dollars consequence have caused the expenditure of thousands and a great waste of time, and all that without establishing any important precedents for guarding the rights and privileges of the public. The present organization of the Vermont judiciary, has had a tendency to the despatch of business, and to prevent a multiplicity of law suits. What the law is has been clearly and substantially expressed in the cases reported. The character of the state vitally depends upon the judiciary, and "the degree of confidence reposed in a government is measured by the rank it sustains." A resolution was introduced and passed by the legislature, remonstrating against the admission of Missouri into the union, with a constitution legalizing slavery and the cruel and unnatural traffic in human blood. The subject of their resolution was, that congress has a right to prohibit any further extention of slavery, as one of the conditions from which any new state may be admitted into the union. They therefore viewed with alarm the attempts of the inhabitants of Missouri to obtain admission into the union, as one of the

United States, under a constitution which legalizes and secures the introduction and continuance of slavery, and also prevents freemen from emigrating and settling in said state, on account of their origin, color and features. The legislature considered the principles, powers and restrictions contained in the reputed constitution of Missouri as anti-republican and repugnant to the constitution of the United States; and further, they resolved to instruct their senators and representatives in Congress to exert their influence and use all legal measures to prevent the admission of Missouri into the union of the states, with such anti-republican powers in her constitution.

The subject was agitated in Congress with great warmth, and at no time had the parties in that body been so marked by a geographical division or so much actuated by feelings so dangerous to the union of the states, as at this time. This controversy was not confined to the seat of the general government, or the state of Vermont, but it attracted the attention of the people in all parts of the Union. Meetings were called in the northern states, and spirited resolutions were passed, expressing their fears of a perpetuation of slavery, and their approbation of the restriction. The restriction was opposed by the southern party, on the ground of self-defence. They alleged that the admission of Missouri without any restriction, would in no degree tend to perpetuate slavery. The number of slaves would not be accumulated by this measure, but they would be diminished by removing from one state to another. They declared that it would be a dangerous and tyrannical act in the federal government, and one that would infringe upon the sovereignties of the states, should the restriction be persisted in and adopted.

After discussing the question through the great part of the session, a bill passed for the admission of Missouri into the Union of the States, without any restriction, but with the inhibition of slavery throughout the territories of the United States north of 36 degrees and 30 minutes north latitude.

1821. The legislature again assembled with governor Skinner at the head of the government. Certain resolutions and reports from committees in the legislatures of

Maryland and New-Hampshire, on the subject of appropriating the public lands for the purposes of education, were submitted for the co-operation of the legislature of Vermont. The people of Vermont, in the language of the governor's speech, "can feel no delicacy in making a claim of this kind, for no one of the United States, in proportion to their ability, contributed more to the acquisition of those rights which were purchased by the toil, distresses and sacrifices of the revolutionary war. Situated upon the frontier, they constituted a barrier between the enemy and the confederated states. Not having then been acknowledged as a member of the confederation, no part of the expense they incurred in the war has been assumed by the general government, while they have participated in the burthens of the public debt."

A resolution was passed declaring that each of the United States had an equal right to participate in the benefits of the public lands, as the common property of the Union, and that the states in whose favor Congress have not made appropriations of land for the purpose of education, will be entitled to such appropriations as shall have been made in favor of the other states. However just such a distribution of the public domain might be in principle, yet in practice it has been considered inexpedient. Another subject of quite a popular character amongst a majority of the people, was, the attempts at revising and ultimately at reducing the fee bill. The items of expenses attending the business of litigation and the salaries of certain officers of the government, were considered extravagant and oppressive upon the people; and in the end would occasion an overthrow of the government of the country.— A reduction of certain items in the taxation of costs and a limitation of the salaries of certain officers of the government, was, after a long and animated debate, enacted into a law of the state. Those employed in the laborious occupations of life, and likewise many others, anticipated much relief from the adoption of this measure. Probably it has operated as a salutary check upon the frequent excesses that had been practiced.

Acts of suspension have frequently been granted by the legislature upon debts due to individuals as well as to the

the state, which are in direct opposition to the constitution, declaring that no law shall be enacted impairing the obligation of contracts. The custom of granting relief to individuals in delaying the fulfilment of their contracts, was entered upon by the legislature and was considered a transcendency of the legitimate powers of the legislative body. The revision of the proceedings of the supreme court and granting new trials after cases have been solemnly adjudicated, upon a full presentation of the evidence, was now regarded as an improper subject of legislation, and but two or three new trials have since been granted.

1822. The meeting of the general assembly was held in October, after a year's recurrence distinguished by no particular prosperity or adversity to the inhabitants of the state. One of the principal topics of public interest and attention was the subject of manufactures.

Vermont, said the committee on the subject of manufactures, "can raise as fine wool as any quarter of the globe—her mountains furnish pasturage of the best kind, and roll down their thousand streams to aid us in its manufacture It also abounds with ores and forests for coal, amply sufficient for the manufacture of iron in all its varieties and equal to the consumption of the state, and for abundant importation. Many materials are found within the state, on which the industry and ingenuity of our citizens might operate to great advantage, and ultimately be sources of revenue, if a capital could be allured to the object by the affinity and patronage of our laws."

An act to prevent usury was, in compliance to the recommendation of governor Skinner, passed. The rate of interest was limited to six per cent. and all contracts whereby a higher rate of interest should be taken or secured, were declared void. The payment of unlawful interest was made recoverable within one year next after such transaction.— Those interested as the receivers of usury could be compelled to disclose the same in a court of chancery. After the amount disclosed should be refunded, the delinquent becomes discharged from any further liability. In some governments, money, like other property, is left to regulate itself in market, and this practice had many advocates in Vermont.

In a government founded upon the avowed principle of securing equal privileges and furnishing equal protection to all, "justice demands of those to whom its administration is entrusted so to provide as that the unsuspecting and unfortunate may be secured against the unjust exactions of the more artful and fortunate. The acquisition of wealth by laudable industry, economy and prudence merits approbation and encouragement; but laws, providing facilities for a few calculating, greedy citizens, to monopolize that property, the produce of the toil and industry of the more useful and deserving, can never be sanctioned by the faithful and intelligent representatives of the people."

Mr. Skinner requested of the freemen of the state not to honor him again with their suffrages, as he deemed it a duty to desire that he might not be considered a candidate for the office.

1823. Judge Van Ness was returned governor elect at the meeting of the assembly this year. A customary speech was delivered by him to the legislative bodies fraught with sentiments of interest and concern for the welfare of the state. "In calling your attention to the immediate concerns of this state, I am not sensible that any material alterations in the laws relating to any department of the government could be beneficially made at this time. The stability of the laws is next in importance to their wisdom; yet so great is the desire of mankind for change and so predominant their ambition for the character of reform, that they are seldom at a loss for subjects to act upon, and after starting upon slight and apparently judicious amendments, their zeal will frequently urge them to overleap the bounds prescribed for themselves in the outset, and in their progress destroy the fairest and most valuable systems." A desire of change and the honors connected with legislative efforts at management and debate, occasion a great expense to the state and controversy among the people.— And further, it produces much uncertainty in the law, and thereby occasions perplexing and expensive law suits, highly detrimental to the prosperity of the state. Few alterations were made in the laws at this session. That species of gambling denominated horse raceing, where a premium in money or any valuable property was bet or hazarded, was prohibited, upon the forfeiture of the horse so kept for running and the loss of the money staked. The influence of gambling has been very deleterious upon national affairs, so far as the citizens of the United States have progressed in practices of this character. The sterling virtues of the Romans were dissipated at their national games, and luxury destroyed the patriotism and energy of the state.

1824. This year the tariff upon cotton goods, which had engaged the attention of the people throughout the United States ever since 1816, was laid upon foreign importations. It had been proved from experience that manufactures needed protection, and that such policy had been pursued by those governments where they flourished.— The English had grown rich by their protecting system; hence other nations could participate in similar privileges.

On the reaccession of Mr. Van Ness to the chair of state, he directed the attention of the legislature to the alteration of the law for choosing the electors of the president and vice-president of the United States. In compliance with this recommendation, an act was passed giving the choice of the electors to the people, by a general ticket, instead of the former method, by a legislative appointment.

Since the close of the late war with Great-Britain, party spirit continued to subside, until the contest for the presidential election excited a spirited opposition, which, however, did not become so general or inveterate as in their former contests. On canvassing the character and qualifications of the respective candidates, at the first election of Mr. Adams, in Vermont, the opposition raised against his claims was very trifling. The pride of New-England, in having one of her sons honored with the highest office in the government, and one who was in every respect competent to discharge the various and important duties annexed to his office by the provisions of the national constitution, actuated the ingenuous and enlightened sentiments of the freemen of Vermont to take a general and decisive stand in favor of the successful candidate. Sectional feelings operated somewhat in his favor; but his long and faithful services in the government, his profound knowledge and political integrity, and above all the rest, as an officer invested with the civil power and authority of the country, his truly legal and philosophic method of deciding on difficult and important subjects of commercial and political interest between this and other nations, by a kind of intellectual calculation founded upon the strictest rules of legal evidence, rather than by the presentiments of habit or the momentary bursts of feeling, gave him a decided preference over any other individual. His qualifications were considered as worthy of succeeding the venerated Washington, and in his administration of the government the expectations of the people have been fully realized.

The arrival of general La Fayette, the early and distinguished benefactor of the American Republic, was hailed with acclamations of joy and festivity throughout the country. On the 17th of August he and his son entered the city of New-York, where they were met by the city authorities and a military escort, and welcomed to the shores of a country whose freedom and happiness he had contributed so much towards establishing. A committee of the general assembly reported, that Vermont, in common with her sister states, would rejoice in the opportunity of manifesting her gratitude by a solemn and public act. The feelings and duty of the state, say the committee, are united in demanding an expression of gratitude which is owed to this worthy patriot of the revolution.— Accordingly the legislative councils of the state voted that the governor should, in behalf of the people of Vermont, invite general La Fayette to extend his tour into the state, and honor its citizens with his presence. In July 4th, 1825, the general crossed the Connecticut and entered the state of Vermont for the first time, at Windsor. Here he met with a friendly and interesting reception from the governor and a numerous body of citizens assembled to participate in the joy and gratitude of the occasion. After the ceremony of an address, and a reply from the Nation's guest were concluded, he proceeded with the governor and a large escort of citizens over the lofty mountains of

Vermont, by the way of Montpelier, to Burlington, where much gratification was experienced in making arrangements and beholding the early and celebrated friend of our country. His reception was the offering of unaffected friendship. Indifferent as the state was for the attendant curiosities of wealthy and populous cities, yet her exhibitions were of a cast as worthy of the character of an enlightened Republic as the more brilliant examples of expensive munificence. With Vermont, the highest commendations of character were an undeviating affection and zeal for the rights and liberties of the country; and such has been her bravery in war and the difficulties of revolutions, that patriotism is not humbled by declaring her a brave and energetic people. During the gloomy period of 1781, says the address, the citizens of this state were violently assailed by two powerful neighboring states, while her bold and inflexible patriots were nobly struggling for self existence and state independence. The waters of yonder beautiful lake were covered with an hostile fleet and powerful army, and all her strong holds in the undisturbed possession of the enemy; but Washington was our mediator and friend. A self created board of war, consisting of eight persons, wielded the destinies of the New-Hampshire grants, then containing thirty thousand inhabitants. I have, says the general in his reply, "the gratification in the sons of the green mountains to find many who have been my intimate companions, and while in the throngs of both sexes and of every age, who so kindly welcome me, I often recognise the features and shall ever recognise the feelings of my American cotemporaries." La Fayette was accompanied through the lake to Whitehall by the governor and other gentlemen from Vermont, where he then proceeded directly to New-York.

An act, before mentioned, was passed giving to the people the power of choosing the electors of the president and vice-president, which had formerly been exercised by the legislature. The progress of the bill was delayed by a motion of amendment, which proposed giving the choice of electors to the people at the approaching election. The present crisis of public affairs was urged in favor of giving the law an immediate effect. This power, the birthright of the people, they asserted had been withheld so long that it should not now be delayed even by the customary rules of legislation. One argument of a leading member was, that such professions of love for the people, without corresponding actions, did not, like Bonaparte's system, amount to much. The motion for amendment was therefore dismissed by 183 in the affirmative and 23 in the negative.

CHAPTER XII.

Proceedings of the General Assembly from the year 1824 to the termination of the year 1830.—Mr. Butler elected governor in 1826.—Great demand for banking privileges.—Legal provisions for the better regulation of common schools.—Mr. Crafts' election for governor of the state in 1828.—Excitement on the subject of the presidential election.—Controversy concerning masonry.—Popular views on the subject.—Flood in 1830.—Election of Mr. Crafts by the house of representatives.—State of parties.

1825. The legislature convened this fall with Mr. Van Ness again at the head of the government. The attention of the legislature was particularly directed to the subject of internal improvements—the navigation of Connecticut river, and the junction of its waters with those of lake Champlain and Memphremagog, were the routes which received the notice of the public. The period may not be far distant when the attention of the state may properly be fixed upon enterprises of this kind; but to what extent, time and the advancing resources of the state only can determine.

Canal commissioners were appointed and an appropriation of five hundred dollars made for their expenses, whose duty it was to assist any commissioner of the United States who should be sent on to ascertain the most practicable route for the erection of canals within this state; and a further sum of seventy-five dollars was also appropriated to aid the subscriptions for proceeding with a survey of the contemplated routes from Montpelier to lake Champlain.

The expediency and benefit of attempting public works of this kind in Vermont, was debated with considerable earnestness and zeal in the house. Calculations were made by the members who favored the contemplated improvements, that the intercourse and trade of the state would be sufficiently facilitated to meet the expense and furnish a revenue equal to the interest and an additional profit upon the capital expended; that the other states engaged in constructing such public works have already witnessed the prosperity which they have tended to produce. The evils of refusing to direct the energies of the country to the subject of internal improvements was portrayed in lively colors. An alienation of amicable feeling—a severance of natural friendship, say they, will pursue the destiny of that country, advancing in one section by its improvements, and in another depressed by an inattention to its interest. The bonds of national union are strengthened by a friendly intercourse and an equal participation of confederate wealth and prosperity. An equalization in improvements only can sustain the health, prosperity and freedom of the political compact of the United States. Should the enterprise and talents of some of the states monopolize the profits which an advancing country might put in requisition, want and dependence will be experienced by the others. The people will emigrate for subsistence, and manufactures will become a source of unimproved wealth. Those who opposed the project were willing that companies should be formed and invested with corporate power for enjoying all the immunities and profits arising from improvements in transportation, either by canals or railways; but they would not consent to have the state become accountable or undertake in the scheme.

The revenue of the state arises from public taxes assessed upon the grand list, except the profits of a certain per cent. upon the banks, and some other state immunities.— The method of making up the grand list of the state having been frequently modified, was repealed at this session, and a new one, upon different principles, substituted.—

According to the provisions of this act, each male person residing in the state, between the ages of 21 and 60 years, shall, on the first day of April, be set in the list in the town where he resides at ten dollars, excepting students of colleges, and such persons as sickness, bodily or mental infirmity ought, in the opinion of the listers, to be exempt from the payment of taxes, and also the polls of the militia equipped shall be exempt, excepting from highway and school taxes. For minors equipped ten dollars is to be deducted from the list of the parent or guardian, and three dollars to be deducted for every horse kept for training, which shall further be free from all taxes, except for highways and schools. Public lands, and those sequestered for public use, shall not be set in the list; but buildings on the above lands and building lots of two acres, shall be assessed and set in the list at 4 per cent. on their real value. Real estate is to be appraised every five years, between the 1st day of May and the 10th day of June. Those towns where the list does not exceed 2000 dollars, which have no representative in the legislature, are not liable to be doomed; but if they neglect to make such returns to the legislature, such town or towns may be doomed. Towns may make an appraisal of real estate, for the purpose of raising highway and school taxes.

1826. Mr. Butler, formerly a member of Congress, and one of the executive council of the state, was elected governor for the ensuing year. In his speech to the assembly, he observed that the legislature of the state had for more than twenty years past uniformly manifested its disapprobation of raising money by lotteries for any purpose whatever. At the last session large sums were offered for the privilege of selling tickets and drawing lotteries in this state, but every proposition of the kind was rejected, and it is believed the great body of our citizens are in sentiment opposed to raising money by that way. Indeed the principles of morality in Vermont must suffer a sad decline before this species of gambling will be sanctioned by the government or approved by the people. The numerous sales of lottery tickets made within the last year had not been a little surprising to many and especially to those who had personal knowledge of all that took place at the last session. If the construction lately given to those grants anciently made by the state, to raise money from lotteries, were correct, it would be difficult to say when the business will stop.

An examination was had upon the subject of granting lotteries and vending lottery tickets at the present session. From the investigation of the subject, it appeared that twenty-four lotteries had been granted in the state, from 1783 to 1804, eight of which were limited as to the time of their operation, and sixteen unlimited. In consideration of the subject, an act prohibiting the vending of lottery tickets, without a license obtained from the county court, was passed after considerable debate, under the penalty of a heavy fine. Applications had been made at the session previous, for liberty to sell lottery tickets in the state. A large sum was offered for this permission, to be appropriated for the benefit of schools; but objections were urged against profits arising from lotteries, that they are acquired by a species of gambling and ought not to be encouraged, however laudably the avails may be appropriated, as the acquisitions made are demoralizing to community, and give constant encouragement to idleness and dissipation. But these objections were answered by asserting that the admission of evils is necessary in the economy of nature. Lotteries are granted in other states and large sums of money pass from this to their benefit, which would be a saving were corporations of this kind chartered in Vermont. The evils in this case would be mitigated, and the benefits exclusively enjoyed. In addition to this, individual happiness is enhanced by the admission of such institutions. The human mind is so constituted that the anticpation of events afford as much pleasure as the actual possession, or at least the feelings are buoyed up under circumstances of wretchedness, want and pain, from the belief and hope that better fortune will ensue. The person who ventures his chance in the lottery lives in a kind of hopeful indulgence, for his prospects of realizing a fortune are equally as certain as others.— A vote was taken on the subject, and the admission of the privilege was decided against. This effectually checked the operation of the state lotteries, and the sale of foreign tickets in Vermont.

The interest of the sciences received the attention of the government. A college of natural history was incorporated in the University of Vermont, and the Vermont agricultural society was also established. This institution has eminently proved, so far as it went into operation, the utility of social communion and the advantage arising from comparing opinions and making the results of individual experience a common stock.

Petitions had for several years been brought before the legislature for the establishment of banks in various places in the state. Seven banking charters had already been granted, which had gone into operation, and others were demanded, with an increased confidence of success in the petitions. The natural effect produced by the fortunate result which attended the petitions for banking institutions has had a tendency to encourage others in the pursuit, and the difficulty of opposing applications supported by arguments that had been urged with much skill and efficiency, was not diminished. The commercial affairs of the state did not, however, require extensive banking institutions, and the resources of the farming interest was but illy calculated to meet the demands and to comply with their necessary regulations. But the consequences which would ensue to the state from the increase of a circulating medium that is not the representative of real wealth, was not discerned.

The zeal and untiring efforts of the applicants produced an acquiescence among a majority of the members for granting their requests. Management then became necessary in many instances for uniting upon the places of location in some counties where banks were granted.— Arguments of this kind were raised in favor of these incorporations, that many of the commercial cities in Europe had for a long succession of years been greatly benefited by them. And further, that the bank of the United States, granted in 1781, had contributed much toward the achievement of the American independence. That the state of Rhode Island, having more than one bank to every town in the state, has raised her reputation and enriched her citizens by this means, and to them is she in a great degree indebted for the unexampled prosperity of her manufactures.

After lengthy and animated debates, most of the petitions for banking charters were sustained by a considerable majority.

1827. Under the executive authority of the former governor, a communication was received from the ordinance department of the United States, respecting the arms for the use of Vermont, which was noticed by the governor. Also a view of the attempt to alter the constitution, so as to prevent the re-election of any one to the presidency, however just, wise and prosperous his administration may have been; but this proposal was commented on as ominous of evil consequences to the government of the Union.

The subject of a common school education engaged much of the attention of the legislature. For investigating the principles which afford the best method of instruction and the more easy and adequate way of discharging the expenses, the legislature employed considerable time and attention. A general plan was finally adopted for establishing a uniform method of instruction, which was, "that each organized town in the state shall keep and support a school or schools, provided with a teacher of good morals, for the instruction of youth in orthography, reading, writing, English grammar, geography, arithmetic, history of the United States, and good behaviour." It was further provided, that each town should appoint a committee at their annual meeting, for the purpose of superintending all the public schools in the town, which are supported at the expense of the public. It is the duty of this board to examine the instructors and visit the corporation—to enquire into the regulations and discipline of the schools, and the habits and proficiency of the scholars. They are to make a report by the third Thursday in October of the number of school districts, the length of time that schools have been taught therein, and the whole number of pupils between the ages of four and eighteen that have been instructed in the course of the year. Teachers are obliged to be examined by this board, and receive of them a certificate of their qualifications for teaching, before they are entitled to pay for their services.

A board consisting of five commissioners was also appointed, whose duty it is to meet annually, and oftener if it should be deemed necessary, to make and prepare a list of school books, from which they shall advise the superintending committees to select the books in the common schools, to procure information on the subjects connected with the education of youth, and examine into the operation and effects produced by the laws of this state for the support of common schools, and see if any alterations in the law are necessary to be made, and make an annual report to the legislature. This board made their first report at the succeeding session of the legislature, which has been anticipated on account of the connected view which it was desirable to present on the subject. "It cannot be necessary (observe the commissioners) to urge upon the consideration of the legislature of a free and sovereign people, the vital importance of making ample provision for the support of common schools. They are the broad and deep fountains from which must issue the streams of knowledge and virtue, that will ensure strength and durability to our political institutions, and give harmony and beauty to all the relations of social life. Experience attests the truth of the maxim that intelligence and morality are essential to liberty. Our constitution and all our legislative enactments are but recorded expressions of the popular will. How necessary is it then that the public mind should be enlightened and the tone of public morals elevated! Love of country can only exist in its true sense where knowledge is cultivated, where the arts and sciences are cherished. It is a source of proud satisfaction to the citizens of Vermont, that her legislature has, by repeated acts and resolves, treated the education of youth as a matter of high public concern, and recognized the expediency and justice of providing for this important object at the public expense." This report contains sentiments which ought to be registered in the memory of every individual in the state.

A resolution proposing an amendment to the constitution of the United States, presented by the state of Georgia, which provided that the president of the United States should be chosen by the freemen generally, was taken up by the legislature, and a resolution passed declaring it inexpedient to amend the constitution of the general government in relation to the mode of election of the president.

1828. Mr. Crafts received a majority of votes over the opposing candidates for governor, and his long acquaintance with public business rendered his accession to the dignified office pleasant and easy. "I congratulate my fellow citizens upon the prosperous condition of our country. At a time of peace with the whole world, the great interests of our nation, adds he, are fostered and protected—our population and resources increasing at a ratio unprecedented in the history of man." The revenue of the government is collected in a manner the least burthensome to the people, and being so abundant as to defray the ordinary expenses of the national government and contribute largely to the permanent defence and internal improvement of the country, and rapidly to reduce the public debt. Our government bears so lightly on the people as to be felt only in the consciousness of the security it gives. "This unexampled prosperity, in connexion with the civil and religious liberty enjoyed under our free institutions, places within the reach of the citizens of the United States greater means for happiness than ever fell to the lot of any other people." Such was then and now is the condition of the American people that they have no occasion to look abroad for liberty, prosperity and peace.

The services and sufferings of the revolutionary soldiers was taken up by the legislature, and a resolution requiring that the senators and representatives in Congress from this state should be requested to exert their influence in procuring a pension for those American citizens who served in the war of the revolution, whether they did or did not need the assistance of their country. The former method of distribution had occasioned feelings of displeasure. Those who were affluent in circumstances among the old soldiers and officers of the revolution, considered pensions as a reward of merit, rather than an actual contribution for the support of the needy. Therefore the distribution made in the pension list appeared partial and invidious. The object of the aforesaid resolutions was to remove all unfavorable impressions from those whose services deserved so well of their country.

After Mr. Adams' induction into office, a vigilant opposition to his administration commenced. The waves of disappointed feelings first broke upon the shores of the middle states, which spread by degrees until the violence of the electioneering campaign became general in its effects. In this political ferment, general Jackson was selected as the proper person for the presidency, because he was inflexible and unsophisticated with political chicanery; and, in the language of many, was declared the second saviour of this country—the only person who would dare to correct the abuses of executive patronage, and accomplish, by the weight of his character, more than his predecessor could with all his exertions properly directed. Since the organization of the government there never had been a political controversy of more virulence or of a more formidable character than the one upon the subject of the last presidential election. The states were separated into two grand political parties, one of whom was in favor of the administration and re-election of Mr. Adams, and the other strenuously engaged in supporting general Jackson's claims to the presidency. Nothing that could be effected by argument, misstatement or ridicule, was unimproved in the irritation and heat of party zeal. Not only the public transactions of the candidates, but the occurrences of their private lives, were severely scrutinized and censured by those who were in favor of one or the other of the candidates, and in like manner prejudiced against the other. The qualifications, talents and character of the favorite of each party was extolled and represented as the most perfect standard of human excellence. Among such a variety of statements and contradictions as the public journals of that period spread before the people, it was impossible to determine from the evidence contained in them what were the merits or faults, talents or inability, integrity or corruption, of the two gentlemen respectively supported for the presidency of the federal government.— The southern, western, and a part of the middle states, were in favor of the character and claims of general Jackson, and succeeded in securing his election by a very considerable majority. Such a scene of confusion and irruption of friendly sentiments is sincerely to be lamented, and every individual friendly to America must desire that it should never transpire again. Temperate exertions, calling forth a suitable degree of emulation, are as necessary in politics as in the laborious or professional pursuits in life; for surely the liberty and independence of the United States would sink into forgetfulness and ruin were inactivity and ignorance to prevail. But the improper proceedings of a relentless and persecuting opposition, produces anarchy and finally the overthrow of republican liberty.

1829. By the votes of the freemen of Vermont, Mr. Crafts was again elected to preside over the state. Among the variety of subjects which came before the house, the report of the sheriff and commissioners of jail delivery was submitted to a committee appointed for that purpose by the legislature, who stated that the whole number of commitments, except in Franklin county, was 4,091, for four years ending with October 1st, 1829. The number discharged during that period was 2,085.

A communication was laid before the legislature by the governor, comprising certain resolutions passed by the legislature of South-Carolina, denying the constitutional power of Congress to regulate duties on imports for the encouragement of domestic industry, in building roads and canals in the states, or in any way to patronize the American colonization society; together with an exposition of the injurious effects of the tariff upon the prosperity of the agricultural states. Also, reports from Georgia, Virginia and Missouri, adopted by the legislatures of these states, upon the same subjects, supporting the constitutional construction maintained by the state of South Carolina. These communications, relating to subjects so closely connected with the great interests and prosperity of the country, and being the deliberate acts of four members of the national confederacy, were received as worthy of that attention and consideration which is due to the importance of the subjects and the high sources from which they emanated.

A committee to whom the resolutions were referred, reported that they were "unable to perceive any constitutional obstacle to such laws, or conclusive evidence of their inexpediency or injurious and oppressive effects upon the southern states, or any other particular section of the country." The legislature thereupon resolved, that they would not concur with the resolutions denying to Congress the constitutional right to regulate the tariff and to make appropriations for internal improvements.

The tempest of the presidential controversy had scarcely ceased agitating the public, when a beacon of approaching danger suddenly arose in the western sky, which soon encircled the horizon with the angry elements of contention. The alleged disclosures of freemasonry, by one William Morgan, of Buffalo, in 1826; his abduction and confinement in a fortress at Niagara, and his secret disappearance immediately afterwards, aroused and agitated the feelings of the public in the immediate vicinity of the transaction, and soon after throughout the United States. In pursuing enquiries respecting the destiny of Morgan, before courts of justice, by committees appointed for that purpose, and in the public journals, no authority or power emanating from the federal or state governments, was discovered or proved to have been employed in taking, confining and disposing of the alleged offender; but the sheriff of Niagara county was convicted, fined and imprisoned for the part he took in the transaction. The will and vengeance of individuals, acting under the phrenzy of a mistaken authority, or under the impression of a high crime committed against the fraternity, or otherwise in pursuance of the secret mandates of the association to which he belonged, and whose principles he professedly disclosed, (as has since been legally proved) secured and disposed of him in a way that seemed to them best.— A strong and powerful combination seized and secretly conveyed him more than one hundred miles, through a very populous part of the country, to the place of tragical exit. Soon after the perpetration of this act, governor Clinton issued a proclamation offering a liberal reward to any individual who would apprehend either or all of the actors in this conspiracy. There was an artful and obstinate resistance in the management of many of the witnesses who were called upon by the government to testify in trials upon this transaction.

Many important facts in the affair were concealed from the public, because the witnesses under oath were not at liberty, as they asserted, according to their masonic obligations, to testify upon certain points of enquiry. The bonds of fellowship between themselves and the lodge, were declared paramount to their allegiance and submission to the government. Some of the witnesses refusing to testify, were fined and imprisoned for disobeying the ordinances of the government, which orders were complied with by the delinquents, rather than to permit an exposure of their knowledge to the dishonor of their brotherhood. From the testimony of others, who disclosed freely whatever they had cognizance of, it appeared that the offender received the punishment of death.

In this secret and unlawful manner perished the professed revealer of the secrets of masonry. Those implicated in aiding and assisting in the transaction, were members of the masonic institution. It was therefore alleged that the masonic obligations universally bound its members to proceed in a similar manner, under a like violation of their rules; and that this act of certain individuals was sanctioned by the masonic oaths and obligations. On the other hand, it has been maintained by members of the institution, that no such regulation ever did exist; that its design and end was for the cultivation of friendship, benevolence, and a species of universal language, which would benefit them in any clime or country wherever masonry might prevail; that the Morgan outrage was as strongly condemned by them as by any portion of the community; that they knew of no regulation in their fraternities for civil preference, punishing with death an offending brother, or secreting any that were guilty of murder or other high crimes. These were some of the arguments and assertions used in their appeals and addresses, which have been made in justification of masonry.*

Evidence, of another and very different character, has been further adduced by the opponents of masonry.— This was of a positive and direct character, furnished by the renunciations of seceding masons. The Le Roy convention of associated masons renounced masonry, surrendered their charters, substantiated the truths of Morgan's illustrations, and declared that the substance of masonry was literally before the world. Numerous individuals of distinguished rank and elevated characters have also added their testimony in confirmation of what has been said, that masonry was revealed, and more than this, that it was a silent conspiracy against the supreme power of the land and the common rights of the American citizens. Partiality of one member towards another in public appointments, and protection given in all cases of danger or crimes, are enumerated as accumulative evidence of the treasonable character of the order. The utterance of such sentiments had a direct tendency to raise up formidable parties in several of the states: masonic and anti-masonic were the badges of party distin .on.— Vermont was not the foremost state in the controversy: her numbers in the outset opposed to masonry were very few, in comparison with the votaries of the order. But during its progress, certain influential individuals avowed their opposition and exerted much influence upon society against such institutions. Men of experience and celebrity in the state have seceded from a membership with the fraternity, and declared it both a useless and dangerous institution, while they gave their testimony to the truth of the disclosures and revelations made respecting masonry. The rancor of feelings elicited upon the subject soon passed from the bickerings of individuals to political canvassings for civil appointments.

The first year, however, that it became a political question in the state, there was no nomination of candidates for state officers made out, but a kind of compromise ticket from those who had never been initiated into the lodge, was got up. A convention was holden in August, 1829, consisting of those opposed to the principles of freemasonry, and resolutions were published expressive of their views of the influence and character of masonry, and recommending certain measures as necessary to be persued in securing its overthrow. Nothing further occurred upon the subject, worthy of notice, until the meeting of the legislature the ensuing fall; when an appeal to the people was issued from the grand lodge in Vermont, signed by 168 masons. Their language was, if they were to remain silent, they should be guilty of inflicting no less an injury upon others than upon themselves, "for were we quietly to submit to the dispensation and dissemination of error, and a political party to be built up on it, destructive of the liberty of the people, when we possess the power to expose the falsity of the representations, we should, to say the least, display an unwarrantable and reprehensible disregard for the safety of the free institutions under which we live." They also declared " themselves guiltless in any manner of entertaining the remotest suspicion that the life of a fellow being was subject to their control." From their remarks, the inference is deducible that it is a scientific, useful and charitable institution, suited to the wants and dignified enjoyments of life.

Sometime in the month of July, a most destructive storm of hail spread over the northern part of Addison county. Commencing in the state of New-York, it passed over lake Champlain, in a direction from the north-west to the south-east, about half a mile in width; and so great was its violence that it destroyed and beat down the grass and all kinds of cultivated vegetables. Hail stones of several inches in diameter fell and broke most of the glass in the buildings opposite to the storm.

1830. The valley of lake Champlain and the adjacent highlands was visited by one of the most severe and remarkable calamities of the kind that was ever experienced in the memory of the oldest inhabitants. A storm of rain, commencing in the afternoon of the 24th of July, continued with but slight abatements till Tuesday noon, and from that time with less violence to Thursday morning.— For several days previous, the weather had been remarkably sultry and dry. The wind changed about the same time the storm commenced from the south to the northwest, and light clouds, attended in some parts with shocks of thunder, passed rapidly through the sky. At first, a slight sprinkling of rain descended, which continued increasing until the water fell in torrents, with scarce an intermission, till morning; at which time the cellars were filled with water, and streams and rivers were swelled to the highest extent of former freshets. It continued raining with unabating violence through Sunday and Monday. The people in the vallies began now to look with fearful anxiety for the safety of their lives and possessions, but were not apprehensive of the awful calamity which awaited them in the dark and dreary hours of midnight. A vast accumulation of clouds settled upon the mountains, from which proceeded every few minutes dreadful shocks of thunder and streams of livid lightning. The aqueous element appeared to descend in streams and rushed in cataracts down the sides of the hills and mountains, bearing away in the raging current, rocks, woods, houses, fences, bridges and mills, and rolled them along on the majesty of the billows. The whole surrounding country to the height of fifteen feet above the natural current of the streams, presented, in the course of Monday evening, one extended sheet of water. All the grain and growing vegitables upon the intervals were beat down and destroyed, and almost every mill and machine propelled by water on the larger streams, together with the fences, bridges and several buildings, passed away like a leaf in the violence of a whirlwind. Houses and barns and other buildings rose upon the water and were soon dashed in pieces.— The force of the storm was experienced in Vermont upon Onion and New-Haven rivers and their tributaries, together with the whole extent of country intervening between them. Great damages were sustained upon the banks of Onion river, as almost the whole produce of it thereon was swept away in the flood. But the most dreadful and melancholy instance of destruction occasioned by the rain, happened at Beeman's Hollow, in New-Haven. New-Haven river had rose to such an unprecedented height, on Monday, that the owners of mills and some of their neighbors had assembled to consult upon their safety. Darkness had now veiled the earth in obscurity, and the rain continued to pour down incessantly: Yet no one had the least suspicion that their lives were endangered, or that the raging element would soon convey them to unexperienced scenes of eternity. It was near the hour of midnight, and none had intelligence that ten or twelve feet of head water was rushing furiously towards them and soon to ingulf them in its bosom. The river at the upper part of the settlement formed a new channel in the road and completely isolated the place where the mills and houses were situated. Twenty-one persons were in and about these buildings, surrounded by water. Two of them plunged into the stream of the new formed channel, and swam safely to the highlands. Some of those remaining attempted to escape upon a raft which they had constructed, but did not succeed. The houses and mills in the upper part of the settlement began to give way, when, suddenly, the whole, except one house, which had just been deserted by several persons for a more secure situation, as they supposed, in a barn, were precipitated in the abyss below. A vast accumulation of flood-wood from the whole length of the river, together with the wreck of buildings and lumber at this place, dashed down the rough and rocky channel of the river, the water in which was more than twenty feet higher than was ever known before.

Nineteen persons were carried along in this torrent every moment exposed to be dashed upon the rocks or bruised between the floating timber. Five of those precipitated into the stream escaped the cold embrace of death, which their remaining associates in this calamity experienced. These providentially preserved their lives—four of them lodging upon rocks and trees about three fourths of a mile from where they were preticipated, and the other, Lemuel B. Eldridge, Esq. who was carried down about the same distance, but happened to float into a cornfield, then flooded several feet deep with a rapid stream of water. He there got on to a rise of land, sufficient, by standing erect, to keep his head out of the water. In this perilous and uncomfortable situation, he continued from about two o'clock until day-light, when, by the assistance of the people collected on the banks of the river, he, with those lodged on eminences near, were rescued at the same time from impending destruction. The bodies of thirteen of those who perished were found at various distances from the scene of this dreadful catastrophe.

Mr. Crafts not having a majority of the votes given in for a governor of the state, was elected by the house of representatives, after a long and obstinate contest. The citizens of the state had been considerably engaged on the subject of election for some time previous to its transpiring. In the present political controversy three parties made their appearance, and presented claims for the election of their candidates, with much earnestness and zeal. On canvassing the votes at the opening of the legislature, the whole number given for the three candidates was 30,686; of these 13,486 were for Crafts, 10,925 for Palmer, the antimasonic candidate, and 6,235 for Meech, the administration candidate. Governor Crafts was supported by the masons, and had a plurality of the votes. Palmer had something more than one third of the whole. The choice of a governor therefore going before the legislative body, the representatives of the parties took an uncompromising stand in supporting a candidate of their particular party. After thirty-two ballotings, governor Crafts was re-elected by a small majority over the other two candidates, and, in like manner, Mr. Richards was chosen lieutenant-governor. The governor's speech to the legislature contained sentiments suited to the dignity of his station and the circumstances of the people.

The law for imprisoning poor debtors, originating in a foreign country and at a remote period, when the civil and political rights of man were imperfectly known and but little regarded, he requested the attention of the legislature to see if some measure could not be taken to relieve this unfortunate class of community. On the subject of education, he observed, that the "mode of instruction adopted in common schools, and in some degree in those of a higher order, is directed more to the improvement of the faculties than to form and fix the character of the youth. To qualify them to perform the high and responsible duties of freemen, they, in addition to the usual course of instruction, should be instructed also in the principles of our free institutions—in the social relations and duties—in a love of country, of order, morality and religion, and whatever shall tend to establish correct habits and principles."— The message throughout was a very sensible and appropriate communication. However, not many of the topics presented were acted upon.

The abolition of imprisonment for debt had for a series of years been attempted, both by the federal and state legislatures. Benevolence, patriotism, and all the finer feelings of the heart have been in favor of a universal emancipation of poor debtors, confined in jail upon judgements obtained on civil contracts. The arguments in favor of such a law, are, that if a person buys a piece of property and engages to pay so much money or other specific articles, he does not, on failure of payment, engage to divest himself of his liberty, or have his body confined in prison, because, unfortunately, he is not able to perform the contract:—That property only should be subject to attachment, not the body. It is repugnant to civil liberty, that men should be confined in consequence of their owing a few dollars, which they have not ability to discharge. The opposition urged against such mild, or at least alleviating measures, was, the ready access to fraudulent practices in changing property into cash or paper security, and also leaving the creditor without any redress or method of securing the debt where no clue could be had for discovering property, without the privilege of examining the debtor upon his oath. After considerable debate, an act was passed, that on all judgements obtained upon debts made after the first day of January, 1831, the debtor may, within two hours after the rendition of such judgement before a court of justice, submit himself to an examination on oath by such court or creditor, or his attorney, touching his situation, circumstances or property, and may be entitled to the benefit of the oath, which shall be administered to such debtor by said court or justice, and a record made thereof, and no execution shall be issued thereon. Many were in favor of extending the provisions of the bill so as to exempt the debtor from arrest in all cases of contract; but the majority decided that the provision now made was a sufficient relief in the present state of affairs.

The petition of Norman Cleveland, now under sentence of death for the murder of Hannah Rose, praying that his punishment might be commuted to a sentence of imprisonment in the state penitentiary, was determined, after an animated debate, in favor of his imprisonment for five years. This was the first instance of the kind, except

Bourn's, who was afterwards proved innocent by the return of Colvin, the supposed dead man, that the power of changing the mode of punishment incident to this branch of the government, was ever exercised. There might be a reason why many people were somewhat surprised that such a crime as was proved in this case should only receive the same punishment as his who had passed a one dollar counterfeit bill.

The usual business of the legislature was accomplished without a continuation of those party exertions which were manifested at the commencement of the session.

On examining the proceedings of the legislature for a long succession of years, there is much anxiety experienced by the writer; fearing lest he should not fully comprehend the views or justly represent the conduct of parties. The business of stating facts correct, is not difficult; but judging of those matters which are the most suitable for historical narration, is troublesome. On giving an account of the legislative assemblies of this country, the minds of men appear to be influenced by the same motives and passions in this as in any other quarter of the globe. "Where their own individual advantage and emoluments are out of view, the men who are clothed with authority will be much influenced by considerations of justice and equity, by moral and social principles."— When their own advancement is dependent on the principles they embrace, it is always expected that they will be in danger of being swayed by their interest, governed by their passions, and irritated by opposition. Let the form of government be what it may, whenever men seek their own wealth and advancement, it is not surprising to find them combined in assisting and supporting each other, and in humbling their opposers. "Their passions rise and rule; their reason loses its influence and force; crime, guilt and shame are divided into equal shares, and no man means or expects to take a large portion to himself. In legislative assemblies, the representatives do not wish to ascertain what will be proper and useful to the state, but how much the people can be made to believe and bear. The facts ought to be otherwise: the person who is chosen for a legislator should be capable of rising above such feelings : he should be qualified for something more than legislative traffic of bargain and sale, or of stipulating by the sale of his vote to carry some measure in favor of himself or his party, without any regard to public expediency.

The only checks upon the legislative branches of the government, are popular sentiments and feelings. So long then as the people are free, intelligent, active and virtuous, they will know and understand the principles of their own government and call to account the conduct of their rulers. The destruction or continuance of the American government does not therefore depend upon the conduct of their representatives, but upon the state and condition of society.

CHAPTER XIII.

Condition of Society.—Different employments of the people.—Agriculture.—Manufactures.—Commerce.—Literature.

Not a century ago the state of Vermont was an entire wilderness, covered with forest trees, shrubbery and various species of wild plants. Antiquities of a former civilized settlement have never been discovered, nor were there the least traces of human existence remaining, except occasional residences of the Indian. The soil had for ages been enriched with decaying vegetables, and the streams had been gradually wearing down the highlands. This was the situation of the country when the emigrants began to make this state the abode of civilization. Lands were very cheap and usually cantoned out in farms from fifty to one hundred acres each. The first business of the husbandman in this new settlement, was to clear the land of timber, sow crops, erect necessary buildings and open roads, and thus form communications between the scattered settlements. A farm of convenient size was purchased with the surplus produce of two or three years labor, beside furnishing the necessary provisions of living for a family. When industry was applied to the soil, a great profit accrued. The first crop generally paid for the labor of raising and increased the value of the land ten times the original cost. An acre of land was made in one year of such value that it would yield annually ten or fifteen dollars worth of produce. The profits of labor in a new settlement are in this way the greatest that can be realized in agriculture. Great wages were obtained in the production of a crop and the addition of a tract of cultivated land to a farm.

Whether agriculture is considered as the means of furnishing the necessaries or luxuries of life—of providing a security against famine and disease, or of engaging the mind in active enterprise or the pursuits of general knowledge, it is the most useful and important of all arts which has ever employed the attention of mankind. The food and raiment of every individual are derived from the land or water, but in this state almost entirely from the land.— Therefore agriculture supports and maintains all other employments, and deserves the greatest encouragement.— Wealth obtained by agriculture is permanent and fixed, as it is generally vested in real estate and is free from those uncertainties attendant upon the business of commerce, and independent of the restrictions of other countries.— Besides the utility of agricultural pursuits, there are pleasures, for a contemplative mind, of the highest order. The causes for advancement are the same in agriculture as in the mechanical or professional pursuits. In the early ages of the world ignorance was an imposing obstruction to an accumulation of agricultural productions, and even operated as a barrier to the progress of population. But necessity and social intercourse awakened the slumbering genius of man and directed his attention to a choice in the management of his flocks and the better cultivation of his fields. Thus men were led to consider the adaptation of labor to the soil a means for obtaining a greater and better production of crops, and introduced methods of improvement highly beneficial to the country.

All other professions, particularly the liberal arts, are of great importance, which man in a civilized state cannot do without. Yet they derive their importance from the imperfections of human nature, and add nothing of themselves to the wealth of nations. The learned professions, the philosopher and the statesman, are engaged in great and important business; yet the learned Dr. Franklin said that he who makes two blades of grass grow where one did before, does more for the benefit of his country than the most distinguished statesman. The one adds nothing to the wealth, but the other furnishes the whole support of human existence. Health may be preserved—property accumulated—morals improved—the understanding invigorated, and proper direction given to the mind by the other arts; but agriculture furnishes the means and gives support to them all. The glory of nations has been more enhanced by this art than by all the discoveries and improvements in science. Hence the ancient Romans esteemed agriculture so honorable an employment, that their most distinguished senators applied themselves at intervals of leisure to the cultivation of the soil; and such was the amiable simplicity of those times, that their greatest warriors and legislators were often called from the active labors of the field to the highest offices in the state. Regulus, the celebrated Roman general, when in Africa, requested of the senate to be recalled, lest his farm might suffer from want of proper cultivation in his absence; and the senate wrote to him for answer that the public would attend to his business. The Emperor of China goes an-annually, on an appointed day, to the field, and there, to show his sense of the inestimable value of agriculture, he personally undertakes the task of holding the plough. A high estimation has been given to the subject of agriculture in many of the kingdoms of Europe. Societies have been formed, and the business has been introduced as a study in the seminaries of learning.

The legislature of this state incorporated the Vermont agricultural society in 1806; and after that, the county societies were chartered. The effect of these societies, so far as the counties acted in pursuance of their corporate privileges, have very considerably increased the prosperity of the state. Better crops, and a more valuable stock of cattle and horses, have been raised by the farmers of Vermont than was done at any former period; and much of the soil which was judged incapable of cultivation has been brought to a very fertile and productive state. The importation of merino sheep into this state from Spain, and more recently, of the Saxony breed, has added much to the value of our flocks. Wool now grown is worth twenty cents more a pound than it formerly was, and the quantity taken from the same number of sheep exceeds very considerably what it used to be. Breeds of every kind of domestic animals have been very much improved within a few years, and great profits have been realized from the same. The soil is such, and the seasons are so uncertain, for the perfection of crops of grain, that grazing is the most sure and profitable branch of agriculture which the farmer of Vermont can attend to with success. And from this source the principal exportations are derived. It is for the pleasure and profitable entertainment of the husbandman's mind, that the nature of his occupation obliges him to contemplate a great variety of objects and things. The state of the soil and climate must be familiar, and what the different parts of his farm will produce. The growth and production of vegetables, grain and fruits, which can be raised with profit, engages his attention.— The constitution, genius and pursuit of animals from which the most profit can be derived, and which can be raised and governed to the greatest advantage, is understood by him. The seasons, winds and weather, so far as can be anticipated from the various operations of nature, become matters of constant observation. These subjects belong to the various sciences of natural history and philosophy, and are familiar to the experience of the husbandman.

The morality of mankind appears to be intimately connected with those employments which are the most useful and necessary. Hence the business of agriculture, which furnishes the support of society, appears to be nearer allied to virtue than any of the arts. Instances have never occurred of a body of farmers becoming debauched and corrupt. Their pursuits have a tendency to make them industrious, moral, and honest. Political demagogues and aspirants for office are the persons most familiar with the practices of corruption and venality. Vermont, being entirely an inland state, must acquire the actual, necessary and fashionable articles of life from agriculture or manufactures. The products for exportation are principally derived from the forest, or animal and vegetable cultivation,—the two latter of these enter principally into the consumption of the people, and probably will in a few years furnish but very inconsiderable quantities for exportation. Horses, cattle and sheep are the only animals that can be raised to much profit in this state, and these, from the decreasing fertility of a long cultivated soil, and from the long duration of cold weather in this section of the Union, are frequently raised with but very little advance from their actual cost. Wool has, since the operation of the tariff upon importations of foreign commodities, yielded the greatest profit on a given capital of any agricultural production; and should the manufacture of woollens still continue to increase, the business may hereafter become more profitable. Wheat, rye, corn, and other grain and vegetables were, upon the clearing of the new lands, much safer crops, more easy to be raised, and altogether more productive than they now are, and the wants of society were much less then than at present. This gave a great and rapid increase to the wealth of the people. Property was then easily accumulated; whereas it now takes much severe labor and hazardous enterprize to gain a competence, and much more to rise to easy and independent circumstances.

MANUFACTURES.—Cotton goods have for some years been extensively manufactured in several towns in this state. The aid of water power and machinery has enabled the manufacturers of this article to compete with the European workshops; but the fabrication might be extended still further, with increasing profit, was the stamping of calico introduced.

Woollen cloths, of which there is a considerable amount imported for the consumption of the state, are manufactured to a great profit, on quite a limited capital. Large quantities might be made, particularly for supplying the wants of the southern parts of the United States. Flax succeeds well in our soil; often, four or five hundred pounds are raised, which before the use of cottons was manufactured in almost every family. The culture of hemp has not, until recently, received much attention, and that on a limited scale. In particular destricts of the state attempts at raising it upon land not properly enriched and prepared, and the method of getting it out by the aid of machinery, have quite checked the cultivation of it. In Europe, where hemp is extensively cultivated, the climate corresponds with the northern parts of the United States. Hence it does not require to be acclimated to a high northern latitude, to come to perfection. It might be a very profitable article for exportation, if it was properly attended to. The manufacture of iron has been and will continue to be a profitable business. Iron is found in large quantities in Swanton, Bristol, Monkton, Brandon, Pittsford, Tinmouth, Bennington, and other places on the west side of the green mountains. The ore is of a redish color, mixed with earth and tinctured with yellow ochre. It is very fusible and yields about one fifth part of iron. In some places there is a kind of rock ore, called hematite, very hard, but of a richer quality than the other. The iron obtained from this ore is very soft and excellent for nails. Most of the ore which has been used in the manufacture of bar iron has been taken from the beds on the west side of lake Champlain, at Arnold's mine, and various other places, as it extensively abounds in this ironbound region. This ore is granular, of a steel color and almost in a state of pure iron, and when prudently managed will yield from fifty to sixty per cent. It makes excellent iron for such articles as are to be drawn length-ways.

The county of Essex, and many parts adjoining, abound with ore of the purest quality. Manufactories have been established, such as furnaces and forges, for the purpose of making iron, in many towns on the western side of the mountain. There are blast furnaces at Highgate, Sheldon, Vergennes, Brandon, Tinmouth, Pittsford, Clarendon, Wallingford, Dorset, Manchester, Bennington and Fairfield, and forges in a large number of towns from Canada line to Massachusetts. On account of the facilities and raw materials in Vermont, nature no doubt has designed this portion of the Union to be a flourishing seat of iron manufacturing.

At Stratford and Shrewsbury there are extensive beds of the sulphuret of iron, from which immense quantities of copperas are manufactured. A considerable depth of earth covers this stratum of ore. Ferruginous petrefactions, which exhibit forms of buds, leaves and limbs of trees in great perfection, are found below this body, which varies very considerable in depth. Under this lies the bed of sulphuret of iron, in a very compact form, and its color varying from that of steel to a bright yellow ore, very brilliant, and in many places diversified by small quantities of green copperas. Some parts of the ore are detached from the bed by blasting, being then broke in pieces and thrown into heaps of different dimensions. In this situation exposure to the action and moisture of the atmosphere occasions spontaneous combustion, and the whole pile is converted from a sulphuret to the sulphate of iron, which process generally requires several weeks. The sulphuret of iron is a combination of iron and sulpher in their primitive state, and the sulphate of iron is a combination of iron and a sulphuric acid or oil of vitriol. By being exposed to the atmosphere, it takes fire and is converted into sulphuric acid; and this acid, as it is thus formed, combines with the iron, and converts it into the sulphate of iron, which is copperas. After this process, it is leached in vats, and the ley passed off to boilers. Here it is boiled to a certain consistence, and is from thence transported to chrystalizers, where the copperas continues to chrystalize for some time, and when that ceases, it is returned to the boilers again to be evaporated. About three hundred tons are manufactured at each place yearly. Pot and pearl ashes are yet made in considerable quantities, although mostly of ashes collected from culinary fires.— Since the state has become generally cleared, but few ashes are made from the burning of timber in the woods. The use of stoves has also diminished them to a much smaller amount.

The manufacture of maple sugar, some years ago, was of very great importance to the state. More than one half of the families in Vermont were engaged in this business, and they manufactured more sugar than was necessary for their consumption. This kind of business is not as much attended to now as formerly, except in the towns on the mountain, where large groves of maple trees still remain. In some towns in the southern parts of the state, a second growth of thrifty maples produce large quantities of saccharine juice, which is of a quality far exceeding that produced by the first growth. Halifax and Guilford, in Vermont, and Colerain, in Massachusetts, probably make more sugar, in good seasons, than the people require for their consumption. Their groves are mostly of the second growth, on lands which have been chopped over or cleared. As soon as the weather is sufficiently warm to thaw the timber in the spring, an incision is made in the tree, either with an auger or axe, into which a spout is inserted, which conveys the juice to a receiver. From thence it is taken to a place fitted up for boiling, either in the lot or at the house. It is there evaporated in a pan of copper or sheet iron, set in an arch, to the consistency of molasses; then filtered and boiled down to sugar. Two or three hundred weight of sugar can be made with a very little trouble or expense from one hundred trees. There is no better sugar than what is made from the maple, and when properly refined has a peculiarly rich, salubrious and pleasant taste. The sap runs plentifully while the trees are frozen at night and thawed through the day. As soon, however, as the buds start the sap ceases to flow. The quantity of maple sugar made in this state has been estimated at 6,000,000 pounds; but this probably exceeds the real amount.

Marble of a very superior quality and of various shades and colors is found in the towns along the margin of lake Champlain, and is manufactured in considerable quantities at Swanton, Middlebury, Pittsford and Vergennes.

Distilleries for extracting spirituous liquors from grain or oils from various species of vegetables, have been put in operation in almost every town in the state. These did a great amount of business during the late war, in making potatoe whiskey; but they have very much diminished within a few years. Other manufactures of various commodities used by the inhabitants of the state, are numerous, and some of them profitable.

COMMERCE.—The commercial business of Vermont has

much increased within a few years past. Large quantities of goods are imported from New-York, Boston, Portland, and some from Canada, into almost every town and section of the state. Various kinds of articles for necessary or fashionable use or dress, and all manner of groceries for accommodation or convenience, and every species of manufacture, whether fanciful or substantial, are imported for sale among the people. Live cattle, horses, hogs, beef, pork, lumber, pot and pearl ashes, bar and pig iron, grain of various kinds, tanned leather, cotton and woollen goods, are exported. An exact amount of the commerce of an inland state cannot be ascertained, nor is it possible to determine what quantity of goods are annually brought into the state, or to what value the remittances generally amount. Trade is valuable to a country to the amount of whatever in produce or domestic manufactures the people have to spare, after reserving a sufficiency for their own consumption. But farther than this commercial business has a tendency to destroy the credit, ruin the funds, and impoverish the circumstances of the people.

New-York is the grand emporium of trade for the valley of lake Champlain, and Boston that of Connecticut river. Before the imposition of duties upon the trade with the Canadas great quantities of produce were annually transported there from the northern part of the state; but the restrictions now almost amount to a prohibition.

The amount of business has increased exceedingly upon lake Champlain, since the opening of the northern canal and the sailing by steam upon its waters. Navigation is open from the city of New-York, for boats of a small burthen, through the river to lake Champlain. The amount of shipping employed in every kind of transportation on the lake is almost incredible. In 1826 the number was ascertained to be three hundred and seventy-eight in all that sailed the lake.

The commerce of the state has been very much promoted within the last thirty years by the establishment of turnpike roads. It was a long time before the legislature would make a grant of the kind, being very much prejudiced against corporations of this kind. But grants have been made from time to time, so that there are now turnpike roads, crossing the green mountains, on Onion river; from Middlebury to Woodstock, from Clarendon to Bellows-Falls, from Chester to Manchester, from Bennington to Brattleborough, from Woodstock to Pittsford, and from Montpelier to Norwich; with various others in different parts of the state. These have increased the facilities of trade and transportation very considerably.— Such is the prevailing spirit of the times for trading in merchandize, and such immense quantities are obtained from the commercial marts, that the business has spread out to a very extraordinary extent; so much so as to hazard the interest and credit of community. Commercial business having more inducements than agriculture or manufactures: therefore numbers have engaged in it from a choice business, rather than from the public demands.

From the eastern part of the state lumber is conveyed to market by means of the Connecticut river, which has been rendered navigable for rafts of timber and flat bottomed boats as far as the fifteen mile falls, at Barnet.— A small steam boat has been sailed up the river, from Hartford, Connecticut, to Windsor, in this state. But its power is not sufficient for the purposes of a general conveyance. A company for improving the navigation of Connecticut river has been incorporated by an act of the Vermont legislature, and also by acts of the other states upon its borders; the design of which is to remove obstructions and erect locks around the falls, so that boats of heavy burthen can be propelled along the stream, and in this way forming a water communication for the conveyance of produce to and from Vermont and the adjacent country. The privileges of their charter remain to be improved in such a manner and to such an extent as the funds and enterprize of the association shall be able to accomplish. Internal improvements, such as connecting the waters of lake Memphremagog by a canal with those of Connecticut river and the waters of lake Champlain by a canal or railway along Onion river to its head waters, and then back to the aforesaid river, have received the attention of the legislature, and surveys of different routes have been made. Corporate powers and privileges have been granted to such as might choose to vest their funds in this kind of public improvement. The vesting of public funds, or the authorizing of state or United States subscription, for the purpose of internal improvements, has, by those opposed to such measures, been considered a transgression to constitutional powers, particularly those of the federal constitution.

The expediency of erecting such works in Vermont depends on the emolument which would accrue to individuals and the utility which would arise to the public.— Should the amount of business done this way afford a profit equal to the interest of the capital, and the appropriations for repairs, then such investments will be advantageous.

LITERATURE.—The general sentiments of the people of Vermont have ever been favorable to the diffusion of common school education. Early provisions were made for the incorporation and maintainance of common schools in every town in the state, and afterwards a section of land in each chartered township was reserved for the furtherance of this object. The fund arising from this source was to be applied to the building of school houses and paying instructors. This amount, with a small contribution paid by each individual, constituted a sufficient provision for educating the youth of the state in the elementary branches of education, which were to learn to read with ease and propriety, to write a plain and legible hand, and be made acquainted with arithmetic, so far as was necessary for the more common and necessary occupations of life. Such a diffusion of information gives a taste for reading periodical publications and newspapers, and at the same time an acquaintance with the laws of the country, the proceedings of the courts of justice, of the general assembly of the state and of the Congress of the U. S. This cultivation of the mind, through the accessible channels of common schools, has brought into exercise sentiments of kindness, civility and patriotism. Reading for amusement, as well as instruction, has, in a considerable measure, superseded the deleterious practice of dissipating diversions. The mind has been conducted to the dignified enjoyment of reason and reflection, and from these emanations has obtained pleasures agreeable to the fancy and instructing to the understanding. Education of this kind is of more benefit to mankind than all the knowledge and disputes that metaphysical logic and scholastic theology have ever produced. For virtue, liberty and public happiness have their foundations in common sense. In whatever light we view education, it presents itself as the most important subject that can engage the attention of mankind. If the ignorance and rudeness of the savage be contrasted with the knowledge and refinements of civilized life, the difference between them is so great that they can scarcely be considered of the species; but compare the infant of the savage with that of the philosopher, and the same high powers of mind are hidden in both: in each the organs adapted to their intellectual capacities are exactly similar. The only difference which is afterwards to distinguish them depends upon the difference of their education. The mind of the savage, left neglected, will scarcely raise him above the brute; while a member of civilized society, whose capacities are unfolded by a proper education, will comprehend in the range of his intelligence the universe of God. All the beauties of creation are open before him; the sacred stores of nature are unlocked, her secret laws revealed, and all the attainments of men are made subservient to his advancement and delight. Such is its importance to mental improvement, and consequently to the happiness of man; but it is not his mental advancement alone that increases the sphere of his enjoyments: it infolds sources of more exquisite delight in the moral and religious tendencies of his nature. The savage, like the beast, acts under the guidance of instinct or from the impulse of appetite or passion: he acknowledges no law but his own will; his enjoyments are as gloomy as they are contracted, seeking gratification only from the fierceness of his passions; his devotion is a feeling of terror, and the fabric of his superstition is raised by his vices. Education raises man above the debasing control of sense, and teaches him to follow reason as the guide of his actions; it convinces him how much individual happiness is promoted by submission to government, and expands his selfishness into patriotism; and it is this also, which gives constancy to his virtues amidst every trial and adversity of life, and security to his mind amidst all its evils. However, these happy effects do not always flow from a well conducted education; vices may prevail in the most enlightened communities. The system of education may be counteracted by unfavorable circumstances; but the failure is not chargeable to education.

Sufficient patronage cannot be afforded among a farming community like Vermont to induce writers of ability and high attainments in the arts and sciences, to devote in a very great degree their time and talents to such pursuits here. Talents of a high order seek a more favored clime to unfold the resources of mental energy. Large cities, where wealth, taste and talents are assembled, furnish motives of sufficient inducement to call the learned and distinguished to a residence within their limits. Men of professional business have risen to great eminence and distinction in the service and practice of their callings.— But active employments leave little time to spend in the researches of science, as few would spend the intervals of leisure or exchange the pleasures of social intercourse for the retirement of the student's closet. Several departments of literature and science have, notwithstanding, been enriched by the explanations and the researches of distinguished individuals.

In history, doctor Williams has given a general narrative of the proceedings and character of the first settlers of this state. Many parts, treating upon the natural history, civil institutions and freedom of America, discover considerable philosophic acumen and labored investigation. The change of climate, on clearing up a new country, he ascribes to the decrease of evaporation, occasioned by the destruction of forest timber, which emitted vast quantities of aqueous fluid that fell in the winter season, in the form of snow, and in the summer descended in rain. The foundations of American freedom he ascribes to popular sentiment. His estimate of the pursuits of a people in the formation of national character, is clearly deducible from the constitution of human nature itself. The style of the work is diffuse, and some topics of description are unreasonably long for the history of a separate state. The colloction of state papers, by William Slade, is a valuable repository of ancient records, exhibited in proper order of time. The first grants and settlement of the state—the commencement of those legislative regulations which then constituted the positive law, embraced in a body of repealed and obsolete acts, have been judiciously commented on by the author. Thompson's Gazetteer is an interesting and useful work, comprising a well arranged and perspicuous view of the natural and political resources of the state. The style and descriptions, so far as the author laid claims to originality, and in some of the articles furnished by others, are perspicuous and well suited to the subject. Several smaller treatises, embracing only general events or placing the accounts in detail sufficiently brief and comprehensive for the understanding and grasp of the juvenile mind, have by different authors been given to the public.

On the subject of law, few of those who have acquired a distinguished eminence for their legal attainments and talents, have contributed any addition to the legal publications of the state. Judge Chipman's reports and forms of government claim a respectful notice, on account of the general correctness of his decisions and the logical method of his reasoning. The influence of party feelings gave no direction to the cool deliberation of his judgement. The decision of his mind was formed from the weight of testimony and a rational construction of the law. His opinions, except upon local and temporary matters, are now regarded as law.

Contracts, payable in specific articles, have been investigated by Daniel Chipman, in a work on that subject.— His constructions of the law are supported by numerous authorities strictly analagous to the points. The clearness and knowledge of the writer claim for the performance a weight of authority not inferior to the best American and European productions. His reports of cases decided in the supreme court of the state, contained in one hundred and thirty-four numbers, afford evidence of much research and discrimination in selection. Other cases adjudged by the supreme court for four years ending with 1819, have been reported from the notes taken by the judges, under an alphabetical arrangement, like some of the ancient reports of the British courts, by judge Brayton.

What the law was, in litigated matters in this state, at the commencement of the nineteenth century, was promulgated by judge Tyler. At this time, trials by jury were had before the supreme court, and many of the decisions were rendered upon a verdict. Several of the cases have since been over-ruled. An attempt at rhetorical embellishments and a wearisome diffuseness of style, characterize this performance. This work was published in 1809, at a time when any one who ventured upon such an undertaking had to meet the whole expense out of his own funds, and endure the criticism of the public.

Two volumes of law reports were published by judge Aiken, the state reporter, in 1827 and '8: also a book of forms, containing some very general and useful matter on the subject of conveyancing of real estate in the several states in the Union. Legal precedents and forms were previously published by Messrs. Simmons and Fessenden, together with the law of patents, by the latter gentleman, which embrace most of the instruments and forms, with some of the most common pleading used in courts of justice in this state. The supreme court, now legally constituted a board for reporting their own decisions, published two volumes of cases for 1829 and '30, in a style not inferior to the best productions of the other states. The opinions of the courts are rendered in clear and perspicuous terms, discovering a variety and extent of legal erudition and a consistency of reasoning easily to be understood and applied to analagous cases.

Matters of litigation are very much lessened in this state. No part of the maratime law is adopted in administering justice or in securing the rights to the citizens of this inland district of country. The alleviating provisions of a general bankrupt law has never been adopted to facilitate the progress of commercial enterprize. And the law relating to real estates has been stripped of those fictions connected with this branch of jurisprudence in England and some of the American states.

Theology has had some able writers. Doctor Burton's work upon the evidences of Christianity, is replete with sound reasoning and extensive learning. The Christian Instructor, containing a summary explanation and defence of the doctrines and duties of the Christian religion, written by reverend Josiah Hopkins, a man of strong mind and considerable learning, is deservedly popular for liberality of sentiment, candor of expression, and force of argument. Other works upon metaphysical divinity, or discussions upon the doctrine of election and fore-ordination, as connected with the freedom of the will, have been advocated in the publications of Osburn, Baylies, Niles and others. The Christian Gazetteer, by reverend W. Chapin, is a work of considerable merit. The discourses of doctor Swift and Haynes discover much thought and purity of sentiment. Those which have been published by other gentlemen of the clerical profession, are descriptive of the duties and high resposibility of the Christian character and the happy prospect of the humble and devout.

Medical science in Vermont has been well supported in the writings of doctor Gallup. His history of epidemic diseases in the state, from its first settlement to 1815, with the causes of their origin and treatment, is full of interest to the practitioner, and gives a full developement of such matters as are useful to the historian, philanthropist and the citizen. That enemy to human health and life, the consumption, which in its inroads upon society has proved the most fatal of all diseases, has been examined in a manner that may lead to an arrest of its progress.

Many individuals in the state have distinguished themselves in the different departments of the healing art.—Of the various publications that have issued from the press, in the form of newspapers or magazines, many articles in them are written with argument, eloquence and taste, as the most approved classics of the age are. Some of the speeches in courts of justice, in the councils of the state and nation, and on occasions of public rejoicing, are replete with energy, persuasion and eloquence.

CHAPTER XIV.

Character of the people.—Poor Laws.—Various Societies for the promotion of the public welfare.—American government.—Constitution and Laws of Vermont. —Counties.—Towns.—Courts, and their jurisdictional powers.—Revenue and expenses of the government.

The first settlers of Vermont were emigrants from New-England, and for the most part of an English origin. At the time of their settlement the territory now embraced in the jurisdiction of Vermont was an unbroken wilderness and exposed to the cruelties of Indian depredations and warfare. Hence none but the spirited and enterprising would place themselves in a situation to encounter these evils; and those who did had most of their time occupied in providing a subsistence for their families, which afforded them but little opportunity for the cultivation of their minds or the improvement of their manners. The character of the people, therefore, like the roughness of their native mountains, was bold and unyielding. Acquiring by their own exertions an ascendency over the perplexing difficulties that beset them, high notions of liberty and independence were entertained, and great confidence placed in their abilities. Such traits of character were fully exhibited in the several controversies which for a series of years unhappily involved them, and always marked their proceedings in the council or the field. Many of the first settlers were men of superior talents, but like the diamond in its native quarry, were unpolished. Being deprived of the advantages of learning themselves, they made early provision for bestowing the invaluable inheritance of a good education upon their posterity.

The inhabitants of a new state, trusting entirely to their own industry, and having nothing to expect from speculations or from the errors of government, directed their views and employments to the best methods of acquiring a subsistence and estate. Hence enterprize and activity in business became almost universal. They applied their attention, with the exception of a few instances of managers, gamblers and beggars, to honest and laborious pursuits. To them no hardships seemed too difficult to be overcome. A few years perseverance generally removed the obstacles that first lay in their way.

Providence has annexed great and immediate blessings to the most essential and necessary duties of man. The great exertions and hard fare which people in new countries often experience, generally tend to better health and greater longevity than the sumptuous living and idle habits of the wealthy. Temperance and labor do more towards preserving health than art or medicine can do. Disorders which wear away the inhabitants of wealthy cities, are almost unknown in the woods: but few deaths take place, except those produced by the unavoidable decays of nature, and the deaths to the births are generally in no higher proportion than 1 to about 5.

Among the first settlers the names of diseases or their remedies were almost unknown; nor did they stand in need of the discoveries and prescriptions of physicians, so long as the author of nature had ordained that health should be found in temperance and industry, which never can in medicine or the healing art.

An equality in rank and property has generally conduced among the citizens of Vermont to the cultivation of friendship and hospitality. Charitable among themselves, they are hospitable and courteous to strangers. Their exertions in the friendly and social intercourse of life were formerly more the result of spontaneous and uncalculating affection and kindness, than at present. The situation of the inhabitants in a new country places them nearest to a state of equality than can possibly happen among mankind. Their situation, feelings and manners will be nearly similar, for the method of obtaining a living and wealth are alike to all; but this is nothing more than an equality of rights and a similarity of business and circumstances. In the social condition of mankind nothing can produce an equality of capacity, power or advantages.— This is effectually prevented by their capacities being created unequal. There is in the state of human existence points of elevation and depression, above and below which none can ever rise or fall: somewhere between these extremes every grade, rank and species of people happen. In the symmetry of their bodies and in their original desires, passions and reason there is a similitude; but it is only a similarity, not an equality, which nature has produced.— A difference in their capacity for judging, genius for investigating, force of reason and discernment, and also a disparity of strength and health has been wisely implanted in the constitution, which was evidently designed for different attainments and pursuits. The condition of mankind, as nature formed and endowed them, tends to the promotion of society. But great changes are perceivable in the habits and customs of the people, as they advance from a new settlement to numbers, wealth and improvements. In the formation of a residence in a new country, the people are at all times exposed to wants and difficulties, which lead them to assist one another; but this could not be expected in an old populous country. As the numbers of society increase, the inability of many to furnish themselves with a support, increases also: therefore it becomes necessary either by private or public assistance to supply their wants. The government of the state have, in consequence of this, provided the means of subsistence for those who are unable to support themselves. By this method the expense is equalized throughout the community. Whereas if individual munificence and charity was the only source from which the sufferings of the poor were relieved, a few only would share the burthen.

Poor Laws.—Each incorporated town is compelled by statute to support all the poor who have a legal settlement within their jurisdiction. A lawful settlement is acquired, according to the statute passed in 1817, by the following way. A married woman has always the settlement of her husband. Legitimate children have always the settlement of their parents. Illegitimate children have that of their mothers. Every child, whose parents have not a legal settlement, shall not gain one by birth in the town where they are born. Every person whose rateable estate, besides his poll, shall be set in the list at $60 or upwards for five years in succession, gains a settlement in such town. Every person who is sworn into the office two years of a town clerk, selectman, overseer of the poor, treasurer of the town, lister, constable or grand juror, or shall be sworn to the faithful discharge of one of these offices one year and another the next, gains a legal settlement thereby.— A settlement may also be obtained by vote of the town legally warned for that purpose. Any person of full age, with a residence of one year in a town, which afterwards is organized, shall thereby gain a settlement; and finally, if any person, having a settlement in any town in the state, shall remove to and reside in any other town for the term of seven years, and shall maintain himself or herself and family, and not be chargeable to either of said towns, shall be adjudged to gain a settlement in the town in which he or she may reside. The way paupers are to be transported and the board before whom they are to be examined, together with other regulations relating to the subject, are determined by the provisions of the law. And further, those persons who are idle, disorderly and squander away their property, the selectmen and civil authority may appoint guardians over to take the management of their property, and make such contracts as are necessary for the preservation and benefit of the person or estate of their wards, and do all other acts necessary in the case. The poor laws have a tendency to increase the applicants for charity. England expends an enormous revenue upon her many impoverished subjects, who are constantly increasing. When a living can be obtained without efforts, no matter if it be in a poor house, increasing numbers will neglect the means of acquiring a living, on account of the certainty of their being supported at the public expense.

Societies.—Humanity, religion, science and benevolence have been encouraged in this state by the associated exertions of individuals. Much has been accomplished by their agency, and the pleasing prospect continues of a more successful and extended operation. The neglected descendants of Ethiopia's sultry clime have received the prospective encouragement, and in some instances the free sons of color have actually participated in the privilege of returning to that country where color is no impediment to their civil and political rights, where they are the proprietors of the government and the general privileges of mankind. The society for colonizing the free blacks has held ten annual meetings since the date of their incorporation, at Montpelier, on the second Thursdays of October.

That invaluable treasure, the bible, originating in the merciful councils of Heaven, has been distributed to the destitute and poor in this and other lands by the aid of the Vermont bible society, which meets yearly, since the date of its charter, in 1812, on the second Thursday of October, at Montpelier. The united exertions of this country, Great Britain and the continent of Europe have lit up the torch of revelation in the shadowed regions of infidelity and barbarism.

The Vermont Sabbath School union was formed in 1825, and meets in different places in the state, in September.— The object of this is the instruction of youth in literature and upon moral and religious subjects, on the Sabbath, throughout the different towns in the state.

The cause of temperance has received that attention, both from the formation of societies and the examples of abstinence among numerous citizens in the state, which its moralizing and useful purposes deserve. The exertions made to check intemperance has probably within the space of one year lessened the consumption of ardent spirits to one half of the former quantity; and should the disuse of it be continued in the same ratio a few years only would be requisite to confine its use to that of medicine. The state society was organized in 1829, being comprised of gentlemen of the first distinction in Vermont

By an act of the legislature, the Vermont Medical society was incorporated in 1813, to regulate a uniform mode of examination and admission of students to practice.— Subordinate to this society are those of the same kind formed in the several counties through the state.

Various other societies, of a more local interest, for moral, religious or social improvement, are formed in most places in the state. Small libraries have been furnished in most of the towns. These are among the best means of improvement that can possibly be employed.— A well selected library should be kept up by such a uumber of individuals as can support the expense. It is by reading books that we avail ourselves of the literary industry of every age and country,—we find an epitome of human knowledge in this repository of intellectual wealth. Here the historian informs, the poet delights, the philosopher instructs, and the orator convinces us. Here, the world, with its customs, is displayed in miniature, and we find an abstract of all the opinions that have ever been promulgated. Much depends upon our judgement in the choice of books; on subjects that are in a state of improvement, such as natural philosophy, chemistry, geography, and natural history, the latest writers should be preferred; but in theology the more ancient.

An act appropriating 3000 dollars a year out of the state treasury for the purpose of assisting those deaf and dumb persons in the state who are desirous of obtaining an education at the American asylum, established for that purpose in the city of Hartford, was passed in 1825. A board of three commissioners are annually appointed by the legislature, who have power to designate and approbate the subjects of the state's bounty—to draw orders on the treasury, pursuant to the provision of the act—to superintend and direct all the expenditures and concerns relating to this unfortunate class of citizens, in their education, at the institution aforesaid.

American government.—The principle upon which the governments of the United States are founded, is representation. The powers exercised by a representation are granted by the people, and defined by written constitutions.

The difficulties which occurred in the ancient democracies, where the whole body of the people assembled to judge and decide upon public affairs, never happens to the representative government of America. However numerous the population, or great the extent of territory, representation is proportioned to it, and thus becomes expressive of public opinion throughout the Union.

The form of government may vary in different states by entrusting more or less to the governor and council or house of representatives, as the situation of any separate state may require. Each of these branches, deriving their power from the people, are accountable to them for the use and exercise they make of it. The security of the people is therefore derived from the accountability and dependence of each part of the government, and not from the application of checks and balances among the different parts of the government, which may be of no disadvantage in the administration of the laws.

The method of a representative government was unknown to the ancients, and was introduced by the European sovereigns, not with the design, however, of favoring the condition of the people, but for the purpose of collecting money from them, which was very cautiously done wherever the rights and privileges of the people were examined or understood. However complete the form of a government may be, it cannot arrive at the highest perfection without embracing in itself the means of its own improvement. Where a society is constantly making improvements in the arts and sciences, and almost every business of life, the form of government which suited them in one period will not apply to another; and unless the government progresses with the gradual improvements of the people, it will be wanting in power and become disrespectable to the country. But where the people are the property of the sovereign, every attempt at improvement is destructive to legalized tyranny and prevented by every possible means from going into execution.

The foundation of the United States government rests entirely upon the common understanding of community, and expects its support and continuance in the progressive improvement of the knowledge and liberty of mankind.— This government is not considered the most perfect standard which can be devised, but the best form that the community of the states have as yet discovered. That the form of our government should not be binding upon posterity, one of its constituent and principal parts is that conventions shall be called at certain periods of time, to change, amend or improve the present constitution of the government, as the situation of society shall require.

Any attempt to check the progress and improvement of government would be as unworthy and impolitic as an attempt to fetter the energies of community in the progress to scientific, literary and other improvements.

Constitution of Vermont.—The constitution of Vermont is of a republican form, and embraces the same principles as the other governments of the states. This instrument was revised in 1786, and in 1792 vesting the supreme legislative power in the house of representatives of the freemen. Every organized town has a right to choose one representative on the first Tuesday of September. These are chosen to meet on the second Thursday of October annually, and are called the General Assembly of the state of Vermont. They have power to elect their own officers; set on their own adjournments; prepare bills and enact them into laws; judge of the elections and qualifications of their own members, but not for causes known to their constituents antecedent to their election; impeach state criminals; grant charters of incorporation; constitute towns, burroughs, cities and counties. In conjunction with the council, they annually elect judges of the supreme, county and probate courts, sheriffs and justices of the peace, and also, with the concurrence of the council, they elect major and brigadier generals, and have all the power necesary for the legislature of a free and sovereign state. But they have no power to add to, alter, abolish or infringe upon any part of the constitution.

The supreme executive power is vested in a governor, lieutenant-governor, and twelve councillors, chosen by the freemen of the state, at the same time they elect their representatives.*

The governor or the lieutenant-governor and council are to commission all officers, and prepare such business

*Note.—I intended to have inserted the names, times of election, and length of service of the governors, lieutenant-governors, treasurers, secretaries of state, judges of the supreme court, and senators and representatives in Congress from this state; but finding the matter would occupy several pages, and that the same was now before the public, in the annual register of the state, I therefore relinquished the plan of their insertion. During fifty-two years since the adoption of the present form of the state government, there has been an election of ten different individuals for governor: four of these are dead, and the longest term of service was that of Thomas Chittenden, a period of eighteen years. Twelve individuals have presided as lieutenant-governors, eight of whom are dead, and the longest term of service of any one was that of Paul Brigham, twenty-two years. The

as may appear to them necessary to lay before the General Assembly. They are to sit as judges to hear and determine on impeachments, taking to their assistance for advice only the judges of the supreme court. They have power to grant pardons and remit fines, and in all cases, except treason and murder, in which they have power to grant reprieves, but not pardon, until after the end of the next session of the legislature; and in cases of impeachment, in which there is no mitigation of punishment, but by an act of legislation. They are to take care that the laws are faithfully executed—may lay embargoes or prohibit exportation of any commodity, for any time not exceeding thirty days, in the recess of the house only. The governor is captain general and commander-in-chief of the forces of the state; but shall not command in person, except advised thereto by the council, and then only so long as they approve. The lieutenant-governor is lieutenant-general of all the forces in the state. To the end that the laws may be more maturely considered and the inconvenience of hasty decisions as much as possible prevented, all bills which originate in the assembly are laid before the governor and council, for their revision and concurrence, or proposals of amendment (if any) in writing, and if the same are not agreed to by the assembly, the governor and council have the power of suspending the

---

secretary of state's office has been bestowed on nine individuals, and the longest term of service was that of Roswell Hopkins, thirteen years. In fifty-two elections forty-eight different individuals have been made judges of the supreme court: the longest period of any one presiding was that of Royal Tyler, twelve years: twenty-eight of these are dead. Twelve persons have been senators to the Congress of the United States, and four of them have deceased: Stephen R. Bradley served fifteen years in this capacity, the longest of any member chosen in this state.— Forty-six different persons have represented this state in Congress; the longest term of service was that of Martin Chittenden, ten years, and thirteen or more of them are deceased.— Benjamin Swan has been the greatest length of time in office of any one: his appointment of treasurer of the state has been continued for thirty years. The next is Isaac Tichenor, who was seven years senator in Congress, eleven governor, and five one of the judges of the supreme court: in the whole twenty-three years.

passage of such bills until the next legislature ; but no negative is allowed to the governor and council.

The constitution provides that a council of censors, consisting of thirteen persons, to be chosen by the people every seventh year, on the last Wednesday of March, shall meet on the first Wednesday of June. The business of their delegation is to enquire whether the constitution has been preserved inviolate; whether the legislative and executive branches of the government have performed their duty, or assumed to themselves or exercised other or greater powers than they are entitled to by the constitution; whether the public taxes have been justly laid and collected, and whether the laws have been duly executed. They have power to send for persons, papers and records; to pass public censures; to order impeachments, and recommend the repeal of such laws as they may deem contrary to the principles of the constitution. These powers may be exercised for the space of one year from the time of their election, and they may call a convention to meet within two years after their sitting, should they deem it necessary.

The constitution of Vermont differs in one respect from that of any other state in the Union, having but one branch of power in the legislature. The whole power of legislation is placed in the house of representatives. The method of transacting public business, on the first establishment of civil authority in the state, was by committees and town meetings. Whatever was therefore ordered by these bodies became the supreme law of the land, subject to the control or revision of no other power. The first assumption of legislation was exercised in their meetings and councils of safety. In the advancing state of society there is no other way than to have the government and society progressive, that both may admit of improvements which are gradually made in human affairs. The advantages anticipated from the council of censors has never been realized in their proceedings. The plan does not seem adequate to the object. Of all the propositions brought forward by the council but one amendment of the constitution has been adopted for the four last septeniries, which is, that no person who is not already a freeman of this state shall be entitled to exercise the privileges of a freeman of this state, unless he be a natural born citizen of this or some one of the United States, or until he shall be naturalized agreeably to the laws of Congress.

Laws.—The first code of written laws in this state was very imperfect, and required changing as the rights, wealth, commerce and population of this territory increased. The most judicious laws are not to be expected in the imperfect commencement of political associations, unaccustomed to the certainty of settled regulations. The influence of sudden and momentary rules depending upon public sentiment, the exasperated and insubordinate feelings of community, had a very counteracting influence on the passage of the early laws of the state. The irregular ideas were also entertained of applying scripture declarations as rules of positive law for determining the boundaries of right and wrong in matters of civil subjection, public and private injuries, and moral obligations. The ten commandments, Connecticut statutes, and the resolutions of the leaders, were the principal laws, until the session of the legislature, in 1778. The compilation of laws, adopted soon after the institution of a state government, in the period above mentioned, are the commencement of that superstructure of statutory laws now in force in Vermont. The history of legislation in this state shows that successive enactments have swept almost every early regulation from the statute book. Improvements in society have so increased topics of legislation that the regulations of the first settlers are but a point in comparison with the fullness of their present condition. The wants of society increase as numbers multiply. Hence subjects of legislative concern become numerous,—prohibitions of crimes; chartered incorporations of literary, banking, insurance, commercial, road and manufacturing companies, and all matters relating to the jurisdiction of different courts of justice, the power and liabilities of ministerial officers and the regulation of ecclesiastical bodies; and finally, the whole unlimited diversity of legislative business, succeeded. There is nothing, however, among the peculiarities of the early laws of Vermont evincive of that fierce, uncultivated spirit, inter-national prohibitions, barbarous expedients and summary vengeance which the Romans first adopted as the laws of their empire. Certain offences against public morality were, according to the legal version of that period, peculiarly punished. Those who withdrew from meeting on Sunday, fast or thanksgiving, or went out into the streets on Saturday evening, were liable to be fined three pounds and sit in the stocks two hours. Whoever was bereaved or disabled in the use of their reason, and discovered it either in their gestures, speech or behaviour, was fined eight shillings, and for want of goods whereon to make distress, could be set in the stocks not exceeding three hours.

Profanity was punished by a fine of six shillings for every offence, and for want of ability would be set in the stocks not more than three hours. By the present law of this state, any one who profanely swears in the presence of a judge or magistrate, may, by a summary conviction, be sentenced to pay a fine.

Blasphemy was punishable with death; likewise an incendiary who in any manner endangered the life or lives of others by his depredations. Slander and defamation was punished by a heavy fine, with costs and damages to the injured party. Disorders and damages, done in the night time, were chargeable upon those who would give no account of themselves, or were out during the same period, and the delinquent party was liable to a pecuniary amercement. The crime of lying received the reprehensions of the public in rather an ignominious way, by a fine and stripes. He who was guilty of secretly taking another's property had to restore threefold and endure thirty-nine stripes at the whipping post.

The people were at that period very fruitful in legal expedients upon various other subjects besides those before mentioned. Relief laws were enacted—paper money was made a legal tender in discharge of all contracts, executions, &c.—personal property and real estate was, on apprizement by the highest authority of the state, ordered to be received in discharge of executions. This provision was afterwards so extended that a payment could be made in such articles as were stipulated in the contract, although the time for its discharge had long elapsed.

Vermont was in fact an independent government at this time, subject to no authority but her own and allied to no power on earth. She raised and paid her own quota of troops for the continental service, laid embargoes, regulated her commerce and intercourse with other nations, granted letters of *marque* and *reprisal*, and pardoned those who were guilty of treason.

The legislature considered themselves invested with transcendent powers. The decisions of the courts were frequently overruled by legislative authority, executions were ordered satisfied and new trials granted. Land causes were tried before commissioners, with powers only delegated for that purpose, and finally they were adjudicated before the governor and council, who had exclusive jurisdiction in such cases. The standard of gold and silver coin was also determined by the law of the state. Such were some of the first laws enacted by the legislature of Vermont, which are now superceded by more comprehensive and enlightened methods of civil policy and legislation.

So much of the common law of England as is applicable to the local situation and circumstances, and is not repugnant to the constitution or to any act of the legislature of this state, is adopted as law within the same. The criminal code of Vermont has been mitigated since the erection of the state penitentiary, and five out of nine of the crimes made capital by a former law of the State, have been repealed.

Treason, murder, perjury, by means of which some person's life is taken away, and arson, effected in such manner that the life of a person is destroyed, are punished with death. Treason consists in levying or conspiring to levy war against the state, or in giving aid to the enemies of the state, by a person owing allegiance to the same. The testimony necessary for conviction is the confession of the party in open court, on the evidence of two witnesses to some overt act of treason. Murder in the first degree is defined to be the malicious, deliberate and premeditated killing of a human being. The destruction of life by perjury is declared to be a wilful misrepresentation of facts, for the purpose of destroying life, which does take effect according to such design; and that by arson, consists in the death of a person by means of burning some buildings that are inhabited. The other high crimes are punishable by imprisonment and fines. The time of imprisonment is proportioned to the enormity of the offence, and fixed at the discretion of the court.—Manslaughter and bearing false-witness, not affecting life, are punishable by confinement in the state's prison during life, or for a term not less than seven years, and a fine not exceeding 1000 dollars. Misprison of treason, by imprisonment not exceeding seven years, and a fine not more than 2000 dollars. Arson, without death; assault, with an intent to rob; forgery, with a disqualification of being sworn to give evidence on a verdict; rape, and perjury, also, are punishable by imprisonment not exceeding seven years, and a fine of 2000 dollars. A second conviction for horse stealing is punished by imprisonment for a term not exceeding fifteen years, and a fine not more than 1000 dollars. Bigamy and robbery, the same punishments as for horse stealing; and a second conviction, imprisonment for life, or a term not less than seven years. Theft, receiving stolen goods, and assault with an intent to know a person, imprisonment not exceeding seven years, and a fine not more than 500 dollars. Breaking jail, counterfeiting metals, swindling and impeding authority, by imprisonment not exceeding three years, and a fine not more than 300 dollars. Adultery, poligamy, incest, illicit intention under certain circumstances, and disintering the dead, by imprisonment not more than three years, and a fine not exceeding 1000 dollars. Fraudulent practices and forging coin, by imprisonment not exceeding five years, and a fine not more than 500 dollars. Counterfeiting bank notes, by imprisonment not exceeding fourteen years, and a fine not exceeding 1000 dollars. Maiming, by imprisonment not less than seven years. Malicious transportation of a citizen of the state, by imprisonment seven years, and a fine not more than 1000 dollars. Rescue of a prisoner, by imprisonment not exceeding ten years, and a fine not exceeding 500 dollars. Guards of the state prison suffering a voluntary escape, imprisonment for one year, and a fine of five hundred dollars.

The term of time for imprisonment is in all instances

except four, and the fine in all cases, is left to the discretion of the court. They can either imprison or fine, or award both at the time of conviction. In all cases except one, imprisonment is accompanied with hard labor, and two only award for life.

Great credit has been given by many writers and friends of humanity to the reformation in the laws of most of the states by substituting confinement at hard labor in place of the disgusting and demoralizing public punishments to which, by former laws, criminals have been subjected.— Had the guilty been generally reformed by this humane method of punishment, a short period only would be necessary to work an entire reformation among the lower classes of mankind. But the records of our states prisons and the presentments of the grand jurors show that the fear of hard labor and confinement does not have a salutary influence upon all who have been subjects of them.— The annual number of convicts to the state's prison for several years has been about twenty-four. Since that time the number has considerably increased. The greater part of these have been sentenced for theft and counterfeiting. There has been but three executions in Vermont, by a sentence of a court of law, since the assumption of the government, in 1777. Dean was the first that was executed, in 1808, at Burlington. Then Godfrey, at Woodstock, in 1818; and Virginia, a man of color, at St. Albans, in 1820. Redding was executed at Bennington before the present form of government was organized, and a number suffered in the time of the war by sentence of court martials.

Counties, Towns and Courts.—Vermont is divided into the following counties. Bennington, Rutland, Addison, Chittenden, Franklin and Grand-Isle, on the west side of the mountain; Windham, Windsor, Orange, Caledonia, Essex, Orleans and Washington on the east side. These are again subdivided into two hundred and forty-six townships and fifteen gores. The judiciary powers of the state are vested in the supreme court and court of chancery, consisting of five judges and a county court in each county, having one of the supreme court judges for a chief justice, and two assistant judges appointed from the county, and a probate court in each district, of which there are nineteen, and justices of the peace in each town, appointed annually by the legislature. The supreme court and court of chancery hold one session a year in each county. This court have original and conclusive jurisdiction in all suits in chancery and petitions not triable by a jury; and have power now given by law to issue and determine all writs of error, habeas corpus, mandamus, scirefacias, and certiorari, and all other writs, agreeable to the usages of law. And either of them, as chancellors, at any county or in vacation, may make interlocutory orders or decrees, issue writs, subpœnas and other processes necessary to be made, and also make any necessary orders of notice in any suit in chancery or law. Appeals are had from the judgement of the county court to the supreme court only for the hearing of some issue of law, determined by such county court. And all questions of law arising upon jury trials, which are placed upon record by the agreement of parties or the allowance of any two of the judges who shall attend the trial, may pass to the supreme court for decision, and as a court of chancery they have power to issue writs of sequestration and to grant new trials. The county courts hold two sessions in each of the counties annually. They have in their respective counties original jurisdiction of all criminal matters of every name or nature, arising within such counties, except such as are made cognizable before justices of the peace, and award sentence on the same; and also have original jurisdiction of all civil matters whatsoever, except such as are by this act made cognizable before the supreme court; and such as are made cognizable before justices of the peace can render judgement and award execution thereon, and have appellate jurisdiction in all pauper causes, probate appeals or petitions from the decisions of justices of the peace.— Justices of the peace within their respective jurisdiction have power to try all actions of a criminal nature, if the fines and forfeitures are within the sum of seven dollars, and to bind over all offenders whose crimes exceed their power to try. They have original and exclusive jurisdiction in civil causes, where the matter in demand does not exceed 100 dollars, except in actions for slanderous words, replevin above the sum of seven dollars, and trespass upon the freehold above the sum of 20 dollars. Action on book account may be brought before them, where the debit of the plaintiff's book does not exceed 100 dollars, and on note, where the sum due does not exceed 100 dollars. No judgement rendered by a justice of the peace can be reversed by a writ of error or certiorari before the supreme court. The adjustment of claims in favor or against the estate of a person deceased, are settled before commissioners appointed by the judge of probate for that purpose, whose decision may, however, be appealed from to the supreme court. Five road commissioners are annually appointed by the legislature, for each county, who have power, upon the application of twenty or more freeholders, and upon a view of the premises, to lay out and establish public roads or to alter and discontinue old ones by whomsoever laid out—to order the building or repairing of roads or bridges, and direct such sum as each town shall be liable to pay for such purposes, and to issue execution for costs. An appeal may be had from the decrees of the commissioners to the county court, where damages are not satisfactorily assessed, who can upon trial of the case order new proceedings to be had on the subject.

Revenue.—Public taxes are the principal source of revenue in this state. Those kinds of property subject to taxation are designated by law, and the rates at which they shall be assessed, and an inventory, is yearly made out in June, and called the grand list, which for 1830 amounted to $1,834,980. Three cents upon the dollar, is generally voted for the support of the government. The sum paid into the treasury for taxes last year, after deducting the expense of collecting, was $39,942 36, and $9,550 09 was derived from other sources, which makes the whole revenue of the state.

Expenses of Government.—The sum paid into the treasury is mostly expended for the yearly administration of the government of Vermont. But there are other occasional and contingent expenses arising almost every year, such as those paid to commissioners, council of censors, and conventions. Taking the census of 1830, the annual sum which each individual in the state pays for the protection of his person and property, and the advantages of a free government, is about twenty cents. Among the salaries paid out by the state, the governor has 750 dollars, each of the judges $1,050, secretary $150, treasurer $400, secretary to the governor and council $250, clerk of the general assembly $375—the lieutenant-governor $4 per day, councillors and representatives $1 50 each per day, engrossing clerk $75, besides $2 50 per day for attendance. So long as the government continue economical in their expenditure the freedom of the country may be preserved. Large salaries and prodigal emoluments are productive of ruinous controversies and political intrigues.— For those in power, who derive their living from the public, will compute the honor and dignity of the government by the sums of public money which they receive.

CHAPTER XV.

Population of the State.—Banks.—Militia.—Colleges.— Religion.

Population.—The following dates show when the several counties were incorporated under the state of New-York, and afterwards by the government of Vermont; also the time when each township was granted or chartered and settled; together with the number of inhabitants in each county, for all the censuses that have been taken in the state, and the last in each town. The territory of Vermont was on the first division, in 1765, formed into four counties: Albany in the south-west, Charlotte in the north-west, Cumberland in the south-east, and Gloucester in the north-east part; but is now divided into thirteen counties.

Windham county contains 24 towns and four gores, was incorporated in 1781, and had a population of 17,693 in 1791, 23,581 in 1800, 26,760 in 1810, 28,457 in 1820, 23,748 in 1830.

	Date of grant or charter.	Settlement.	No. inhab.
Acton	February 23, 1782	1800	176

HISTORY OF VERMONT.

Athens	March 11,	1780	1779	415
Brattleborough	December 26,	53	24	2741
Brookline	October 30,	94	77	376
Dummerston	December 26,	53	34	1592
Dover	December 20,	1810	87	831
Grafton	April 6,	1754	68	1439
Guilford	April 4,	54	54	1760
Halifax	May 11,	50	61	1562
Jamaica	November 7,	80	80	1523
Londonderry	February 30,	70	74	1302
Marlborough	September 21,	61	63	1218
Newfane	May 11,	72	74	1441
Putney	December 6,	53	53	1510
Rockingham	December 28,	52	53	2272
Somerset				245
Stratton				312
Townshend	June 20,	53	61	1386
Vernon	September 5,	53	53	681
Westminster	November 9,	52	42	1737
Wardsborough	November 7,	80	80	1148
Whitingham	March 23,	80	70	1477
Wilmington	June 17,	63	70	1367
Windham	February 30,	70	74	847

Bennington county, containing 17 towns, was incorporated in 1781, and had a population of 12,554 in 1791, 14,617 in 1800, 15,893 in 1810, 16,125 in 1820, 17,470 in 1830.

Date of grant or charter.			Settlement.	No. inhab.
Arlington	July 28,	1761	1763	1207
Bennington	January 3,	49	61	3419
Dorset	August 20,	61	68	1507
Glastonbury	August 20,	61	70	52
Landgrove	November 8,	80	69	385
Manchester	August 11,	61	64	1525
Peru	October 13,	61	73	455
Pownal	January 8,	60	61	1835
Rupert	August 20,	61	70	1318
Readsboro'				662
Sandgate	August 13,	61	63	933
Searsboro'	February 23,	81		40
Shaftsbury	August 20,	61	63	2143

HISTORY OF VERMONT.

Stamford	March 6, 1753		563
Sunderland	July 30, 61	1765	463
Winhall	September 15, 61	61	571
Woodford	March 6, 53	96	395

Rutland county was incorporated in 1781, and contains 26 towns, with a population of 15,565 in 1791, 23,813 in 1800, 29,487 in 1810, 29,975 in 1820, 31,293 in 1830.

	Date of grant or charter,	Settlement.	No.inhab.
Benson	May 5, 1780	1783	1493
Brandon	October 20, 62	83	1940
Castleton	September 20, 61	61	1783
Chittenden	March 16, 80	85	610
Clarendon	September 5, 61	78	1585
Danby	August 27, 61	68	1362
Fairhaven	October 27, 79	83	675
Hubbardton	June 15, 64	74	865
Ira	May 31, 79	79	442
Mendon	February 23, 81	1806	432
Mount Holly	October 31, 92	1781	1318
Mount Tabor	August 28, 61		210
Middletown		86	919
Orwell	August 8, 63	83	1598
Pawlet	August 26, 61	61	1965
Pittsford	October 12, 61	68	2005
Pittsfield	July 29, 81	86	505
Poultney	September 21, 61	71	1909
Sherburn	July 7, 61	85	452
Shrewsbury	September 4, 63	85	1289
Sudbury	August 6, 61		812
Tinmouth	September 15, 61	75	1049
Wallingford	November 27, 61	73	1740
Wells	September 15, 61	68	880
West-Haven	October 27, 79	83	724
Rutland	September 7, 61	70	2753

Windsor county was incorporated in 1781, containing 23 towns and one gore, and had a population of 15,748 in 1791. 26,944 in 1800, 34,877 in 1810, 38,233 in 1820, 40,623 in 1830.

	Date of grant or charter.	Settlement.	No.inhab.
Andover	October 16, 1761	1776	975

HISTORY OF VERMONT. 301

Baltimore	October 19,	1793	1763	179
Bethel	October 27,	79	80	1667
Barnard	July 17,	61	75	1881
Bridgewater	July 10,	61	79	1311
Cavendish	October 12,	61	71	1498
Chester	February 4,	66	64	2320
Hartford	July 4,	61	64	2044
Hartland	June 15,	82	63	2505
Ludlow	September 16,	61	84	1227
Norwich	July 4,	"	63	2316
Plymouth	July 6,	"	76	1237
Pomfret	July 8,	"	70	1867
Reading	July 6,	81	72	1409
Rochester	August 30,	81	83	1392
Royalton	August 3,	70	63	1893
Sharon	August 17,	61	82	1459
Springfield	August 20,	"	82	2749
Stockbridge	July 21,	"	84	1333
Weathersfield	February 20,	"	77	2213
Weston	March 3,	1800	76	172
Windsor	July 6,	1761	64	3934
Woodstock	July 10,	"	68	3044

Orange county was incorporated in 1792, and contains 17 towns, with a population of 7,334 in 1791, 16,318 in 1800, 21,724 in 1810, 24,169 in 1820, 27,285 in 1830.

Date of grant or charter. Settlement. No. inhab.

Bradford	January 22,	1791	1761	1507
Braintree	November 2,	80	83	1209
Brookfield	November 6,	80	79	1677
Chelsea	November 2,	80	83	1958
Corinth	February 4,	64	78	1953
Fairlee	September 9,	61	68	656
Newbury	May 18,	63	64	2252
Orange	November 6,	80	93	1016
Randolph	November 2,	80	77	2743
Stratford	August 12,	61	74	1935
Thetford	August 12,	"	64	2113
Topsham	June 17,	63	81	1384
Tunbridge	September 2,	63	76	1920
Vershire	November 7,	80	80	1260
Washington	November 6,	80	92	1374

West Fairlee   September 9, 1761   1768   841
Williamstown   November 6,   80   84   1487

Addison county was incorporated in 1787, containing 22 towns and 1 gore, and had a population of 9488 in 1791, 13,417 in 1800, 19,993 in 1810, 20,469 in 1820, 24,907 in 1830.

Date of grant or charter.		Settlement.	No.inhab.
Addison	October 14, 1761	1731	1306
Bridport	October 10, '	68	1774
Bristol	June 20, '	84	1247
Cornwall	November 3, '	74	1264
Ferrisburgh	June 24, 62	85	1822
Goshen	February 23, 82	1800	555
Hancock	November 7, 80	1788	472
Kingston	November 7, '	86	403
Leicester	October 20, 63	90	638
Lincoln	November 7, 80	90	639
Middlebury	November 2, 61	66	3468
Monkton	June 24, 62	55	1334
New-Haven	November 2, 61	69	1834
Panton	November 3, 64	70	605
Ripton	April 13, 81	1808	278
Salisbury	November 3, 61	1775	907
Shoreham	October 8, 61	66	2137
Starksborough	November 7, 80	80	1342
Vergennes	October 23, 88	66	999
Waltham	96	73	330
Weybridge	November 3, 61	74	850
Whiting	August 6, 63	72	653

Chittenden county, incorporated in 1787, contains 16 towns and 1 gore, and had a population of 3918 in 1791, 9563 in 1800, 14,684 in 1810, 16,055 in 1820, 21,775 in 1830.

Date of grant or charter.		Settlement.	No.inhab.
Bolton	October 27, 1794		452
Burlington	June 7, 63	1775	3526
Charlotte	June 24, 62	76	1702
Colchester	June 7, 63	74	1489
Essex	June 7, 63	83	1664
Hinesburgh	June 21, 62	83	1669
Huntington	June 7, 63	86	929

HISTORY OF VERMONT. 303

Jerico	June	8,	1763	1774	1654
Mansfield	June	'	63	1800	279
Milton	June	'	63	1783	2100
Richmond	October		93	75	1109
Shelburn	August	18,	63	70	1117
St. George	August	'	63	84	135
Underhill	June	8,	63	86	1052
Westford	June	'	63	84	1290
Williston	June	7,	63	74	1608

Washington county was incorporated by its present name in 1814, embracing 18 towns, and had a population of 711 in 1791, 5703 in 1800, 10,190 in 1810, 14,725 in 1820, 21,376 in 1830.

Date of grant or charter.   Settlement. No.inhab.

Barre	August	12,	1781	1796	2012
Berlin	June	7,	63	86	1664
Calais	October	21,	80	7	1539
Duxbury	June	7,	63	9	652
Elmore	August	21,	81	90	442
Fayston	February	25,	2	98	458
Marshfield	June	8,	63	1800	1271
Middlesex	June	'	63	1781	1156
Montpelier	August	14,	81	6	3065
Moretown	June	7,	63	90	816
Northfield	November	6,	80	88	1412
Plainfield	October	27,	8	94	874
Roxbury	August	6,	1	89	737
Stow	June	8,	63	93	1570
Waitsfield	February	25,	82	89	958
Waterbury	June	7,	65	4	1650
Warren	October	20,	89	97	766
Worcester	June	8,	63	97	434

Caledonia county was incorporated in 1792, has 19 towns and 3 gores, with a population of 2047 in 1791, 7566 in 1800, 14,966 in 1810, 16,669 in 1820, 2,967 in 1830.

Date of grant or charter.   Settlement. No.inhab.

Barnet	September	15,	1763	1770	1764
Burke	February	26,	82	90	866
Cabot	August	17,	81	85	1304
Danville	October	31,	86	84	2681
Groton	October	20,	89	87	836
Hardwick	August	19,	81	90	1216

HISTORY OF VERMONT.

Kirby	October 27, 1790	1799	401
Lyndon	November 20, 80	88	1822
Newark	August 15, 81	1800	257
Peacham	December 31, 63	1775	1351
Ryegate	September 8, 63	74	1119
Sheffield	November 7, 80	92	720
St. Johnsbury	November 1, 86	86	1592
Sutton	February 6, 82	91	1008
Walden	August 18, 80	89	827
Waterford	November 8, 80	87	1358
Wheelock	June 14, 85	90	834
Woodbury	August 16, 81	1800	824
Bradleyvale	January 27, 91	"	21
Goshen gore	November 1, 98	01	209
Harris' gore	October 30, 81	21	19

Essex county was incorporated in 1792, contains 17 towns and 3 gores, and had a population of 588 in 1791, 1479 in 1800, 3087 in 1810, 3334 in 1820, 3917 in 1830.

Date of grant or charter.   Settlement. No.inhab.

Brunswick	February 26, 1782	1790	116
Canaan	July 29, 63	85	373
Concord	September 15, 81	88	1031
Ferdinand	October 13, 61	uninhabited	
Granby	October 10, 61	1800	97
Guildhall	October 10, 61	1764	481
Lemington	June 29, 62	1800	183
Lunenburgh	July 5, 63	1770	1054
Lewis	June 29, 62	uninhabited	
Maidstone	October 12, 61	1770	236
Minehead	June 29, 62	1800	150
Averill	June 23, 62		1
East Haven	October 22, 90		23
Norton	62	uninhabited	
Random	August 13, 81	23	105
Wenlock	October 13, 61	23	24
Victory	September 6, 81	21	53

Orleans county was incorporated in 1792, has 23 towns and 1 gore, with a population of 119 in 1790, 1384 in 1800, 5671 in 1810, 6819 in 1820, 13,980 in 1830.

Date of grant or charter.   Settlement. No.inhab.

Albany	June 26, 1782	1800	683
Barton	October 20, 96	1796	729
Brownington	October 2, 90	"	412
Craftsbury	November 12, 90	91	982
Charleston	November 8, 80	1803	564

HISTORY OF VERMONT. 305

Derby	October 29, 1779	1795	1469
Eden	August 28, 81	1802	461
Glover	November 20, 83	1797	902
Greensboro'	August 20, 81	88	784
Holland	October 26, 89	1800	422
Hydepark	August 7, 81	1787	823
Irasburgh	February 23, '	99	860
Jay	November 7, 92	1812	196
Kellyvale	June 7, 91	06	314
Morgan	November 6, 80	00	331
Morristown	August 24, 81	1790	1315
Newport	October 30, 1802	"	284
Salem	August 18, 1781	98	230
Troy	October 13, 92	1800	608
Westfield	May 15, 80	"	353
Woolcot	August 22, 81	"	492
Westmore	August 17, 81	02	32
Coventry	October 23, 85	00	728
Coventry gore granted same time			6

Franklin county was incorporated in 1792, and contains 19 towns and 2 gores, had a population of 1939 in 1791, 7582 in 1800, 16,427 in 1810, 17,192 in 1820, 24,525 in 1830.

	Date of grant or charter.	Settlement.	No.inhab.
Bakersfield	June 25, 1791	1789	1087
Belvidere	November 4, 91	91	185
Berkshire	June 22, 81	92	1308
Cambridge	August 13, '	83	1613
Enosburgh	May 15, '	97	1560
Fairfax	August 18, 63	83	1729
Fairfield	August ' 63	8	2270
Fletcher	August 20, 81		793
Franklin	March 19, 89	9	1129
Georgia	August 17, 63	4	1897
Highgate	August 17, 63	4	2038
Johnson	January 2, 92	4	1079
Montgomery	October 8, 89	93	460
Richford	August 21, 80	90	704
Sheldon	August 18, 63	90	1427
Sterling	February 25, 82	99	183
St. Albans	August 7, 63	85	2395
Swanton	October 17, 63	7	2158
Waterville	October 26, 88—called Coit's gore		488
Avery's Gore	June 23, 96	1817	22

Grand Isle county was incorporated in 1802, contains

5 towns, with a population of 1155 in 1791, 2498 in 1800, 3145 in 1810, 3527 in 1820, 3696 in 1830.

	Date of grant or charter.	Settlement.	No.inhab.
Alburgh	February 23, 1781	1782	1239
Grand Isle	October 27, 79	3	459
North Hero	October ʻ 79	3	688
South Hero	October ʻ 79	4	717
Vineyard	October ʻ 79	5	648

The aggregate amount of each description of persons, by classes, in the state of Vermont, are:—

FREE WHITE PERSONS:

Males under five years of age	21689
five and under ten	19410
ten and under fifteen	17596
fifteen and under twenty	15805
twenty and under thirty	24200
thirty and under forty	15761
forty and under fifty	10443
fifty and under sixty	7052
sixty and under seventy	5192
seventy and under eighty	2204
eighty and under ninety	603
ninety and under one hundred	48
one hundred and upwards	3
	140,006
Females under five years of age	21326
five and under ten	18633
ten and under fifteen	16877
fifteen and under twenty	15776
twenty and under thirty	25167
thirty and under forty	16257
forty and under fifty	11035
fifty and under sixty	7157
sixty and under seventy	4723
seventy and under eighty	2089
eighty and under ninety	656
ninety and under one hundred	87
one hundred and upwards	5
	139,788
	279,794

FREE COLORED PERSONS:

Males under ten years	125
ten and under twenty	114

Males twenty-four and under thirty-six	78	
thirty-six and under fifty-five	68	
fifty-five and under one hundred	48	
one hundred and upwards	2	430
Females under ten years	121	
ten and under twenty-four	126	
twenty-four and under thirty-six	78	
thirty-six and under fifty	70	
fifty and under one hundred	56	
one hundred and upwards	4	455

280,679

Of white persons included in the above, who are deaf and dumb, under particular ages, there are:—Under fourteen years of age, 37—fourteen and under twenty-five, 58—twenty-five and upwards, 54. Blind persons, 49. Colored persons, of all ages, deaf and dumb, 2.

There are in the state, aliens and foreigners not naturalized, 3420.

	In 1820.	In 1830.
Windham county	3	6
Bennington "	6	58
Rutland "	45	163
Windsor "	29	75
Orange "	13	23
Addison "	151	400
Chittenden "	217	822
Washington "	6	49
Caledonia "	272	55
Essex "	4	1
Orleans "	5	145
Franklin "	145	1107
Grand Isle "	39	516
	935	3420

The colored population has decreased from 903 to 885.

According to the census of the towns in 1820, compared with that of 1830, fifty-one towns have decreased in numbers within the last ten years. Burlington has the most inhabitants of any town in the state; Middlebury is the next in size. Five towns have over three thousand inhabitants; twenty-two towns over two thousand, and one hundred and five over one thousand; fifty-three towns over five hundred. Fourteen towns have only four hundred and forty-nine inhabitants: that is, under one hundred in each. One hundred and thirty-eight towns were chartered by the government of New-Hampshire, and the remainder one hundred and eight under the authority of Vermont. Ninety-five towns were settled before and during the war of the American Independence. Four towns and two gores have been settled within the last ten years.— The least number of people in any town is one. Three towns and nine gores are yet uninhabited. The number of post offices in Vermont, before her admission into the Union, which were established and controlled by the authority of the state, were five, located at Bennington, Rutland, Brattleborough, Windsor and Newbury. The present number is about one hundred and eighty-five.

Among the numerous villages in Vermont, three have a population exceeding one thousand, and seven exceeding five hundred. Between seventeen hundred and two thousand mills and machines are propelled by water in the state.

Banks.—The first banking incorporation chartered in the state was in the year 1806. Two branches were established, one at Woodstock, and the other at Middlebury. The next year two additional branches were granted, at Burlington and Westminster. The management of this institution was under the direction of thirteen directors, and the state were the exclusive proprietors of all the property and profits of the bank. The concerns of the institution became bankrupt, and the bills were consequently withdrawn from circulation.

Ten banks have been incorporated in Vermont, from 1817 to 1829. Windsor bank was incorporated with a capital of $100,000, in 1817; and Burlington, with a capital of $150,000, in 1818. The next bank was established at Brattleboro', Nov. 5, 1821, with a capital of 100,000 dollars. Rutland bank was chartered in 1824; Caledonia, Montpelier and St. Albans banks, in 1825; Vergennes bank in 1826, and Orange and Bennington banks in 1827, all with a capital of 100,000 dollars. Their charters are limited to the term of fifteen years, and the number of directors having the management of these institutions to five, except Burlington and Rutland, which have seven. These banks pay into the state's treasury, six per cent. of all the profits, and the proceedings of the directors of each bank are inspected annually by a committee appointed by the legislature. The banking system has in many and frequent instances produced very heavy losses to the public. This originates in the want of other security than the corporate funds. If the stockholders were obliged to secure the amount of stock they take up, by mortgaging real estate, no losses could be sustained. The stockholders, as the case now is, either from unexpected misfortunes or by mismanagement or dishonesty, may render every dollar of paper currency now in circulation worth no more than a dividend of capital and the profits gained by the operation of the bank, which with many of them would occasion an overwhelming loss. A branch of the United States bank has lately been located and gone into operation at Burlington.

Three fire insurance companies have been incorporated, two of them with capitals of 200,000 dollars each, one fixed at Middlebury, in 1824, and the other at Windsor, in 1825. The mutual fire insurance company was incorporated at Montpelier in 1827: this is founded upon very different principles from the others. Every person who insures becomes a member of the company.

Militia.—The military force of this state consists of all the able-bodied males, with the exception of those who are exempted by law, between the ages of 18 and 45 years. Each military subject is required to provide himself with such arms and equipments as are necessary for actual service, which exempts his poll from taxation. They are divided into four divisions, and these again into brigades, regiments and companies. The companies elect the captains and subalterns. The field officers are chosen by the captains and subalterns. Brigadier and major generals are appointed by the legislature. The governor is captain general and commander-in-chief, and with the advice of the council is to arrange the whole militia into divisions and brigades, and may from time to time, make such alterations as shall seem proper. By a law passed in 1829, regimental and company's reviews, except one in June by the respective companies of militia, are abolished. Each division is commanded by a major general, with a division inspector, a quartermaster and two aids : each brigade by a general, inspector, quartermaster, and one aid : each regiment by one colonel, two lieutenant colonels, one major and the usual staff, and each company by a captain, lieutenant and ensign, with the usual number of non-commissioned officers. Several companies of artillery and cavalry are connected to the several regiments in the state.— The militia of Vermont have frequently distinguished themselves for their perseverance and bravery in times when the soil of freedom was haughtily invaded by a tyrant's forces.

Colleges.—Colleges are established at Burlington and Middlebury; the first in 1791, and the other in 1800; both of them are well endowed and under the direction of faculties distinguished for their talents, virtues and learning. Instruction was commenced at Middlebury college, under Rev. I. Atwater, who was succeeded by Henry Davis, D. D. in 1809. He continued until 1818, when the charge of the institution was committed to Rev. Joshua Bates, D. D. the present incumbent. This institution is in a very flourishing condition. The present number of students is nearly one hundred. The old building erected before the college was incorporated, contains the public rooms. In 1814 a new edifice was built of granular limestone, 106 feet long and 40 wide, four stories high, and contains forty-eight rooms for students. The library belonging to this institution exceeds 1500 volumes. The University of Vermont, at Burlington, has suffered very much since instruction was commenced in it under Rev. Daniel C. Saunders, in 1803, by the calamities of war and fire. Splendid edifices have been erected on the site where the former building was consumed. Rev. James Marsh is the president of the institution, and its prospects are brightening and bids fair to become a flourishing seat of learning. Medical institutions connected with these seminaries have been incorporated and gone into successful operation.

Religion.—The constitution declares that no person shall be compelled to erect any place of worship, or maintain any minister, contrary to the dictates of his own conscience. All denominations, by the same instrument, are enjoined to observe the Sabbath and keep up some kind of religious worship, which to them shall seem most agreeable to the revealed will of God. The various denominations of Christians in this state, are Congregationalists, Methodists, Baptists, Free-will Baptists, Presbyterians, Episcopalians, Christians, Universalists, Unitarians, and Quakers. The number of clergymen employed by the Congregational and Methodist churches are about equally numerous, being something more than one hundred in each connection. The number of clergymen in every denomination was 350 in 1827. No new sect has sprung up and prevailed generally through the state; but one, of a very limited number, under the name and style of Dorrilites, appeared in 1798, in the town of Guilford. The founder of this sect was Dorril, a refugee of Burgoyne's army. He assumed to possess supernatural powers, by which he was shielded from the evils and injuries of human life. The consumption of clothing or food obtained at the expense of life, was forbidden to those who embraced his creed, and assurance was given to those who were steadfast and faithful to him, that they should never die. The leathern garniture of the feet was exchanged for shoes of wood and cloth. Bellows of cloth were used, by a blacksmith, and all of them subsisted upon milk and vegetables. The authority of all revelation, except Dorril's, was discarded, and their conduct, as they asserted, was governed wholly by the light of nature. The worship at their weekly meetings consisted in eating, drinking, singing, fiddling, and dancing, and in attending Dorril's lectures, who was well qualified for the business. By a covenant entered upon among themselves, a large portion of their property was placed in common stock, and the blacksmith became their treasurer. Proselytes were easily gained, and Dorril soon found himself surrounded by numbers of disciples, of both sexes, from some very respectable families in Vermont and Massachusetts. People from the adjoining towns went to see the marvelous proceedings of Dorril and his associates. At one of their meetings, when Dorril was delivering a lecture, and having come to that portion of the doctrine, treating of his miraculous powers, a gentleman by the name of Ezekiel Porter no sooner heard him say that no arm could hurt his flesh, than he rose, indignant at his blasphemy, and knocked him down with his fist—repeating his blows until Dorril cried for mercy, and renounced his doctrine in the hearing of his astonished followers. With this transaction terminated the impious fanaticism of this bold impostor and his deluded followers. The settlement and support of the ministers of religion was encouraged by governor Wentworth, in the earliest grants of townships, with a reservation of certain rights of land for religious purposes. Three rights were reserved in each town:— one to the society for propagating the gospel in foreign lands, another for a glebe designed for the use of the Episcopal clergy, and a third, for the benefit of the first settled minister. In those townships granted by the government of Vermont, two rights have been reserved for the benefit of the ministry: one held as an unalienable parsonage in the right of the town, and the other became the property of the first settled minister, whatever might be his persuasion. The propagation rights have by an act of the legislature been granted for the purpose of schools in the several towns where they are located. The glebe rights were disposed of in the same manner, until the Episcopal church, for whose use they were designed, recovered the lands by an action at law, tried before the supreme court of the United States, and decided in their favor. A law was passed in 1787, making contracts valid which the people may voluntarily enter upon for the purpose of settling and suporting a minister. Since the revisal of the constitution, in 1792, no religious test is required of any member of the legislature. The government of Vermont has secured to the people those rights and privileges which render them free, enlightened and happy. Though their way has often been beset with difficulties, yet liberty, like a polar star, has attracted their attention and received their noblest efforts for her preservation. Probably republican honor and virtue will never rise to greater splendor than was the case in the long and difficult struggle for American Independence.

CHAPTER I.

Situation. Extent. Mountains. Rivers. Lakes. Bays. Climate. Forest trees. Esculent and Medicinal plants. Quadrupeds. Birds, Fishes, Insects, Mineralogy and Geology. - - - - - - - 7

CHAPTER II.

The discovery of Vermont. Situation of Indian Tribes. Surrender of Canada to Great-Britain. - 23

CHAPTER III.

View of the Civil Policy from 1760 to 1775. First Settlement in Vermont. Grants from New-Hampshire. General Montgomery invades Canada. Americans retreat from Canada. Their defeat upon lake Champlain.— Burgoyne's invasion. Surrender of the British - 42

CHAPTER IV.

Indian depredations upon the early settlers. Destruction of Royalton. Political Affairs in Vermont, from the commencement of the revolution in 1775, until its termination in 1783. Meeting of Conventions. Declaration of the Independence of Vermont. Transactions of New-York. Acts of Congress. Controversy and claims of New-Hampshire, New-York, and Massachusetts. Commissioners open a negotiation with Vermont. Proceedings of Vermont. Measures pursued by Congress. Management of the British Agents. Resolutions of Congress. Transactions between Vermont, New-York and New-Hampshire. Washington's communication. Congress defer the admission of Vermont into the Union. - - - - - - 71

CHAPTER V.

A survey of the political affairs of Vermont from the year 1783, to her admission into the Union of the States.— Proceedings at Guilford. Commotion in the southern part of the State. Measures pursued by the New-York Legislature. Resolutions of Congress. Protest of the government of Vermont against them. Cessation of hostilities with Great-Britain. Vermont averse to an union with the Federal Government. New Constitution of the United States. New-York proposes an adjustment of the controversy. Settlement of the same. Boundaries of the State established. Vermont admitted into the Union. Consequences of the controversy. - - - - - - - - 117

CHAPTER VI.

A Sketch of Politics from the year 1791 to the American Embargo in the year 1808. Prosperity of Vermont on her union with the States. Annual proceedings of the Legislature of the State. Effect of the Revolution in France upon the policy of this country. Resignation and death of governor Chittenden. Mr. Tichenor elected governor. His proceedings. Civil affairs of the State, and measures pursued by the General Assembly at Vergennes, Windsor, Middlebury, Newbury, Burlington, Westminster, Windsor, Rutland, Danville, Middlebury, and Woodstock, embracing a period of eleven years from 1798 to 1808. Outrage committed by the British ship Leopard upon the United States frigate Chesapeake. - - - - - - 131

CHAPTER VII.

A review of the legislative proceedings from the year 1808 to 1815. Embargo laid by Congress upon the vessels of the United States. Disturbances under that law in 1808. Flood in July, 1811. John Henry's mission.— United States declaration of war against Great-Britain, June 18th, 1812. Riotous proceedings at Georgia.— Correspondence between governor Chittenden, James Monroe, generals Strong, Newell and Macomb. Hartford Convention. - - - - - - 163

CHAPTER VIII.

Condition of the United States at the commencement of hostilities with Great-Britain in 1812. General Dearborn appointed commander-in-chief. Northern campaign for 1812. Expedition against Canada, under the command of general Hull. Surrender of his Army.— Attack upon Queenstown by general Van Rensselaer.

INDEX.

Disorderly conduct of the militia. Capture of the American forces. Exploits of Captain Wool. Proceedings of general Smythe. Abandonment of his enterprise against the British provinces. Military operations at Champlain. Overtures for peace by the American government. Termination of the campaign for 1812. - - - - - - - 192

CHAPTER IX.

Northern Campaign for 1813. Battle and Massacre at Frenchtown. Siege at fort Meigs. Surrender of York. Death of general Pike. Fort George taken. Capture of generals Chandler and Winder. Proceedings at Sacketts Harbor. Repulse of the British at Fort Stephenson. Perry's Victory on lake Erie. Battle at the Thames. Defeat of the British Army. Commodore Chauncey captures the British Squadron on lake Ontario. Wilkinson takes the command of the center Army. Engagement at Williamsburg. Affair at Chateaugay. Americans defeated at Black Rock. - 202

CHAPTER X.

Proffered mediation of Russia declined by the British government. Opinions of Great-Britain on the prosecution of the War. Unsuccessful attempt at La Colle.— Oswego attacked by the British. Battle of Chippewa. Engagement at Bridgewater. The British repulsed in their attack upon fort Erie. Successful sortie of general Porter against the British garrison near fort Erie.— Capitulation of the eastern part of Maine to the enemy. Sir George Prevost marches his army into the States.— Invasion of Plattsburgh. McDonough's Victory over the British squadron, September 11th, 1814. Retreat of the English army. Sequel to the history of the war with Great-Britain. A general treaty of peace concluded at Ghent. - - - - - - 214

CHAPTER XI.

A Narrative of the Legislative Proceedings from the year 1814 to 1824. Unusual cold summer in 1816. President Monroe's Tour through the State. Governor Galusha's resignation in 1819. Mr. Skinner elected governor in 1820. Resolutions upon the question of admitting Missouri into the Union. Election of Judge Van Ness governor of Vermont in 1823. General La Fayette's visit to Vermont. His reception among the people. - - - - - - - 230

CHAPTER XII.

Proceedings of the General Assembly from the year 1824 to the termination of the year 1830. Mr. Butler elected governor in 1826. Great demand for banking privileges. Legal provisions for the better regulation of common schools. Mr. Crafts' election for governor of the state in 1828. Excitement on the subject of the presidential election. Controversy concerning masonry.— Popular views on the subject. Flood in 1830. Election of Mr. Crafts by the house of representatives. State of parties. - - - - - - 246

CHAPTER XIII.

Condition of Society. Different employments of the people. Agriculture. Manufactures. Commerce. Literature. - - - - - - - 265

CHAPTER XIV.

Character of the people. Poor laws. Various Societies for the promotion of the public welfare. American government. Constitution and Laws of Vermont. Counties. Towns. Courts, and their jurisdictional powers. Revenue and expenses of the government. - 281

CHAPTER XV.

Population of the State. Banks. Militia. Colleges. Religion. - - - - - - - 298

ERRATA.—Page 11, ninth line from bottom, for Missisque read Lamoille. Same page, 10th line from bottom, for Lamoille read Missisque. Page 12, 2d line from top, read Shelburn for Selburn. Page 97, 3d line, for cecession read cessation. Page 271, 1st line, for Stratford read Strafford. Page 274, 16th line, for choice business read choice in business. Page 307, 37th line, read Windsor has the largest population, instead of Burlington.

INDEX OF NAMES

ADAMS, 136 137 140 143 145 146 149 243 254
    John 138 John Quincy 214 Mr 138 William 214
AIKEN, Judge 279
ALLEN, 46 102 106 119 Col 12 50 93 102 103 104
    Ethan 46 48 74 89 91 92 101 102 107 119 Gen 95
    Heman 83 I 119 Ira 87 97 103 107 Lt 228
AMHERST, 40 Gen 12 38 39
ANGUS, Lt 199
ANNE, Queen 29 31
ANTHONY, 185
APPLING, Col 224
ARMS, Josiah 119
ARMSTRONG, 164
ARNOLD, 49 52 53 54 55 58 65 69 193 Col 48 Gen 57
ATLE, 94
ATWATER, I 310
BACKUS, Col 206

BAINBRIDGE, Commodore 228
BARCLAY, Commodore 207 229
BARKER, 185 Joseph 73 Mr 73 Mrs 73
BARNUM, A W 188
BARRON, Commodore 161
BATES, Joshua 310
BAUM, Col 65
BAYARD, James A 214
BAYLIES, 280
BEACH, Samuel 184
BEADLE, Col 55
BELKNAP, Simon 76
BENZELL, 46 74
BLANCHARD, Col 34
BLODGET, 185
BLOOMFIELD, Brigadier Gen 193 196
BLYTHE, Capt 228
BOERSTLER, Col 199 205 Lt Col 205

INDEX OF NAMES

BONAPARTE, 163 164 179 216 246
BOURN, 264
BOYD, Gen 210
BOYDEN, Maj 119
BRADLEY, S R 119 Stephen R 97 289
BRAYTON, Judge 279
BRECKENRIDGE, Maj 76
BREYMAN, Col 65
BRIGHAM, Paul 288
BRISBANE, Gen 188 224
BROCK, Gen 194 195 197
BROKE, Capt 228
BROOKS, Col 69
BROWN, Col 67 Gen 200 205 206 210 215 217 218 219 221 229 Jonothan 76 Maj 50 51
BROWNSON, Capt 104 Col 104 Timothy 107
BUDD, Lt 189
BURGOYNE, 60 62 63 67 69 86 Gen 12 60 61 64 66 68 70 223
BURNS, Col 205
BURR, 151 Col 146 147
BURROWS, Lt 228
BURTON, Dr 279
BUTLER, 248
BUTTERFIELD, 55
BUTTON, 76
CAMILLUS, 236
CAMPBELL, Col 53 195

CARDEN, Capt 228 I 7
CARLETON, 50 51 52 54 Gen 57 60 Gov 49 Maj 73
CARPENTER, Nathaniel 119
CARVER, Mr 29
CASSIN, Lt 189
CASTLEREIGH, Lord 200
CHAMPLAIN, 10 27 Samuel 23 28
CHANDLER, Gen 205
CHAPIN, W 280
CHARLES II, 43
CHATHAM, Lord 37
CHAUNCEY, Commodore 203 205 209
CHIPMAN, Daniel 278 Judge 278 Nathaniel 129
CHITTENDEN, 180 181 185 189 230 Gov 88 95 103 106 110 111 113 132 134 135 136 186 187 188 212 213 224 Martin 289 Mr 134 135 188 224 Thomas 83 107 115 288
CHRISTIE, Col 196 197
CLARK, Carpus 180 181 Mr 181
CLAY, Gen 203 Henry 214
CLEVELAND, Norman 263
CLINTON, 68 69 Gov 91 92 93 256
COCKBURN, 46
COLDEN, Gov 43

INDEX OF NAMES

COLIGNI, Jasper 28
COLLINS, I 7
COLUMBUS, Christopher 28
COLVIN, 264
CONGER, 185
CORLEAR, 28
CORNWALLIS, 59 105 108 Lord 104
COURCELLES, M 28
COVINGTON, Gen 211
CRAFTS, 253 255 261 262 Gov 262
CROGHAN, Maj 206
CURTIS, Elias 77
D'AILLEBOUT, 30
DACRES, Capt 228
DAVIS, Henry 310
DEAN, 48 167 295
DEARBORN, Gen 196 200 202 203 204 209 229 Henry 193
DEBELINE, M 32
DECATUR, Commodore 228
DEE, 185
DELAPLACE, Capt 48
DELLIUS, Godfrey 42
DENNET, John 184
DEROUVILLE, 31
DEWY, Rev 45
DIDWIDDIE, Gov 34
DIESKAU, 40 Baron 35
DORRIL, 311

DOWNIE, Commodore 226 227 229
DRUMMOND, Gen 217 221 222 229 Lt Gen 218
DUDLEY, Col 203
DUNCAN, Lt 225
EASTON, Col 51
ELDRIDGE, Lemuel B 261
ELKINS, Col 76
ELLIOT, Capt 207 208
ENOS, Gen 104
ERSKINE, 174
EVEREST, Benjamin 74 Mr 74
FARNSWORTH, 72 Commissary Gen 119 Gen 119
FASSET, John 107
FASSETT, Col 188
FAY, James 46 Jonas 83 86 114 Joseph 103 107 Maj 104 Stephen 46
FESSENDEN, 279
FIFIELD, Col 234
FISCHER, Col 221
FISK, Lt 119
FOSTER, Capt 55
FRANCIS, 62 Col 61
FRANKLIN, Dr 267
FRAZIER, 60 Gen 62 68
FRENCH, 129
FRONTENAC, 31
GAFFIELD, Benjamin 72
GAINES, Gen 221 229

INDEX OF NAMES

GALLATIN, Albert 214
GALLUP, Dr 280 Oliver 163
GALUSHA, 167 173 176 230 Gov 170 232 236 Mr 236
GAMBIER, Lord 214
GANSEVOORT, 112
GATES, 56 Gen 58 65 68 69 70
GEORGE II, 7 29 32
GEORGE III, 7
GERMAIN, George 111 Lord 108
GIBBS, Gen 229 Giles 76
GIBSON, Col 222
GODFREY, 231 295
GOFF, Col 40
GOLBOURN, Henry 214
GORDON, Gen 76
GRANDY, Elijah 73 Mrs 74
GREGG, John 141
GRIFFITH, Adm 222
GRISWOLD, Nathan 74
GROUT, Hilkiah 72
HALDIMAN, Gen 109
HALDIMAND, Gen 103 106 Gov 106
HALL, 62 Gen 193 212
HAMILTON, 60
HAMPTON, Brigadier Gen 193 Gen 202 210 211
HARDY, Commodore 222
HARMER, 209
HARRISON, Gen 195 202 203 208 210 211 229

HASKELL, 75
HATHAWAY, 184
HAVENS, Robert 76
HAVILAND, Col 40
HAWKINS, Thomas 13
HAWKS, Col 33
HAYES, Dr 280
HAZEN, Richard 7
HEMINGWAY, Asa 74
HENDRICK, 34 Col 35
HENRY, 174 Clinton 108 John 174
HERRICK, Col 75
HERRINGTON, James 163
HILL, Col 63
HILLYAR, Commodore 228
HINKLY, Thomas 73
HOLCOMB, Joseph 74
HOLMES, Capt 217
HOPKINS, Gen 195 Josiah 280 Roswell 289
HORTON, Lt 76
HOUSE, 78 John 77
HOWARD, 29
HOWE, Caleb 72 Gen 59 Lord 38
HUBBELL, Mrs 185
HULL, Brigadier Gen 193 Commodore 228 Gen 194 195 208 209
HUTCHINSON, John 76
HYDE, Mrs 185
INDIAN, Roundhead 202 Splitlog 202 Tecumseh

INDEX OF NAMES

INDIAN (Continued) 195 203 208 209 229
IZARD, Gen 211 222 223
JACKSON, Gen 229 254
JEFFERSON, 145 146 147 148 149 150 151 154 159
JESSUP, Col 220
JOHNSON, 40 72 Captive 72 Col 67 208 209 Gen 34 Mrs 72 William 34
JONES, Commodore 228 Reuben 83
KENT, John 77
KING, Capt 199
KNEELANDS, Joseph 76
KNIGHTS, Capt 120
KNOWLES, Charles 33
LABAREE, 72
LACORNE, Chevalier 36
LAFAYETTE, 245 Gen 244
LAMBERT, Capt 228
LAWRENCE, Capt 228
LEONARD, Capt 225
LEVI, M 36
LEWIS, Col 202 Gen 210
LINCOLN, Gen 64 66 68
LIVINGSTON, Maj 51
LORING, Capt 39
LOUIS XIV, King Of France 29
LOUIS XVIII, 216
LYMAN, Gen 34
M'DONOUGH, Commodore 216 226

M'FARLAND, Maj 221
MACDONOUGH, Commodore 213
MACOMB, Gen 187 188 189 224 225 229
MADISON, 126 169 174
MAN OF COLOR, Virginia 295
MANNERS, Capt 229
MAPLES, Capt 228
MARSH, James 310 William B 163
MASON, John 87 Peter 77
MCCLURE, Gen 212
MCDONALD, Capt 197
MCDONOUGH, Capt 189 190 Commodore 12 189 229
MCGINNES, Capt 35
MCLEAN, Col 51
MCREA, Miss 66
MEECH, 262
MELVIN, Capt 72
MILLER, Col 203 220 Gen 221 222
MILLS, Col 206
MITCHELL, Col 217
MONROE, Mr 161 200 Col 36 James 187 189 President 234
MONTCALM, 36 37 40
MONTGOMERY, 52 Gen 50 51 53
MOOERS, Gen 188 224

INDEX OF NAMES

MORGAN, 184 257 258
  William 256
MORRIS, Lewis R 129
MORRISON, Lt Col 210
MUNROE, 182
MURRAY, Col 212
NELSON, Capt 229
NEWELL, Gen 187
NEWTON, 75 Christopher 28
NICHOLSON, Gen 31
NILES, 280
NOADIE, Capt 225
OGLEVIE, Capt 197
OSBURN, 280
PACKENHAM, Gen 229
PAINE, Lt Gov 112 Mr 112
PALMER, 262
PARSONS, 48
PEMBER, 76
PERRY, Commodore 207 229
PHELPS, Capt 48
PHILIPS, 60 Gen 68
PIKE, Col 200 Gen 204 229
PINCKNEY, 182 Gen 146
  Thomas 193
POOR, 56
PORTER, 222 Commodore 228 Exekial 311 Gen 193 198 217 218 220 221
POWELL, 60
POWERS, Gen 75 224
PRESCOT, Gen 51
PRESTON, Lt Col 204 Maj

PRESTON (Continued) 51
PREVOST, Gen 226 George 229 Gov 223 224
PRINDLE, Mr 73
PRINGLE, Capt 57
PROCTER, Gen 228
PROCTOR, 206 208 Col 202 Commander 209 Gen 203
PURDY, Col 211
PUTNAM, Maj 37
QUEBEC, Bishop Of 49
REDDING, 295
REED, Col 46
REGULUS, Gen 267
REIDESEL, Gen 62 68
REIDSEL, 60
RIALL, Gen 218 220 221 229
RICHARDS, Lt Gov 262
RIPLEY, Gen 218 219 220 221 222 229
RITCHIE, Capt 221
ROBINS, Aaron 73 George 73
ROBINSON, 185 Beverly 101 Col 102 Moses 107 114 185 Samuel 45
ROGERS, 39 Maj 38
ROSE, Hannah 263
ROSS, Gen 229
RUSSEL, Jonathan 214
RUSSELL, 200 Col 195
RUSSIA, Emperor of 214
SAFFORD, Samuel 107

INDEX OF NAMES

SAUNDERS, Daniel C 310
   Dr 15
SCHUYLER, 56 63 64 Gen
   49 50 60 65 Maj 30
SCOTT, Col 205 221 Gen 218
   219 220 221 229
SHAFTSBURY, 236
SHEAFFE, Gen 197 203
SHERBURN, 55
SHERWOOD, J 103
SHUTLAND, Capt 231
SIMMONS, 279
SINCLAIR, Commodore 222
SKEEN, Col 46 81 Maj 49
SKINNER, 242 Gov 238 239
   241
SLADE, William 278
SMITH, 160 Israel 159 172
   Lt 189 213 Nathan 74
SMITHS, 73 74
SMYTHE, Alexander 198
   Gen 196 198 George 103
SPENCER, Mr 163
SPERHT, 60
SPERRY, 184
SPOONER, Paul 114
SAINTCLAIR 63 Gen 61 63
SAINTLEDGER, Col 60 Gen
   104
SAINTVINCENT, Col 205
STARK, 56 Brigadier 66 Gen
   64 65 66 87
STEVENS, Capt 32 33 Gen
   77
STEWART, Commodore 228
STONE, Mr 73
STRICKER, Gen 229
STRONG, Gen 187 188 189
   223 Samuel 188
STURDIFIT, 73
SULLIVAN, 56 Gen 55
SUMPTER, Lt 227
SWAM, Benjamin 289
SWARTWOUT, 210
SWIFT, Dr 280 Gen 219
   Samuel 188
THOMAS, Gen 54
THOMPSON, 278 Gen 55
TICHENOR, 149 157 165
   Gov 137 140 141 159 233
   Isaac 114 289 Judge 136
TOTTEN, Lt 197
TOWSON, 217 220
TUPPER, Sgt 104
TYLER, Judge 279 Royal
   289
VANNESS, 243 246 Judge
   242
VANRENSSELAER 197 Col
   196 Gen 196 196 197 198
   229 Solomon 196
VAUGHAN, 70 Capt 225
WALBRIDGE, Col 112
WALES, Capt 229
WALLIS, 70
WARD, 73
WARNER, 46 62 Col 51 64
   65 70 74 84 85 86 Seth 46

WARNER (Continued)
  49 61
WARREN, J B 200 201 John
  B 200
WASHINGTON, 65 109 110
  113 145 149 236 244 245
  Gen 60 64 109 111 124
  144 George 34 President
  136
WATERBURY, Gen 58
WATERS, Capt 119
WAYNE, 56
WEARE, 87 88
WEBB, Gen 36
WELLINGTON, 215
WENTWORTH, Gov 43 312
WHINYATES, Capt 228
WHIPPLE, Gen 64
WHITCOMB, Lt 76
WHITING, Col 34 35

WILKINSON, Brigadier Gen
  193 Gen 209-211 215 216
WILLIAM, King Of England
  29
WILLIAMS, Col 34 35 Dr 7
  277 Rev 31
WINCHESTER, Gen 202 228
WINDER, Gen 205
WITHERSPOON, Dr 94
WOLFE, 52
WOOD, Col 222
WOODBRIDGE, Col 67
WOOL, Capt 197 Maj 224
  225
WOOSTER, 48
WRIGHT, 75
YORK, Duke Of 43 44
YOUNG, 86 Maj 212 Thomas
  85

www.ingramcontent.com/pod-product-compliance
Lightning Source LLC
Chambersburg PA
CBHW071956220426
43662CB00009B/1157